New Trends in Financing Civil Litigation in Europe

NEW HORIZONS IN LAW AND ECONOMICS

Series editors: Gerrit De Geest, *Washington University in St. Louis, USA*; Roger Van den Bergh, *Erasmus University Rotterdam, The Netherlands*; and Thomas S. Ulen, *University of Illinois at Urbana-Champaign, USA*.

The application of economic ideas and theories to the law and the explanation of markets and public economics from a legal point of view is recognized as one of the most exciting developments in both economics and the law. This important series is designed to make a significant contribution to the development of law and economics.

The main emphasis is on the development and application of new ideas. The series provides a forum for original research in areas such as criminal law, civil law, labour law, corporate law, family law, regulation and privatization, tax, risk and insurance and competition law. International in its approach it includes some of the best theoretical and empirical work from both well-established researchers and the new generation of scholars.

Titles in the series include:

New Trends in Financing Civil Litigation in Europe

A Legal, Empirical, and Economic Analysis

Edited by

Mark Tuil

Postdoctoral Researcher, The Rotterdam Institute of Private Law (RIPL), Erasmus University Rotterdam, The Netherlands

Louis Visscher

Associate Professor in Law and Economics, Rotterdam Institute of Law and Economics (RILE), Erasmus University Rotterdam, The Netherlands

NEW HORIZONS IN LAW AND ECONOMICS

Edward Elgar
Cheltenham, UK • Northampton, MA, USA

Published by
Edward Elgar Publishing Limited
The Lypiatts
15 Lansdown Road
Cheltenham
Glos GL50 2JA
UK

Edward Elgar Publishing, Inc.
William Pratt House
9 Dewey Court
Northampton
Massachusetts 01060
USA

A catalogue record for this book
is available from the British Library

Library of Congress Control Number: 2010927658

ISBN 978 1 84844 685 4

Typeset by Servis Filmsetting Ltd, Stockport, Cheshire
Printed and bound by MPG Books Group, UK

Contents

Acknowledgements

This project, both the conference held in Rotterdam in April 2009 and the current volume, would not have been possible without the contribution of many people. We explicitly would like to thank the Erasmus Trustfonds and the research programme 'Behavioural Approaches to Contract and Tort' for their financial support for the organization of the conference, and the people working at Edward Elgar for their assistance in the publication of this book.

Tables

Contributors

Michael Faure is Professor of Comparative Private Law and Economics at the Rotterdam Institute of Law and Economics (RILE) of the Erasmus University Rotterdam and Professor of Comparative and International Environmental Law at the Maastricht University.

Paul Fenn is Norwich Union Professor of Insurance Studies at the Nottingham University Business School.

Fokke Fernhout is Associate Professor Metajuridica at Maastricht University.

Deborah R. Hensler is Judge John W. Ford Professor of Dispute Resolution and Associate Dean for Graduate Studies at Stanford Law School, fellow of the American Academy of Arts and Sciences and the American Academy of Political and Social Science, as well as a member of the board of overseers for the RAND Institute for Civil Justice.

Sonja Keske is European Doctor in Law and Economics (EDLE) with a Ph.D. on Group Litigation in European Competition Law.

Niels Philipsen is Associate Professor of Law and Economics at the Maastricht University.

Andrea Pinna is attorney with the law firm Bredin Prat in Paris, as well as Research Director at Institut de Droit des Affaires Internationales (IDAI).

Andrea Renda is Senior Research Fellow at the Center for European Policy Studies (CEPS) in Brussels and Lecturer at LUISS Guido Carli University in Rome, as well as a Senior Research Fellow at LUISS's Law and Economics Lab.

Neil Rickman is Professor of Economics at the Department of Economics of the University of Surrey, Research Affiliate at the CEPR and director of the RAND Europe's Institute for Civil Justice Europe.

Tom Schepens is a Ph.D. researcher at the Tax Law Department of Ghent University.

Mark Tuil is Postdoctoral researcher at the Rotterdam Institute of Private Law (RIPL) of the Erasmus University Rotterdam.

Willem H. van Boom is Professor of Private Law at the Erasmus University Rotterdam and Director of the Rotterdam Institute of Private Law (RIPL).

Roger Van den Bergh is Professor of Law and Economics and Director of the Rotterdam Institute of Law and Economics (RILE) of the Erasmus University Rotterdam.

Louis Visscher is Associate Professor of Law and Economics at the Rotterdam Institute of Law and Economics (RILE) of the Erasmus University Rotterdam.

1. Introduction

Mark Tuil and Louis Visscher

1. THE PROBLEM OF FINANCING CIVIL LITIGATION

Due to several factors not every meritorious claim is brought to justice. One of these factors is the costs that need to be incurred, which might be too high to make the claim feasible in practice. Such barriers to the effectuation of a claim are problematic for the following reasons: firstly, they effectively frustrate access to justice; secondly, civil litigation is the driving force behind private enforcement; and thirdly, the behavioural incentives that actors may derive from the legal rules are reduced by the financing problem. Traditionally this funding problem is overcome in part by government-subsidized legal aid. However, the budget available for legal aid in most European countries and indeed worldwide is limited and is under threat of reduction.

Many techniques other than government subsidized legal aid may also overcome the aforementioned problem. Parties can buy legal expense insurance, both 'before-the-event' and 'after-the-event'. Result-based fees for lawyers such as contingency fees and conditional fee arrangements enable plaintiffs to initiate a claim without bearing a financial risk. Collectivization of claims into class actions, collective actions, and/or representative actions might substantially decrease the costs per plaintiff. Cost shifting arrangements exist, such as the English Rule or the inclusion of extra-judicial costs in the determination of damages. Finally, several 'market solutions' can be distinguished, such as the Cartel Damage Claims (CDC) whereby victims of antitrust law infringements can sell their claim to CDC for a fixed price plus an additional percentage of the realized damage claims. The auctioning of claims can also be regarded as a possible market solution.

With the decrease in government budgets for legal aid, the importance of these techniques has increased and they have been gradually introduced to a more or lesser extent into the various European legal systems. The introduction of these solutions to the funding problem into the European legal systems poses a number of interesting questions. The first question is, of course, whether these solutions actually provide access to justice in cases where such access would have been lacking under the conventional system. From a legal point of view the most important question is whether these solutions are allowed. Here it is also important to ask whether such solutions *should* be allowed. In this respect it is important to assess whether these solutions do not create problems in their own right. For example, in many European jurisdictions the introduction of result-based fees for lawyers is regarded as problematic, as this could provide the lawyer with incentives not to act in the best interests of his client. For this reason the European Bar Association (CBBE) for example forbids the *pactum de quata litis* in paragraph 3.3 of their code of conduct. Moreover, the fear is often voiced that introducing result-based fees will have harmful effects on society as a whole, because it would lead to a 'claim culture', that is a culture where disputes are overlitigated. Both with respect to harmful effects for the individual litigants and the effect for society as a whole, reference is often made to the US situation.

These kinds of questions cannot be adequately answered from any single perspective. This book aims at analyzing different possible solutions to the financing problems from a legal, empirical, and law and economics point of view. The legal analysis focuses on the question of which financing techniques are legally available and how they are embedded in the existing legal frameworks. The empirical analysis investigates to what extent the theoretically available instruments are actually applied in practice and what effects these instruments have on the behaviour of parties. The law and economics analysis focuses on the strengths and weaknesses of the distinguished instruments from the point of view of maximizing social welfare.

2. METHODOLOGY

As has been explained above, in this book multiple methods are used to address the questions raised by the (prospective) introduction of new solutions to increase access to justice. The approach taken as a whole may therefore be classified as multidisciplinary. This does not mean to say that every author in this book employs a multidisciplinary approach, rather it is arrived at by combining the different approaches taken by the contributors. Three main approaches may be distinguished.

● The legal approach is employed to address the question of what solutions are allowed to the funding problem and what principles underlie allowing or prohibiting a certain instrument. As mentioned above, many European jurisdictions prohibit certain result-based fee arrangements for lawyers. A legal approach may be used to describe to what extent result-based fees for lawyers are allowed within a certain legal system and what principles are served by the prohibition of a certain result-based fee arrangement.

● The law and economics approach analyses the behaviour of parties from the point of view of maximizing social welfare. Applied to the topic of financing civil litigation, it analyses the reasons why rational people may not start a claim (for example, because they assess that the costs of the claim are higher than the expected outcome), as well as the way in which the various instruments affect the whole dispute resolution process.

● The empirical approach is a necessary addition to both the legal and the law and economics perspective, because these disciplines are in the end concerned with the actual behaviour of parties. The predictions that law and economics makes on the basis of a model should be tested against empirical data and, if necessary, the model needs to be changed or refined. For example, the predictions of law and economics are often based on certain assumptions or estimates about the relative size of certain, often countervailing, effects. An empirical approach may provide greater insight into the size of these effects, thereby offering the possibility of increasing the accuracy of the predictions.

Similarly, a legal rule is not a purpose in and of itself. It exists to control or facilitate the behaviour of parties. If it is shown that the behaviour the rule is meant to control is absent or that the rule creates problems of its own, the rule may be changed. An empirical approach is therefore a necessary addition to both law and economics as legal scholarship.

3. FRAMEWORK OF THE RESEARCH

This book is the result of the conference 'New Trends in Financing Civil Litigation in Europe' held on April 24, 2009. This conference was organized as part of the research programme 'Behavioural Approaches to Contract and Tort: Relevancy for Policymakers' of the Erasmus School of Law at the Erasmus University Rotterdam. This programme strives to incorporate insights from the behavioural sciences such as Economics, Psychology and Sociology into the study of Contract and Tort Law.

4. STRUCTURE OF THE BOOK

As was described above, many different solutions exist to the litigation funding problem, all of which are studied in detail by the contributors to this book. Before this detailed analysis, Visscher and Schepens start with a general introduction into these solutions from a law and economics point of view. They begin by introducing the law and economics perspective on legal rules in their capacity of providing actors with behavioural incentives by allocating costs which arise out of different activities. However, if the costs of starting litigation to effectuate these rules are too high, the rules will not be effectuated because the person who should start a claim remains rationally apathetic. The effect is that the behavioural incentives, which the law intends to provide, do not reach the party they are aimed at.

Visscher and Schepens analyse three possible ways of overcoming this rational apathy problem: cost shifting, fee arrangements and legal expenses insurance. All of these approaches shift (some of) the costs of civil litigation to a party other than the plaintiff. Cost shifting entails that (part of) the litigation costs of a successful plaintiff are transferred to the defendant. Fee arrangements lead to the result that the plaintiff only bears attorney costs if he wins. Legal expense insurance shifts the costs to the insurer, in exchange for a premium. By lowering the financial hurdles of bringing a claim, all instruments may provide solutions to the problem of financing civil litigation, thereby improving the behavioural incentives that the legal system can provide.

Visscher and Schepens analyse the possible impact of cost shifting, fee arrangements and legal expenses insurance not only on the number of suits being brought, but on all stages in the dispute resolution process: (1) filing a claim, (2) possibly dropping the claim due to new information, (3) settlement negotiations and (4) adjudication. They investigate the impact of the various instruments by comparing them with the situation where the plaintiff himself bears the costs.

Faure, Fernhout and Philipsen explore the role of result-based fees for lawyers. They note that in Europe these fee arrangements are very controversial. They outline the debate by listing the arguments in favour and against result-based fees for lawyers. They then give strict definitions of different types of result-based fees and go deeper into the law and economics theory behind these fee schemes. They give a comparative overview of the possibilities to agree to result-based fees in Belgium, Denmark, England and Wales, France, Germany, Greece, Ireland, Hong Kong and the Netherlands.

Keske, Van den Bergh and Renda analyse the role of the collectivization of claims as a means to alleviate the funding problem. They first describe the advantages and disadvantages of collective actions. In Europe there is much resistance against the American style class action. Instead, the European commission promotes the 'European model' of the representative actions by consumer associations. Keske, Van den Bergh and Renda analyse the advantages and disadvantages of this model compared to the American model, as well as the role of fee arrangements and private and public funding on collective actions.

Van Boom addresses the role of Legal Expenses Insurance (LEI) as an option to solve the funding problem. He analyses both Before-The-Event Insurance (BTE) and After-The-Event Insurance (ATE). In doing so, Van Boom describes the market for BTE and its legal context, the LEI directive. This directive stipulates the free choice of counsel for legal expense insurance policy holders. Van Boom describes how legal expense insurers strive to keep the costs of legal services down and how the free choice of counsel conflicts with this goal of keeping costs down. When discussing ATE, Van Boom distinguishes between ATE as a form of third-party funding and ATE as an add-on to an English style conditional fee arrangement.

Pinna addresses the possibility of dealing with the funding problem by way of the assignment of a liability claim to an investor, who would 'acquire' the claim and bring a claim in compensation in its own name and on his own behalf. Pinna argues that this model would in principle be a sound solution. He then examines the legality of the assignment of a liability claim under English and French law. Pinna takes position in favour of the assignment of liability claims, especially as a solution to the absence of other techniques, such as mandatory damage insurance, compensation schemes or class actions, which already aim at finding an alternative to the traditional way of seeking compensation for an injured party by an individual claim in court. He also notes that the option of assignment has the added benefit that the liability claim may be securitized.

Fenn and Rickman survey recent research on the empirical analysis of the effects of litigation finance. Drawn in particular from econometric studies of England and Wales and the US, it touches upon contingency fees, hourly fees, legal aid, conditional fees and legal expenses insurance. Fenn and Rickman present a theoretical model to demonstrate the kinds of factors that litigation finance may be expected to influence, in particular case screening, case outcome (including any settlement amount), settlement timing, the volume of litigation, and potential conflicts between lawyer and client. They find that finance plays a statistically significant role in litigation and, for this reason alone, should be taken seriously by policy makers.

As was noted before, much of the debate on financing litigation is conducted against the background of 'the American experience'. However, to what extent the statements about this experience are accurate, or the fear of 'American situations' is justified, remains unclear. Hensler addresses the American system of financing, both non-mass and mass litigation (the latter both via class actions as otherwise) and the role of contingency fees in this respect. She also tackles the difficult question of whether the US legal financing rules lead to excessive litigation.

2. A law and economics approach to cost shifting, fee arrangements and legal expense insurance

Louis Visscher and Tom Schepens

1. INTRODUCTION

In this chapter, we will provide an overview of the economic literature regarding cost shifting, fee arrangements and legal expense insurance. In the economic analysis of law, legal rules are regarded as instruments which can provide actors with behavioural incentives. In essence, private law (torts, contracts, property, etc.) allocates the costs which arise out of different activities. Those costs may only be borne by the party causing them if the party initially suffering from them brings suit. Problems in financing civil litigation may effectively hinder such lawsuits, so that the behavioural incentives which the law intends to provide do not reach the party causing the harm.

For example, tort law is regarded as an instrument that induces people to take care. The prospect of being held liable after negligently having caused losses may induce a potential tortfeasor to take due care, because taking due care (thereby avoiding liability) is less costly than taking too little care (and being liable). Contract law is seen as a device that enables people to increase welfare by engaging in voluntary transactions. The remedies of contract law (specific performance and damages) induce the debtor to fulfil his contractual duties when this is less costly than breaching the contract and facing the sanction. If the victim of a tort or the creditor in a contractual setting does not bring a claim against the tortfeasor or the debtor, neither the tortfeasor nor debtor would face any expected sanction. This would not confront them with the costs they have caused and hence they would not receive the desired incentives. After all, in deciding how to behave, rational actors do not look at the costs they may cause, but only at the costs they may have to bear (Schäfer 2000, p. 184).

Many reasons exist that explain why actors such as the victim of a tort or the creditor in a contract may not effectuate their claim. The first reason, which forms the topic of this chapter, is that the costs of bringing a claim may outweigh the expected benefits. In such cases, a rational victim would decide not to effectuate the claim, because that would cost more than it yields in expected benefits. In economic terms, the victim stays *rationally apathetic* (This concept was introduced by Downs (1957). Also see Schäfer 2000, p. 184). Besides rational apathy, other reasons exist for why actors may not bring suit. They might not know that a law infringement has occurred to which they can react. In a typical tort setting, the victim often knows that he has been injured, and he knows the injurer or the costs of identifying the injurer are low (Landes and Posner 1975, p. 31). With infringements of safety regulations, for example, this may be different. It may be difficult for individual victims to recognize unsafe products, and violations of safety standards might go undetected until harm occurs. Even after harm has materialized, it may prove to be difficult for the individual victim to prove violation of the relevant safety rules (Van den Bergh and Visscher 2008, p. 40). The burden of proof constitutes another reason why victims do not always bring a claim. If they assess that they will not be able to prove negligence, causation, legally relevant losses, et cetera, they could very well decide not to start a procedure, given that they do not expect to prevail. Finally, strategic behaviour may bar claims from being brought. If the victim is not the only one who suffered losses, he may try to take a free ride on the efforts of other victims. If a group of people suffers from, for example, noise or smell from a nearby factory, an action for an injunction would benefit all victims. Each individual victim prefers someone else to bear the costs of the lawsuit, because after a successful procedure, he will also benefit from the injunction. If too many victims behave as free riders, the necessary law suit may not be brought in the first place, leaving all victims worse off.

We will focus our attention on the issue of rational apathy. We will analyse three possible ways to overcome this problem: cost shifting, fee arrangements and legal expense insurance. All of these approaches shift (some of) the costs of civil litigation to a party other than the plaintiff. Cost shifting entails that (part of) the litigation costs of a successful plaintiff are transferred to the defendant. Fee arrangements lead to the result that the plaintiff only bears attorney costs if he wins. Legal expense insurance shifts the costs to the insurer, in exchange for a premium. By lowering the financial hurdles of bringing a claim, all instruments may provide solutions to the problem of financing civil litigation, thereby improving the behavioural incentives that the legal system can provide. This may ultimately even lead to fewer cases being tried because fewer violations occur (Miceli and Segerson 1991, Katz 2000, p. 76 ff.).

The aim of this chapter is to provide an overview of the economic literature dealing with these instruments. We believe this literature provides valuable insights which help to assess the potential of and the limits to these instruments to overcome or decrease the rational apathy problem. This is obviously very relevant for a volume which discusses new trends in financing civil litigation from a legal, empirical and economic point of view.

We will analyse the possible impact of cost shifting, fee arrangements and legal expense insurance not only on the number of suits being brought, but on all stages in the dispute resolution process: (1) filing a claim, (2) possibly dropping the claim due to new information, (3) settlement negotiations and (4) adjudication. We investigate the impact of the various instruments by comparing them with the situation where the plaintiff himself bears the costs. In Section 2 we briefly describe the dispute resolution process and indicate the economic decision-making process in each stage. In Section 3 we analyse the impact of cost shifting, more specifically applying the so-called English Rule instead of the American Rule. In Section 4 we investigate the influence of fee arrangements by comparing a system of hourly fees with a system of contingency fees. In Section 5 we analyse the impact of legal expense insurances in each stage of the dispute resolution process. In Section 6 we summarize and conclude.

2. THE DISPUTE RESOLUTION PROCESS

The economic theory of litigation was developed in the early 1970s. It still serves as the standard model and also constitutes the basis of our approach (Landes 1971, Gould 1973, Posner 1973. Also see Cooter and Rubinfeld 1989, Kobayashi and Parker 2000, Shavell 2004, pp. 389–418).

The economic theory of litigation does not only encompass the different stages of dispute resolution, but also the stage before a dispute has even arisen. In other words, the phase in which actors decide how to behave is also included in the analysis. It is assumed that actors behave rationally. That is, they are assumed to maximize their expected utility, given their beliefs and their available information. Hence, the behaviour in the first stage of the model depends on a weighing of expected costs and benefits. Expected liability is a relevant factor in this weighing process. By taking adequate care, by fulfilling contractual obligations, et cetera, parties can reduce the probability of being held liable or they can avoid liability altogether. The level of expected liability and hence the expected utility of the potential wrongdoer is influenced by whether or not the potential victims respond to an infringement. If they remain rationally apathetic, the potential wrongdoer faces no expected liability. This provides him with inadequate behavioural incentives, compared to the social optimum where he incorporates the effects of his behaviour on others.

At the second stage, the plaintiff, who in the first stage suffered losses due to the behaviour of the defendant, decides whether or not to file a claim. This stage is called the *filing stage*. It is important to note that the filing stage encompasses both formal and informal ways of bringing a claim. Shavell describes it as follows: 'Bringing suit is interpreted as any action which results ultimately in settlement or in trial. Thus, we would consider a mere threat to initiate formal proceedings as a suit if the threat resulted in a settlement' (Shavell 1982, 56 nt. 5). Given that filing a claim costs time and/or money, a plaintiff will only do so if he has a credible threat to go to trial. Generally speaking, this is the case if the expected value of the claim (the expected judgment, multiplied by the probability of prevailing) exceeds the expected costs. Such cases are referred to as positive net expected value claims. In the absence of such a credible threat, the potential defendant does not fear trial and does not incorporate expected liability into his decisions. However, it is recognized in the literature that negative expected value suits may also be brought if they can induce the defendant to settle (Bebchuk 1996, Kobayashi and Parker 2000, p. 14). This could happen if, for example, the defendant's costs of going to trial outweigh the costs of settlement, even if the defendant is certain to prevail in court. We will not incorporate this situation in our analysis.

After a plaintiff has filed a claim, new information which influences the expected outcome may become available. If a claim that previously seemed to have a positive net expected value, after incorporation of the new information turns out to have a negative expected value, the plaintiff may decide to drop it in the third stage of the dispute resolution process. For example, the plaintiff's losses may be lower than he originally assessed, so that the expected damages if successful also decrease. It is also possible that the new information becomes available at another stage of the whole procedure, for example after the defendant refuses to offer to settle (P'ng 1983, p. 540, P'ng 1987, pp. 62–63. Also see Kobayashi and Parker 2000, p. 14). In this chapter, however, we only deal with a drop stage between filing the claim and engaging in settlement negotiations.

In phase four, settlement negotiations may take place. Due to the high costs, risks and duration of going to trial, parties may prefer to settle their dispute. If both parties would be better off by settling, there exists a *settlement surplus*, resulting in a positive settlement range. The plaintiff would be better off if the settlement exceeds the expected outcome of trial minus the expected litigation costs he has to bear. The defendant would be better off if the settlement amount falls short of the expected judgment at trial plus the expected litigation costs he has to bear. The settlement surplus equals the sum of both parties' litigation costs minus the amount by which the plaintiff's estimation of the expected judgment exceeds the defendant's estimation (Cooter and Rubinfeld 1989, p. 1075). For example, if the plaintiff assesses the outcome of trial at 100, the defendant at 80 and the litigation costs would amount to 25 for each party, the settlement surplus is $(25 + 25 - 20) = 30$. The plaintiff would be better off if the settlement exceeds $(100 - 25) = 75$, and the defendant if the settlement is less than $(80 + 25) = 105$. The difference of 30 between both limits is the settlement surplus. The settlement range runs from 75 to 105. Whether or not a settlement will actually be reached depends on the information both parties possess and on the bargaining process, where the possibility of strategic behaviour is important (P'ng 1983, Shavell 1982, Hay and Spier 1998, Daughety 2000). The chance that a settlement is reached, increases with the size of the settlement surplus.

If the parties do not reach a settlement, the case proceeds to the fifth stage: trial. Each party will spend rationally on litigation up to the point where an additional investment no longer improves the expected outcome by more than the additional costs. The optimal expenditure for each party is found there, where its marginal costs equal its marginal benefits.

3. COST SHIFTING

3.1 Introduction

Different arrangements regarding litigation costs exist. Under the so-called *English Rule*, the prevailing party recovers some or all litigation costs from the unsuccessful party. In contrast, under the *American Rule*, each party bears its own expenses. In order to be able to fully focus on the impact of cost shifting, in this section we compare the English Rule, where all costs are shifted, with the American Rule and disregard the more complicated intermediary possibilities where only some costs are shifted. The theoretical effects we distinguish in the analysis below will in practice be less pronounced if not all costs are shifted.

3.2 Trial Expenditure

In economic literature, it is argued that trial expenditure will be greater under the English Rule than under the American Rule (Braetigam, Owen and Panzar 1984, pp. 180–181, Katz 1987, p. 159 ff., Hause 1989, p. 166). After all, given that under the English Rule the unsuccessful party has to bear the litigation costs of the prevailing party (so that there is more at stake), the marginal benefits of additional investment in trial expenditure outweigh those under the American Rule. It is optimal to invest until the marginal costs equal the marginal benefits, and due to the higher marginal benefits this point is reached later under the English Rule. In addition to the higher marginal benefits, the marginal costs are lower under the English Rule, because parties only expect to bear litigation costs if they lose the trial.

It is difficult to isolate this effect empirically. Hughes and Snyder have studied the introduction of the English Rule to medical malpractice claims during the period 1980–85 in Florida. This research reports an increase in defence expenditure of 108 per cent for litigated claims and 150 per cent for settled claims (Hughes and Snyder 1998, p. 51). Kritzer, however, argues that it is hard to isolate the impact of fee arrangements. He states that 'this does not mean that fee arrangements do not matter; rather, it is indicative of the complexity of the effects of fee arrangements. The various effects tend to cross-cut in significant ways. The result is often that clear evidence of effects is difficult to find' (Kritzer 2002, p. 1983).

3.3 Level of Suit

The likely effect of cost shifting on the level of suits depends on several interrelated factors. These effects are most clearly shown when compared to the benchmark where the cost-allocation rule does not matter: the plaintiff assesses his probability of winning at 50 per cent; both parties are expected to spend the same amount on litigation; the English Rule does not lead to greater trial expenditures and both parties are risk neutral. By subsequently changing one of these four conditions, its effect on the level of suit can be assessed.

The first issue is the plaintiff's assessment of his chance of prevailing. The higher his estimated probability of success, the higher the expected benefits of the suit. The expected value of the claim (net of litigation costs) therefore increases with the probability of success, which results in a higher willingness to sue (Shavell 1982, pp. 59–60. Also see Rickman 1995, p. 331). This effect is stronger under the English Rule, because under the American Rule a successful plaintiff still has to bear his own litigation costs.

The second relevant factor is how much both parties are spending on litigation. All other things being equal, if the plaintiff expects to outspend the defendant, he is more likely to bring suit under the English Rule than under the American Rule. After all, given the estimated probability of success of 50 per cent, under the English Rule the plaintiff expects to have to bear half of both parties' costs, which by definition (due to the outspending) is less than having to bear his own costs fully under the American Rule (Hause 1989, pp. 167–168, Snyder and Hughes 1990, p. 349). The opposite result holds if the plaintiff expects to be outspended by the defendant.

The third factor relates to Section 3.2 above. There it became clear that parties are expected to spend more on litigation under the English Rule. This greater expenditure lowers the claim's expected value, which results in a lower level of suit as compared to the American Rule (Hause 1989, pp. 167–168, Snyder and Hughes 1990, p. 351, 352).

Finally, the risk attitude of parties matters. A risk neutral actor is only concerned with the expected value of a certain project and not with the possible magnitude of the outcome. (S)he therefore is indifferent between a project with a certain outcome of €100 and a project with a 50 per cent probability of €200. A risk-averse actor on the other hand is also concerned with the possible magnitude of the outcome and prefers the certainty of €100 over the 50 per cent possibility of €200. This risk attitude is caused by the decreasing marginal utility of wealth, due to which a loss in wealth leads to a more than proportional loss in utility. The plaintiff's risk aversion leads to a lower level of suit, given that litigation entails uncertainty. This effect is stronger under the English Rule than under the American Rule, because the consequences of winning or losing are larger (Shavell 1982, pp. 61–62). The greater expenditures effect of the English Rule reinforces this.

The four effects are interrelated and depend on the circumstances of the case. It is therefore not possible to determine a general overall effect on the level of suit of a shift from the American to the English Rule.

3.4 Quality of the Claims

The first effect of a shift to the English Rule that we have described in Section 3.3 encourages the filing of high-merit claims. After all, the higher the probability of success, the lower the probability of having to bear the litigation costs under the English Rule, whereas under the American Rule the plaintiff would still bear his own costs. This effect is very clear in the extreme situation of certainty of winning the case. Under the American Rule, the plaintiff still has to bear his litigation costs, and hence refrains from filing the claim if its value is lower than these costs, even if he is certain to win. Under the English Rule he would file the claim, because he is certain that he does not bear the litigation costs himself (Shavell 1982, p. 59, Rosenberg and Shavell 1985, pp. 5–6). However, the second effect we have described in Section 3.3 (outspending) may mitigate the encouragement of high-merit claims under the English Rule: in case the defendant sufficiently outspends the plaintiff low value claims are discouraged, even if they are of high merit. The third effect (greater expenditures) and introduction of risk aversion may also hinder the encouragement of strong but small claims under the English Rule (Hause 1989, pp. 167–168, Snyder and Hughes 1990, p. 349 ff.).

Cost-shifting discourages the filing of weak claims, because the probability that the plaintiff who files a weak claim also has to bear the litigation costs of the defendant is relatively high. The greater expenditures effect, risk aversion and outspending by the plaintiff reinforce this discouragement.

Hence, the English Rule entails a selection effect in favour of high merit claims, even of relatively low value. This effect is, however, mitigated by greater expenditures, increased risk and possible outspending by the defendant. Due to these mitigating effects, there is a critical probability of success and a critical value of the claim below which the plaintiff will not sue. This leads to a selection effect in the direction of high merit and high value claims (Snyder and Hughes 1990, p. 349). Empirical research indeed suggests that the probability for plaintiffs to prevail increases under the English Rule (Hughes and Snyder 1995, p. 238).

It should be noted that if a plaintiff is judgment proof so that he cannot pay the litigation costs of the defendant in the case of losing the trial, he may also file weaker claims (Di Pietro, Carns and Kelley 1995, p. 101). Furthermore, the plaintiff's subjective assessment of the merits of the claim determines his behaviour. Given that under the English Rule he may have to bear the litigation costs of both parties, he will have an incentive to screen claims more carefully (Mause 1969, p. 32).

3.5   Drop Rate

Whether a plaintiff drops a claim depends on his assessment of the expected value of the claim. Given the quality enhancing features of the English Rule, which were discussed above, one would expect a lower drop rate than under the American Rule. Fewer low quality claims, which may eventually reach the drop stage, are brought under the English Rule in the first place. However, whether or not a claim is dropped ultimately depends on the type of information that becomes available after the claim is brought and, more in particular, the way in which the information affects the claim's expected value under either one or both rules. It is theoretically impossible to know what information will become available. Therefore, it is also impossible to predict the overall effect on the drop rate.

Despite the theoretical impossibility of predicting the overall effect, there is empirical research that found an increase in the drop rate of 10.4

per cent (Snyder and Hughes 1990, p.364). This may be explained by the low filing costs: plaintiffs file a claim without carefully ascertaining its quality, with the purpose of acquiring more information (Snyder and Hughes 1990, p.377). The claim selection characteristic of the English Rule apparently occurs at the drop stage rather than at the filing stage.

3.6 Settlement Rate

When the literature on the effects of the English Rule on settlement behaviour is analysed, it becomes clear that no unambiguous results exist. Given that the English Rule increases litigation expenditure, it increases the settlement surplus. Settlement hence becomes more attractive because it can avoid higher litigation costs (Bowles 1987, p.177 ff., Hause 1989, p.167). Risk aversion strengthens this tendency, because by settling, parties can avoid the risky trial (Shavell 1982, p.68).

On the other hand, in as far as parties have a tendency to overestimate their probability of success, the English Rule leads to fewer settlements. Over optimism reduces the settlement surplus because it increases the difference in the parties' expectations of the outcome of the trial. The English Rule strengthens this effect because the over optimism also extends to the litigation costs (Shavell 1982, pp.65–66, Katz 1987, p.157 ff.).

The overall effect of cost shifting on the settlement rate cannot be determined theoretically, because it depends on the relative size of the two distinguished effects. Empirical research suggests that the over optimism effect dominates, for it has found a decrease in the settlement rate of 9.6 per cent (Snyder and Hughes 1990, p.366).

3.7 Level of Adjudication

All the above-described effects determine the overall influence of cost shifting on the level of adjudication. It is impossible to draw general conclusions on this issue on a theoretical level. Empirical research found that the probability for a filed claim to be adjudicated decreased by 5 per cent as a result of the English Rule. This effect consists of a decrease of 9.4 per cent due to the selection effect, which leads to a higher drop rate on the one hand, and an increase of 4.4 per cent due to less settlements as a result of over optimism on the other hand (Snyder and Hughes 1990, p.364 ff.).

3.8 Duration of Claims

The decision whether or not to drop a claim is made on the basis of its expected value. As soon as this value becomes negative, the claim will be dropped. New information leading to a lower estimation of the merits of the claim under the English Rule also increases the assessed probability of having to bear the other party's litigation costs. Hence, the expected value decreases more quickly under the English Rule as such information becomes available, leading to an earlier drop than under the American Rule. The greater expenditure effect strengthens this tendency (Hughes and Savoca 1997, p. 264). Empirical findings corroborate this view (Hughes and Savoca 1997, p. 269).

The English Rule also shortens the duration of the settled claims. Due to the selection effect, the claims that proceed to the settlement stage are, on average, of higher quality. If parties indeed settle, the over optimism effect has turned out not to be prohibitively large. Under these conditions, the plaintiff has a credible threat to go to trial, and given the relatively high quality of the case, the defendant faces a good possibility of having to bear all litigation costs. It is therefore in his best interest to quickly settle the case (Hughes and Savoca 1997, pp. 264–265, 269).

The adjudication phase, finally, is expected to take longer under the English Rule, due to the greater expenditures effect. The possibility of having to pay the other party's litigation costs does not counter this effect, because parties are overly optimistic about their prospects (otherwise, they would have already dropped or settled the claim). Each party hence expects that the other party will have to bear the litigation costs (Hughes and Savoca 1997, p. 294).

4.   FEE ARRANGEMENTS

4.1   Introduction

Lawyer's fees constitute a large part of the costs of pursuing a legal claim (see for example Williams and Williams 1994, p. 79 ff.). Broadly speaking, besides fixed fees, two forms of payment for legal services exist: hourly fees and contingency fees. Under hourly fees, the party hiring the attorney has to pay the fee, regardless of the outcome of the case. Under contingency fees, on the other hand, the lawyer's reward often depends on two contingencies. First, if the case is lost, the lawyer receives no compensation ('no cure, no pay'). Second, if the case is won, the fee is often a prefixed percentage of the obtained award ('*quota pars litis*').

In many European countries, contingency fees are prohibited, whereas in the United States these are commonly used (also see Chapter 3 by Faure, Fernhout and Philipsen and Chapter 8 by Hensler). Article 3.3 of the Code of Conduct for Lawyers in the European Union explicitly states that 'A lawyer shall not be entitled to make a *pactum de quota litis'*. However, the traditional European resistance seems to be weakening. In the United Kingdom, conditional fees were adopted in the 1990s. The main difference between contingent and conditional fees is the idea of *quota pars litis*, which is not present under conditional fees. Under such conditional fees the lawyer receives a premium (not related to the amount at stake) if the case is won and nothing if the case is lost. According to Emons, in Belgium and the Netherlands such conditional fees also exist. Furthermore, 'Spain, France, Italy, and Portugal are considering the introduction of conditional fees. Germany has also relaxed some restrictions by means of third party contingent contracts (. . .). In Greece contingent fees of up to 20 per cent as well as conditional fees are permitted' (Emons 2007, pp. 89–90. See Faure, Hartlief and Philipsen 2006a and 2006b and Chapter 3 in this book for an overview of conditional fees in several European countries and Hong Kong).

In this section, we will analyse hourly fees and contingency fees from an economic point of view. Both the dispute resolution model as well as the principal–agent theory is relevant in this respect. Both will be subsequently discussed.

4.2 Level of Suit

In the literature it is generally argued that contingency fees lead to an increase in the level of suit. The first reason, which lies at the core of this chapter and even the entire book, is the fact that contingency fees can be used to finance the attorney costs of pursuing a claim. After all, the costs are only paid after a positive result has been achieved. In essence, the plaintiff borrows money from his lawyer while the case is pending. This allows him to bring suit also in cases where an hourly wage might have been prohibitively costly.

Second, contingency fees essentially contain an insurance policy which shifts the risk of not obtaining a sufficient award to cover the attorney costs from the plaintiff to the lawyer. Risk-averse plaintiffs will hence be less often deterred from bringing a claim, because their financial risk is lower under contingency fees (Posner [1973] 2003, p. 584). Given that lawyers can diversify their portfolio of cases, they are likely to be less risk-averse than their clients. This reduces the overall costs of risk borne by the plaintiffs and lawyers. Hourly fees do not allow for such beneficial risk sharing (Gravelle 1998, p. 383).

Whether or not these two effects lead to an overall increase in the level of suit depends on the existence of overcapacity in the market for legal services. If there is no excess capacity and lawyers in some cases shift from hourly wages to contingency fees, the total number of cases would decrease if they spend more time on these contingency fee cases than they would have spent under a system of hourly fees. There is (limited) empirical literature suggesting that contingency fee lawyers spend fewer hours on small cases than hourly fee lawyers, but more hours on cases with a higher value (Kritzer et al. 1985, pp. 266–267).

The percentage that is agreed upon in the contingency fee arrangement determines the share of the judgment that the plaintiff receives after deduction of the lawyer's fee. In his decision of whether or not to bring suit, the plaintiff compares his expected benefits with the other costs involved in litigation, which he still bears himself. After all, contingency fees only regard the attorney fee. The agreed percentage itself therefore also influences the level of suit. On the one hand, the higher this percentage the less often a plaintiff will bring suit because the expected benefits decrease. On the other hand, in as far as a higher percentage induces the attorney to devote more effort to the case (see Section 4.5 below), the probability of winning and/ or the magnitude of the award may increase, leading to higher expected benefits. The overall effect cannot be predicted theoretically.

4.3   Quality of the Claims

It is often argued that contingency fees encourage meritless litigation, because the plaintiff does not bear the risk of having to pay the attorney fee if he loses. Hence, under the simplifying assumption that there are no litigation costs besides the attorney fee (which better allows us to focus on the difference between hourly fees and contingency fees), the plaintiff would be willing to start a claim as soon as there is a positive probability of success, no matter how small.

However, this line of reasoning overlooks the crucial role of the attorney. He will only be interested in trying the case if there is a large enough probability of winning, because only then will he receive the agreed percentage (Dana and Spier 1993, pp. 349–350, Miceli 1994). Given that a lawyer is a repeat player who ordinarily can better assess the quality of a case than the plaintiff, he will also be better able to screen cases and distinguish the low-quality from the high-quality cases. In that sense, contingency fees are expected to increase the overall quality of the cases being brought (Clermont and Currivan 1978, pp. 571–572). Empirical research verifies this gate-keeping role of lawyers working on a contingency fee basis, but it also shows that lawyers turn down cases with a relative low value (Kritzer 1997, p. 26 ff.). A report on the profitability of conditional fees in the United Kingdom suggests that specialization as well as screening cases on their probability of success has a positive impact on the profits of a firm (KPMG 1998). Other research indicates that under a system of hourly fees lawyers have fewer incentives to provide the plaintiff with an unbiased assessment of the quality of their claim than contingency fee lawyers (Dana and Spier 1993).

4.4 Drop Rate

Given that the remuneration of a contingency fee lawyer depends on the outcome of the case, we can expect him to screen information that becomes available after the suit was brought more carefully than hourly fee lawyers. In deciding whether or not to continue the case, the contingency fee lawyer requires a sufficiently high expected return. This so-called *screening effect* leads to more cases being dropped under contingency fees.

However, there is an opposite *selection effect*, which is caused by less screening by hourly fee lawyers in the filing stage, which was discussed in Section 4.3. Hourly fee lawyers have fewer incentives to avoid low quality claims from being filed so more of such claims reach the drop stage. The probability that clients will decide to drop a claim as a result of new information suggesting a negative expected value is therefore higher under hourly fees than under contingency fees.

Theoretically it is impossible to predict the overall effect of contingency fees on the drop rate. Danzon and Lillard (1983, p. 363) in their empirical research found that the selection effect outweighs the screening effect. Limitations on contingency fees lead to an increase in the drop rate of 5 per cent.

4.5 Settlement Rate

Different strands of literature provide different predictions regarding the impact of contingency fees on the settlement rate. In the first strand it is argued that contingency fees lead to more settlements, because this way the lawyer secures his share of the settlement without having to invest additional time and effort. Given that the lawyer is interested in his share of the settlement rather than in the client's share, he may advise to settle for an amount that is too low, as this increases the likelihood that the defendant accepts the settlement offer (see for example Schwartz and Mitchell 1970, Miller 1987, Thomason 1991 and Gravelle and Waterson 1993).

The second strand of literature incorporates the effect of fee arrangements on attorney effort. Contingency fee lawyers in essence weigh their costs of additional efforts against the expected increase in their own reward, which is only a fraction of the total benefits of increased efforts.

This induces them to spend less time on a tried case than is in the best interest of their client. Only if the contingency fee percentage is 100 per cent (hence, if the lawyer *buys* the claim from his client), would this problem be avoided. This, however, is prohibited in most US states (Santore and Viard 2001). Incorporating this effect on attorney effort, the expected cost of the defendant of going to trial is lower, making it less likely for him to accept any given settlement demand. The costs of the plaintiff's attorney of going to court are also lower because he spends less than optimal efforts on it. This can result in the contingency fee lawyer proposing a settlement offer that is too high, resulting in fewer settlements, so that the case goes to trial (Polinsky and Rubinfeld 2002, p. 222 ff. Also see Miceli 1994, Bebchuk and Guzman 1996 and Rickman 1999).

Empirical evidence corroborates the findings of the second strand of literature. The settlement rate turns out to increase if limits on contingency fees are introduced, and the settlement amounts decrease (Danzon and Lillard 1983, p. 363, Snyder and Hughes 1990, p. 366).

4.6 Level of Adjudication

In the previous sections, we have seen that under hourly fees the drop rate of claims as well as the number of settled cases is higher than under contingency fees. Hence, relatively fewer claims are adjudicated under hourly fees. It is also shown empirically that limitations on contingency fees tend to decrease the probability that a claim proceeds to trial (Snyder and Hughes 1990, p. 360).

4.7 Duration of Claims

When discussing the drop rate, we saw that under contingency fees the lawyer is the primary decision taker, whereas under hourly fees it is the client. Both want to avoid spending resources on a case with an expected value that is too low. Given the superior information of the lawyer in this respect, we expect filed cases to be dropped sooner under contingency fees. We do not know of any empirical studies regarding this specific issue.

Regarding the settlement phase, a contingency fee lawyer does not gain by prolonging the negotiations any further than necessary. Hourly fee lawyers, however, can increase billable hours by dilatory tactics. Settlements are therefore expected to take longer under hourly fees. This also shows empirically (Helland and Tabarrok 2003, p. 536 ff.).

With the same line of reasoning, we expect adjudication to take longer under hourly fees than under contingency fees.

4.8 Attorney Costs

Contingency fee lawyers will charge a premium for the de facto financing and insurance services they provide, so that the expected hourly wages of contingency fee lawyers will exceed those of hourly fee lawyers (Brickman 1996, p. 270). This effect may be mitigated because contingency fee lawyers can use the contingent fee in the competition process, in order to attract more clients. However, it is an empirical question if the market for lawyers' services is competitive enough for this downward tendency. Another possible reason for a decrease in contingency fees is the fact that high-quality lawyers with a relative large success rate are able to ask for a lower percentage than lower quality lawyers. By charging a relative low fee, high quality lawyers can signal their quality, thereby attracting more clients. The danger, however, exists that clients view the low fee as a signal of low rather than high quality, in which case the signal would not be able to separate high quality and low quality lawyers (Brickman 2003, pp. 100–101).

4.9 Principal–Agent Issues

Implicit in the above analysis, we have already encountered a number of issues regarding the principal–agent relationship of clients and lawyers. The common ground of these issues is that the interests of lawyers and clients are not necessarily well-aligned. The client has an interest in winning the case against as low costs as possible, whereas the lawyer has an interest in earning an as high as possible fee.

This tension appeared in Section 4.3, where we argued that hourly fee lawyers have fewer incentives to provide the plaintiff with an unbiased assessment of the quality of their claim than contingency fee lawyers. Given the tendency of clients to choose contingency fees whenever there is a possibility of losing the case, a contingency fee lawyer may advise his client to take the case on a contingency fee basis, where in fact an hourly fee would have been better for the client (Kritzer 1998, p. 305). Also, given the fact that the lawyer can better assess the risks, he may negotiate a percentage that is higher than the case justifies (Halpern and Turnbull 1983, p. 14). Both possibilities for opportunistic behaviour are curtailed somewhat in rules governing fee negotiations in the United States and in the possibility of having the reasonableness of the fees evaluated by the court.

In Section 4.7 we discussed the effects on the duration of the case. The client often does not have adequate information to evaluate the amount of time an hourly fee lawyer claims is required for the case. This may induce the lawyer to allocate too many hours to the case. In Section 4.5

we already saw that the opposite is true for a contingency fee lawyer, who is not expected to spend enough time on the case, given that he bears the full costs of additional effort, but only receives a fraction of the benefits thereof. An additional problem with hourly fee lawyers is that they could bill for more hours than they have actually put in. Contingency fees may reduce this moral hazard problem (Danzon 1983, Gravelle and Waterson 1993, Emons and Garoupa 2006).

5. LEGAL EXPENSE INSURANCE

5.1 Introduction

The last instrument in combating the financing problem discussed in this chapter is legal expense insurance. This instrument introduces an additional player into the analysis: the insurance company. Given that the interests of the insurer are not identical to those of the parties (plaintiff and defendant), and the interests of the lawyers involved are yet different, the full picture becomes rather complicated. This holds even more if one realizes that each player may possess different information. The multitude of principal–agent relationships opens many possibilities of strategic behaviour, which are dealt with in the following sections.

5.2 Level of Suit

Due to several reasons, legal expense insurances are expected to increase the level of suit. First, the insured plaintiff does not bear the full litigation costs, which increases the claim's expected value. Second, the insurance covers the plaintiff's risk, so that it induces risk-averse plaintiffs also to bring suit. Third, it solves a plaintiff's possible liquidity problem (Kirstein 2000, Van Velthoven and Van Wijck 2001).

An additional, more problematic reason why the level of suit may increase is formed by the typical informational problems of insurance contracts: moral hazard and adverse selection. These problems, if not adequately addressed, may cause the market for legal expense insurance to fail (Bowles and Rickman 1998, p. 197). Due to adverse selection, mainly high-risks will take the insurance, increasing the likelihood that it will actually be used. Due to moral hazard, the insured may take fewer measures which could have avoided the conflict in the first place, again increasing the probability of using the insurance.

However, several instruments exist which allow insurance companies to confront both problems, such as risk diversification, exclusion of certain risks, deductibles et cetera. Empirical data from Germany and the Netherlands suggest that insurers are successful in this respect because, notwithstanding a rapid increase in the number of legal expense insurances, the number of claims per 100 policies remained practically constant in the Netherlands in the period 2000–2008 (Verbond van Verzekeraars 2005, pp. 26–27 and 2009, pp. 94–95) and only increased by 4–8 per cent in Germany (Kilian and Regan 2004, p. 242. The period is not mentioned).

5.3 Quality of the Claims

Legal expense insurance could theoretically cause a flood of unmeritorious litigation, now the plaintiff does not bear the full costs of litigation. Claims could also be of low value, although the deductibles which are present in most policies reduce this problem.

However, the way in which insurances function in general reduces the scope for unmeritorious claims. In order for a risk to be insurable, the insurer needs a large enough volume of business, but he also needs to limit adverse selection (leaving moral hazard aside for the moment). The premiums collected should be high enough to cover the costs, but they should not be too high to be attractive for the potential insured. The higher the proportion of unmeritorious claims becomes, the higher the premiums have to be to cover the costs, inducing the good risks to terminate the insurance policy. Hence, in order to keep the insurance profitable, the insurer will pose limits on the coverage of unmeritorious claims. This can be done through, for example, only providing coverage if there is a reasonable chance of success (Rickman and Gray 1995, p. 311, Kilian 2003, p. 46) and through the general obligation of good faith, which allows an insurer to deny coverage for groundless or unreasonable claims. Given that the insurer, being a repeat player, is better equipped to screen a case on its merits than the plaintiff himself, who is likely to be a one-shotter, this screening will likely increase the overall quality of the claims being brought.

Empirical research suggests that there is only limited difference in the value of claims issued by insured and uninsured litigants. Furthermore, the percentage of insured litigants winning their case is only 3 per cent higher than that of uninsured (Prais 1995, p. 439). This could be caused by more careful screening of the insurer, but it is not clear whether this indeed is the case.

5.4 Drop Rate

Insured plaintiffs are less likely to drop their case, now they do not bear the full costs themselves (Bowles and Rickman 1998, p. 197). However, the insurer can also influence the decision to drop a claim, by withdrawing coverage.

Two counteracting effects determine the overall impact of legal expense insurance on the drop rate. We do not have adequate data to determine the overall effect. The better screening of the insurer which we discussed in Section 5.3 results in fewer low-quality cases reaching the drop stage in the first place, leading to a lower drop rate (selection effect). On the other hand, if the insurer acquires new information suggesting a lower value of the claim, he may decide to withdraw coverage. As we have argued in Section 4.4, hourly fee lawyers on the contrary have few incentives to correctly advise their clients in the drop phase. This suggests that the drop rate may be higher with legal expense insurance than without it (screening effect).

5.5 Settlement Rate

Looking at the parties involved in the dispute, legal expense insurance covers their litigation costs and hence reduces the settlement surplus as well as the likelihood of settlement (Kirstein 2000, Van Velthoven and Van Wijck 2001). Also, the positive impact of risk aversion on the willingness to settle is removed by the insurance. However, the insurer still can benefit from settlement because it avoids the higher litigation costs. Hence, if allowed, the insurer may settle a case where the insured party would have preferred to go to trial.

If a plaintiff has legal expense insurance, his bargaining position is better than without the insurance, because he can more credibly threaten to go to trial. This implies that if a settlement is reached, the amount settled for is expected to be higher (Heyes, Rickman and Tzavara 2004, p. 109).

Empirical research in Germany suggests that settlement is discouraged by legal expense insurance, because 5–8 per cent more litigants proceed to trial (Prais 1995, p. 439).

5.6 Level of Adjudication

The overall impact on the level of adjudication depends on the foregoing factors and cannot be predicted theoretically. According to Prais, a German study found that 'legal expenses insurance enabled the insured to issue proceedings more readily and to pursue those proceedings to judgment more tenaciously than if he did not have insurance', but this increase was 'only between 5 and 10 per cent' (Prais 1995, p. 439).

5.7 Duration of Claims

Under the assumption that the (professional) insurer is better able to evaluate the quality of a claim than the (often non-professional) plaintiff, and given the better incentives of the insurer as compared to hourly fee lawyers, we expect low-quality claims to be dropped sooner if the plaintiff uses a legal expense insurance.

Regarding settlements, the better incentives for the insurer as compared to hourly fee lawyers again predict quicker settlements. This is confirmed empirically (Fenn et al. 2006, p. 26).

Regarding the duration of trial, two distinct principal–agent issues play a role. First, under an hourly fee system, an uninsured client has an incentive to monitor his attorney, given their diverging interests (see Section 4.9). If the client is insured, he no longer has this incentive. It is even in the immediate interest of the client if the lawyer spends more time on the case, if this improves the chances of success (Bowles and Rickman 1998, p. 200). The use of deductibles, co-payments and maximum coverage, as well as the possible increase in insurance premiums caused by the increase in lawyers fees, may however reduce this problem. Second, the insurer has an interest in limiting the duration of trial, but he has only limited options in doing so. If the insurer provides counsel, he may have incentives available to avoid delay. If the client has free choice of counsel, this no longer holds (also see Chapter 5 by Van Boom in this book). The superior information of the insurer as opposed to the insured, however, may still enable the former to better control the behaviour of the lawyer.

5.8 Attorney Costs

Finally, also regarding attorney costs, insurers face principal–agent issues. In countries where attorney fees are regulated (such as the German BRAGO system), attorney costs are more predictable so that costs are more controllable. Employing in-house lawyers is another way to control and reduce costs (Kilian 2003, p. 42). The effect may be limited due to the right of the policyholder to choose its own counsel. Finally, insurers may invest in building a lasting relationship with a selected number of lawyers and law firms to handle their legal expense insurance cases. In such a relationship, costs are more controllable, due to the desire to maintain this relationship.

6.   SUMMARY AND CONCLUSIONS

In analyzing the impact of cost shifting, fee arrangements and legal expense insurance, economic literature addresses a multitude of effects. At the outset, improving private enforcement serves the goal of providing better behavioural incentives to the parties involved, so that they take better care, refrain from infringements, fulfil their contractual obligations, et cetera. Given that these incentives are often provided in the form of damages to be paid to the plaintiff, the question of to what extent civil law actually leads to compensation for the plaintiff obviously is relevant in this respect. The problem of rational apathy may frustrate private enforcement. Cost shifting, fee arrangements and legal expense insurance are possible solutions to this problem. In this chapter, their impact on the different levels of the dispute resolution process is analysed from an economic viewpoint.

Cost shifting influences the level of suit in several ways. If a plaintiff assesses his chances of winning to be relatively high, he will sue more often under the English Rule than under the American Rule. The same holds if the plaintiff expects to spend more on litigation than the defendant. However, risk aversion poses a stronger restriction on the level of suit under the English Rule, as does the fact that trial expenditures increase under this rule. The overall effect is unclear. Contingency fees are expected to increase the level of suit because it solves the financing problem and it shifts the risk to a party who is better able to bear it. Legal expense insurance also is expected to increase the level of suit; because the plaintiff does not bear the costs, he is shielded from risk and his liquidity problem is solved. Furthermore, moral hazard and adverse selection, if not properly addressed, may increase the level of suit. Empirical research suggests that the increase is limited.

Cost shifting creates a selection effect towards higher-quality claims, because the lower the quality, the higher the probability of having to bear the other party's litigation costs. Risk aversion strengthens this effect. Empirical research corroborates these theoretical findings. Fee arrangements are also expected to increase the quality of the claims, because the lawyer acts as a gate keeper. This argument is supported by empirical research. The fear for meritless litigation that is often expressed when discussing contingency fees therefore seems unwarranted. The same fear is expressed regarding legal expense insurances but, here as well, the insurer will limit such claims, for example through merit tests or the general obligation of good faith. Hence, all three instruments have the potential to increase the quality of the claims.

All three instruments show two countervailing effects on the drop rate:

on the one hand, the higher quality of the claims may lead to a lower drop rate because the weaker claims have not even been filed (selection effect). On the other hand, the cases that were filed may be screened better so that an increase in the drop rate is possible (screening effect). Empirical research regarding cost shifting suggests that the latter effect dominates there, whereas the former effect seems to dominate in fee arrangements. We do not know of empirical research regarding the overall effect in case of legal expense insurance.

The effect of cost shifting on the settlement rate again is determined by several factors. The English Rule increases litigation expenditure and hence the settlement surplus, which makes settling more attractive. Risk aversion increases this tendency. However, overestimation of the probability of success causes a counter-effect. Empirical research suggests that the latter effect dominates, so that cost shifting decreases the settlement rate. Fee arrangements and legal expense insurance, according to the recent theoretical and empirical literature, show the same tendency.

Given all the previous effects, the impact of the instruments on the level of adjudication cannot be predicted theoretically. Empirical research indicates that introduction of the English Rule leads to an overall decrease in adjudication, which is mostly caused by the higher drop rate. Contingency fees, on the other hand, tend to increase the level of adjudication. Legal expense insurance also leads to an increase, albeit a moderate one.

The total duration of the claim may be shortened by the English Rule, because it leads to an earlier drop and quicker settlements. However, adjudication may take longer because the trial expenditures tend to increase. Contingency fees also lead to a quicker drop, due to the superior information of the lawyer. Because a contingency fee lawyer does not gain from dilatory tactics, settlement and trial are expected to be finished quicker than under hourly fees. Legal expense insurance also leads to a quicker drop due to the better information of the insurer. Settlements will be quicker because the insurer does not gain by delay (different from an hourly fee lawyer). The trial will probably also be shorter, but the insurer only has limited possibilities of influencing the duration.

Finally, fee arrangements and legal expense insurance have an impact on the relationship between the different players (principals and agents). Contingency fees give the lawyer an own interest in winning the case, which better aligns his incentives with those of the client. However, he may advise contingency fees where an hourly fee would be more in the client's interest, and he may negotiate a too-high percentage. Legal expense insurance reduces the client's incentives to avoid conflicts from arising in the first place. If they arise, the client will start legal proceedings more readily and he has fewer incentives to monitor his lawyer. However, through instruments such as deductibles, co-payments and maximum coverage, insurers combat these problems. In their relation with lawyers, insurers try to control and reduce costs by employing in-house lawyers, or to invest in building a lasting relationship with selected lawyers.

It seems that cost shifting, fee arrangements and legal expense insurance are all able to lower the financial hurdles in pursuing a legal claim. The English Rule, however, still leaves the financial risk of losing the case with the plaintiff, and even increases the costs if the case indeed is lost. Contingency fees remove this risk altogether, and legal expense insurance reduces it to the deductible, co-payment or amount exceeding the maximum cover. This reduction of financial obstacles, combined with the selection effect towards higher quality claims, which all instruments show, has the potential to improve the behavioural incentives provided by the legal rules, because norm violators are better confronted with the consequences of their behaviour. This, in the economic analysis of law, is not regarded as merely a desirable side-effect of civil litigation, but as its main goal. The desire to improve the accessibility of civil litigation is hence not only important in the legal view focussing on fairness, but equally so in the welfare-oriented economic view.

REFERENCES

Bebchuk, Lucian A. (1996), 'A New Theory Concerning the Credibility and Success of Threats to Sue', *Journal of Legal Studies*, **25**, 1–26.

Bebchuk, Lucian Arye and Andrew T. Guzman (1996), 'How Would You Like to Pay for That? The Strategic Effects of Fee Arrangements on Settlement Terms', *Harvard Negotiation Law Review*, **1**, 53–64.

Bowles, Roger A. (1987), 'Settlement Range and Cost Allocation Rules', *Journal of Law, Economics, & Organization*, **3**, 177–184.

Bowles, Roger A. and Neil Rickman (1998), 'Asymmetric Information, Moral Hazard and the Insurance of Legal Expenses', *The Geneva Papers on Risk and Insurance. Issues and Practice*, **23**, 196–209.

Braeutigam, Ronald, Bruce Owen and John Panzar (1984), 'An Economic Analysis of Alternative Fee Shifting Systems', *Law and Contemporary Problems*, **47**, 173–185.

Brickman, Lester (1996), 'ABA Regulation of Contingency Fees: Money Talks, Ethics Walk', *Fordham Law Review*, **65**, 247–335.

Brickman, Lester (2003), 'The Market for Contingent-Fee Financed Tort Litigation: Is it Price Competitive?', *Cardozo Law Review*, **25**, 66–128.

Cooter, Robert D. and Daniel L. Rubinfeld (1989), 'Economic Analysis of Legal Disputes and Their Resolution', *Journal of Economic Literature*, **27**, 1067–1097.

Clermont, Kevin M. and John D. Currivan (1978), 'Improving the Contingent Fee', *Cornell Law Review*, **63**, 529–599.

Dana, James D. and Kathryn E. Spier (1993), 'Expertise and Contingent Fees: The

Role of Asymmetric Information in Attorney Compensation', *Journal of Law, Economics, & Organization*, **9**, 349–367.

Danzon, Patricia M. (1983), 'Contingent Fees for Personal Injury Litigation', *Bell Journal of Economics*, **14**, 213–224.

Danzon, Patricia, M. and Lee Lillard (1983), 'Settlement Out of Court: The Disposition of Medical Malpractice Claims', *Journal of Legal Studies*, **12**, 345–377.

Daughety, Andrew F. (2000), 'Settlement', in: Boudewijn Bouckaert and Gerrit De Geest (eds), *Encyclopedia of Law and Economics, Volume V. The Economics of Crime and Litigation*, Cheltenham, UK and Northampton, MA, US: Edward Elgar, 95–158.

Di Pietro, Susanne, Theresa W. Carns and Pamela Kelley (1995), *Alaska's English Rule: Attorney's Fee Shifting in Civil Cases*, Anchorage, AK, US: Alaska Judicial Council, www.ajc.state.ak.us/reports/atyfee.pdf, accessed 27 July 2010.

Downs, Anthony (1957), *An Economic Theory of Democracy*, New York, NY, US: Harper and Row.

Emons, Winand (2007), 'Conditional Versus Contingent Fees', *Oxford Economic Papers*, **59**, 89–101.

Emons, Winand and Nuno Garoupa (2006), 'The Economics of US-Style Contingent Fees and UK-Style Conditional Fees', *Managerial and Decision Economics*, **27**, 378–385.

Faure, Michael G., Ton Hartlief and Niels J. Philipsen (2006a), *Resultaatgerelateerde beloningssystemen voor advocaten. Een vergelijkende beschrijving van beloningssystemen voor advocaten in een aantal landen van de Europese Unie en Hong Kong*, The Hague: Wetenschappelijk Onderzoeks- en Documentatie Centrum/Ministry of Justice, www.wodc.nl/images/1347_volledige_tekst_tcm44-59425.pdf, accessed 27 July 2010.

Faure, Michael G., Ton Hartlief and Niels J. Philipsen (2006b), 'Funding of Personal Injury Litigation and Claims Culture. Evidence from the Netherlands', *Utrecht Law Review*, **2**, 1–21, www.utrechtlawreview.org/publish/issues/2006-02/index.html, accessed 27 July 2010.

Fenn, Paul, Alastair Gray, Neil Rickman and Yasmeen Mansur (2006), *The Funding of Personal Injury Litigation: Comparisons Over Time and Across Jurisdictions*, London: Department for Constitutional Affairs, www.dca.gov.uk/research/2006/02_2006.pdf, accessed 27 July 2010.

Gould, John P. (1973), 'The Economics of Legal Conflicts', *Journal of Legal Studies*, **2**, 279–300.

Gravelle, Hugh S.E. (1998), 'Conditional Fees in Britain', in Peter Newman (ed.), *The New Palgrave Dictionary of Economics and the Law*, London, UK: Macmillan Reference Limited and New York, NY, US: Stockton Press, 382–386.

Gravelle, Hugh S.E. and Michael Waterson (1993), 'No Win, No Fee: Some Economics of Contingent Legal Fees', *The Economic Journal*, **103**, 1205–1220.

Halpern, P.J. and S.M. Turnbull (1983), 'Legal Fees Contracts and Alternative Cost Rules: An economic analysis', *International Review of Law and Economics*, **3**, 3–26.

Hause, John C. (1989), 'Indemnity, Settlement, and Litigation, or I'll be Suing You', *Journal of Legal Studies*, **18**, 157–179.

Hay, Bruce L. and Kathryn E. Spier (1998), 'Settlement of Litigation', in: Peter Newman (ed.), *The New Palgrave Dictionary of Economics and the Law*,

London, UK: Macmillan Reference Limited and New York, NY, US: Stockton Press, 442–450.

Helland, Eric and Alexander Tabarrok (2003), 'Contingency Fees, Settlement Delay, and Low-Quality Litigation: Empirical Evidence from Two Datasets', *Journal of Law, Economics, & Organization*, **19**, 517–542.

Heyes, Anthony, Neil Rickman and Dionisia Tzavara (2004), 'Legal Expenses Insurance, Risk Aversion and Litigation', *International Review of Law and Economics*, **24**, 107–119.

Hughes, James W. and Elizabeth Savoca (1997), 'Measuring the Effect of Legal Reforms on the Longevity of Medical Malpractice Claims', *International Review of Law and Economics*, **17**, 261–273.

Hughes, James W. and Edward A. Snyder (1995), 'Litigation and Settlement Under the English and American Rules: Theory and Evidence', *Journal of Law and Economics*, **38**, 225–250.

Hughes, James W. and Edward A. Snyder (1998), 'Allocation of Litigation Costs: American and English Rules', in: Peter Newman (ed.), *The New Palgrave Dictionary of Economics and the Law*, London, UK: Macmillan Reference Limited and New York, NY, US: Stockton Press, 51–56.

Katz, Avery W. (1987), 'Measuring the Demand for Litigation: Is the English Rule Really Cheaper?', *Journal of Law, Economics, & Organization*, **3**, 143–176.

Katz, Avery W. (2000), 'Indemnity of Legal Fees', in: Boudewijn Bouckaert and Gerrit De Geest (eds), *Encyclopedia of Law and Economics, Volume V. The Economics of Crime and Litigation*, Cheltenham, UK and Northampton, MA, US: Edward Elgar, 63–94.

Kilian, Matthias (2003), 'Alternatives to Public Provision: The Role of Legal Expenses Insurance in Broadening Access to Justice: The German Experience', *Journal of Law and Society*, **30**, 31–48.

Kilian, Matthias and Francis Regan (2004), 'Legal Expenses Insurance and Legal Aid – Two Sides of the Same Coin? The experience from Germany and Sweden', *International Journal of the Legal Profession*, **11**, 233–255.

Kirstein, Roland (2000), 'Risk Neutrality and Strategic Insurance', *The Geneva Papers on Risk and Insurance. Issues and Practice*, **25**, 251–261.

Kobayashi, Bruce H. and Jeffrey S. Parker (2000), 'Civil Procedure: General', in: Boudewijn Bouckaert and Gerrit De Geest (eds), *Encyclopedia of Law and Economics, Volume V. The Economics of Crime and Litigation*, Cheltenham, UK and Northampton, MA, US: Edward Elgar, 1–26.

KPMG (1998), *Conditional Fees – A Business Case*, Report for the Lord Chancellor's Department.

Kritzer, Herbert M. (1997), 'Contingency Fee Lawyers as Gatekeepers in the Civil Justice System', *Juridicature*, **81**, 22–29.

Kritzer, Herbert M. (1998), 'The Wages of Risk: The Return of Contingency Fee Legal Practice', *DePaul Law Review*, **47**, 267–319.

Kritzer, Herbert M. (2002), 'Lawyer Fees and Lawyer Behavior in Litigation: What Does the Empirical Literature Really Say?', *Texas Law Review*, **80**, 1943–1984.

Kritzer, Herbert M., William M.F. Felstiner, Austin Sarat and David M. Trubec (1985), 'The Impact of Fee Arrangement on Lawyer Effort', *Law & Society Review*, **19**, 251–278.

Landes, William M. (1971), 'An Economic Analysis of the Courts', *Journal of Law and Economics*, **14**, 61–107.

Landes, William M. and Richard A. Posner (1975), 'The private enforcement of law', *Journal of Legal Studies*, **4**, 1–46.

Mause, Philip J. (1969), 'Winner Takes All: A Re-Examination of the Indemnity System', *Iowa Law Review*, **55**, 26–55.

Miceli, Thomas J. (1994), 'Do Contingent Fees Promote Excessive Litigation?', *Journal of Legal Studies*, **23**, 211–224.

Miceli, Thomas J. and Kathleen Segerson (1991), 'Contingent Fees for Lawyers: The Impact on Litigation and Accident Prevention', *Journal of Legal Studies*, **20**, 381–399.

Miller, Geoffrey P. (1987), 'Some Agency Problems in Settlement', *Journal of Legal Studies*, **16**, 189–215.

P'ng, Ivan P.L. (1983), 'Strategic Behavior in Suit, Settlement, and Trial', *Bell Journal of Economics*, **14**, 539–550.

P'ng, Ivan P.L. (1987), 'Litigation, Liability, and Incentives for Care', *Journal of Public Economics*, **34**, 61–85.

Polinsky, A. Mitchell and Daniel L. Rubinfeld (2002), 'A note on settlements under the contingent fee method of compensating lawyers', *International Review of Law and Economics*, **22**, 217–225.

Posner, Richard A. (1973), 'An Economic Approach to Legal Procedure and Judicial Administration', *Journal of Legal Studies*, **2**, 399–458.

Posner, Richard A. (2003), *The Economic Analysis of Law*, 6th ed., New York, NY, USA: Aspen Publishers.

Prais, Vivien (1995), 'Legal Expenses Insurance', in Adrian A.S. Zuckerman and Ross Cranston (eds), *Reform of Civil Procedure: Essays on 'Access to Justice'*, Oxford: Clarendon Press, 431–446.

Rickman, Neil (1995), 'The Economics of Cost-Shifting Rules', in Zuckerman, Adrian A.S. and Ross Cranston (eds), *Reform of Civil Procedure: Essays on 'Access to Justice'*, Oxford: Clarendon Press, 327–345.

Rickman, Neil (1999), 'Contingent fees and litigation settlement', *International Review of Law and Economics*, **19**, 295–317.

Rickman, Neil and Alastair Gray (1995), 'The Role of Legal Expenses Insurance in Securing Access to the Market for Legal Services', in Adrian A.S. Zuckerman and Ross Cranston (eds), *Reform of Civil Procedure: Essays on 'Access to Justice'*, Oxford: Clarendon Press, 305–325.

Rosenberg, David and Steven Shavell (1985), 'A Model in Which Suits are Brought for Their Nuisance Value', *International Review of Law and Economics*, **5**, 3–13.

Santore, Rudy and Alan D. Viard (2001), 'Legal fee restrictions, moral hazard and attorney rents', *Journal of Law and Economics*, **44**, 549–572.

Schäfer, Hans-Bernd (2000), 'The Bundling of Similar Interests in Litigation. The Incentives for Class Action and Legal Actions taken by Associations', *European Journal of Law and Economics*, **9**, 183–213.

Schwartz, Murray L. and Daniel J.B. Mitchell (1970), 'An Economic Analysis of Contingent Fee and Personal-Injury Litigation', *Stanford Law Review*, **22**, 1125–1162.

Shavell, Steven (1982), 'Suit, Settlement, and Trial: A Theoretical Analysis Under Alternative Methods for the Allocation of Legal Costs', *Journal of Legal Studies*, **11**, 55–81.

Shavell, Steven (2004), *Foundations of Economic Analysis of Law*, Cambridge, Massachusetts: The Belknap Press of Harvard University Press.

Snyder, Edward A. and James W. Hughes (1990), 'The English Rule for Allocating

Legal Costs: Evidence Confronts Theory', *Journal of Law, Economics, & Organization*, **6**, 345–380.
Thomason, Terry (1991), 'Are Attorneys Paid What They're Worth? Contingent Fees and the Settlement Process', *Journal of Legal Studies*, **20**, 187–223.
Van den Bergh, Roger J. and Louis T. Visscher (2008), 'Optimal Enforcement of Safety Law', in: Richard D. de Mulder (ed.), *Mitigating Risk in the Context of Safety and Security. How Relevant is a Rational Approach?*, Rotterdam: Erasmus University Rotterdam, 29–62.
Van Velthoven, Ben C.J. and Peter W. van Wijck (2001), 'Legal Cost Insurance and Social Welfare', *Economics Letters*, **72**, 387–396.
Verbond van Verzekeraars (2005), *Verzekerd van Cijfers. Dutch Insurance Industry in Figures*, www.verbondvanverzekeraars.nl/Cijfers/Verzekerd van Cijfers/ Cijfers 2005.aspx. Accessed on 27 July 2010.
Verbond van Verzekeraars (2009), *Verzekerd van Cijfers. Dutch Insurance Industry in Figures*, www.verbondvanverzekeraars.nl/UserFiles/File/cijfers/VvC2009. pdf, accessed 27 July 2010.
Williams, Philip L. and Ross A. Williams (1994), 'The Cost of Civil Litigation: An Empirical Study', *International Review of Law and Economics*, **14**, 73–86.

3. No cure, no pay and contingency fees

Michael Faure, Fokke Fernhout and Niels Philipsen

1. INTRODUCTION

In many European countries lawyers are prohibited in one way or another from charging fees on the basis of the outcome of the case. Such prohibitions can be found in statutes as well as in codes of conduct of law societies and comparable organizations. These prohibitions are mostly rooted in a firm belief that lawyers – especially lawyers who represent their clients in litigation, like solicitors and barristers – can only maintain their independence and can only serve justice if their private interests are not in any way affected by the outcome of a case (Faure, Fernhout and Philipsen 2009, p. 19).

However, recent developments show that conflicting points of view are adopted by those responsible for policy in matters with European implications. On the one hand, the object of attaining free competition and free movement of services is responsible for an impulse towards abolishing all restrictions on lawyers' fees, as was reflected in 2004 in the Report on Competition in Professional Services issued by the European Commission (COM 2004, 83, 9 February 2004).[1] Apparently, according to the European Commission, lawyers' fees should be liberalized and unimpeded by state and professional regulations. On the other hand, the Council of the Bars and Law Societies of the European Union (CCBE) still requires its member organizations to proscribe the 'quota pars litis' agreement and has its doubts about 'no win no fee' agreements (for a precise definition of these terms see below). If these regulations are state-controlled and in the public interest, they fall, for the time being, within the ambit of restrictions on free competition allowed by art. 81 EC.[2]

These clashing views find their counterpart in the great variety of regulations on lawyers' fees that can be found in the Member States of the European Union. Although in most cases some restrictions on result-based compensation exist, the scope and contents of such prohibitions are to a large extent rather divergent. Still they have in common that adopting those rules usually was the outcome of a fierce debate on the possible undesirable effects of allowing result-based fees. In the recent past, such discussions took place in, for example, England and Wales, Germany, France, Ireland and the Netherlands. This debate was in most cases fuelled by cutbacks on legal aid, since access to justice could be assured to a certain extent if 'no cure no pay' agreements were allowed.

In the European debate on whether or not to allow (particular forms of) result-based fees for lawyers, a whole variety of arguments has been presented in favour or against the use of result-based fees. From the Dutch debate[3] the following – sometimes conflicting – arguments in favour and against could be derived:

Arguments 'against', related to the due administration of justice
1) Lawyers who represent parties in litigation occupy a special position, since they have a (more or less) exclusive right to represent clients in court. This entails a double duty; to act in the interest of their clients and to act in the interest of justice, and hence the necessity of a double independence. Therefore, lawyers should not have a personal financial interest in the outcome of the case.
2) Contingency fees could harm the lawyer-client relationship, since clients will not know if their lawyers are acting out of self-interest or not. In addition, it will be difficult for clients to know if fees are reasonable, since they lack the information needed to estimate their chances to win. Therefore it is not unthinkable that clients will not trust their lawyer anymore.
3) Lawyers who took bad decisions under contingency fee arrangements (thus losing cases and lacking income) might be tempted to resort to illicit practices to compensate for the loss.

Arguments 'against', related to (consequences of) access to justice
4) Result-based fees are no cure for the access to justice problem. Lawyers will still refuse to take on weak cases on a contingency fee basis, because they do not want to take the financial risk of starting a procedure in those cases (especially since in the Netherlands damages are only awarded in moderate amounts).
5) Weak cases have a risk of being taken to court too easily, since there is no financial incentive for clients to refrain from starting a procedure.

Arguments 'against', related to economical consequences
6) Fees in general will rise, since lost cases have to be covered by the cases won. The only possibility for compensating lost cases is raising fees.
7) Lawyers will tend to increase their clients' claims in court, which might lead to an undesirable change in case law in personal injury cases.
8) Lawyers will be tempted to advise settlements sooner, thus trying to earn their fees by working less than the case normally would require.
9) Contingency fees only work if the opponent is well-resourced and the case is such that there is a reasonable prospect of recovering costs.
10) Insurance companies may become an easy prey for indigent plaintiffs who

realize that settlements will be accepted if cost recovery is impossible, thus starting frivolous procedures.

Arguments 'in favour', related to the due administration of justice
1) The existing practice of charging on an hourly rate might tempt lawyers to work more than necessary; it is better to replace this by a fixed result-based fee.

Arguments 'in favour', related to (consequences of) access to justice
2) Allowing result-based fees will guarantee access to justice for the 'sandwich class', that is, those who are too wealthy for free legal aid but not wealthy enough to finance a personal injury case they might lose.
3) Allowing result-based fees will strengthen the position of personal injury victims with regard to insurance companies, since they will no longer refrain from taking the insurance company to court for financial reasons.
4) By introducing result-based fees, weak cases will no longer be accepted by lawyers. By all means, the risk of losing the case should not be too great for a lawyer. This means that courts will deal with stronger and better cases and no time will be wasted on hopeless claims.

Arguments 'in favour', related to economical consequences
5) Claim agents are not subject to any kind of regulations. They are not restricted in concluding fee agreements and lawyers should therefore be permitted to compete with them in this market.
6) Forbidding contingency fees favours insurance companies, since they will have to deal with a smaller number of claims.

However, the validity of these arguments is hardly ever tested. Therefore this chapter, after devoting Section 2 to definitions of the various types of result-based fees, examines the regulation of lawyers' fees and more particularly result-based fee arrangements from an economic perspective (Section 3). Next is a comparative overview of the regulations concerning result-based lawyers' fees in eight European countries and Hong Kong, the latter being included because of its remarkable experiment of financing legal aid by a Supplementary Legal Aid Scheme based on contingency fees charged by a governmental institution (Section 4). In Section 5 the results of this comparative overview of rules on result-based fees will be evaluated in the light of economic theory. Section 6 presents some concluding remarks.

2.   DEFINITIONS

In legal literature, as well as in politics and in legal practice, different definitions have been used, sometimes implicitly, in the discussion of result-based fees. The rather liberal use of concepts such as 'contingency fees', 'no cure no pay', 'no win no fee' and 'success fees' may give rise to many misunderstandings. Therefore it is important to first define these concepts in more detail, as they will be used throughout this chapter.

In relation to the question of which fees can be charged by a lawyer, two possible scenarios can be distinguished: either a case is won or it is lost. The concepts 'no cure no pay' and 'contingency fees', taken according to their meaning in ordinary language, refer to only one of these scenarios. Nevertheless, by using these terms the speaker usually implies something about the other scenario, without expressly saying so. A debate about result-based fees thus risks being infected by misunderstandings.[4]

Here we will limit ourselves to the four main forms of result-based fees, although in practice variations are possible. In the negative scenario (that is, when a case is lost), result-based fee agreements between lawyers and their clients either stipulate no fee at all, or a fee that is moderated to an amount that is lower than the ordinary fee but still allowed under domestic law. In the positive scenario, a lawyer winning his case could be entitled to a percentage of the outcome or to an uplift on top of the ordinary fee. In every particular case, parties to the agreement have to agree on the exact amounts and percentages. In addition to any form of contingency fee agreements, the lawyer sometimes agrees to fund part of the costs, like court fees, expert expenses and other disbursements.

The following terms will be used throughout this chapter to indicate the four forms of result-based fees. In the negative scenario, 'no cure no pay' (NCNP) appears to be the term that is most frequently used to indicate what it says.[5] 'No win less fee' (NWLF) describes the situation when still some fees have to be paid even if the case is lost. In the positive scenario, the Latin term 'quota pars litis' (QPL) is often used for a fee as percentage of the sum that will be recovered.[6] A 'success fee' designates a mark-up (bonus), either in the form of a flat fee or in the form of an additional percentage to the ordinary fee (which might be a flat fee or a fee according to an hourly rate).

Departing from these definitions, a *contingency fee agreement* can then be defined as a combination of NCNP and QPL.[7] A *conditional fee agreement* (CFA) will be used for any combination of NCNP and a success fee, being a special case of a contingency fee agreement.[8] The combination of NWLF and QPL or an unrestricted success fee will be called the *Dutch agreement*,[9] even though it can be found in France as well.

3.   A LAW AND ECONOMICS ANALYSIS

Various studies of result-based fees can be found in the law and economics literature that analyses the regulation of professional services, such as legal services. On the one hand, there are studies that analyse the behaviour of players in the market for legal services (lawyers, plaintiffs and defendants). Key questions in this branch of literature are, for example, whether lawyers, as a result of contingency fees, are encouraged to invest more or fewer hours in a case, and whether they have more or fewer incentives to settle out of court. On the other hand, there are studies that are aimed predominantly at the volume of litigation and hence analyse the question of whether result-based fees increase access to justice by removing wealth barriers or even lead to a so-called claims culture (Stephen and Love 1999, p. 1001).

3.1 Conflicts of Interest

Generally one may expect that a lawyer who bears his own costs and who is driven by self-interest will accept a settlement offer sooner – and for lower amounts – under a NCNP system than under an hourly fee system. After all, by settling the case he can save on costs (including time invested in cases) of further bargaining and costs of an additional procedure in court. By demanding a low amount, the lawyer can furthermore encourage the defendant to accept the settlement offer (see also Miller 1987 and Gravelle and Waterson 1993). There is hence a potential conflict of interest between the lawyer and his client, because the net proceeds received by the lawyer equal his fee (hourly or result-based) minus his costs, while the client's net proceeds equal the settlement or court award minus the fees paid to his lawyer. This potential conflict of interest has given rise to some criticism on contingency fee systems.

One should realize, however, that also under an hourly fee system a conflict of interest arises, albeit in the opposite direction. A lawyer who bears his own costs and who is driven by self-interest will be less inclined to accept a settlement offer under an hourly fee system, because he is paid by the hour. Moreover, the validity of all the arguments presented here strongly depends on the degree to which a lawyer actually places a greater weight on his own interests than those of his client (see, for example, Gravelle and Waterson 1993).[10] If lawyers behave altruistically, the argument that contingency fees would lead lawyers to settle cases earlier and for lower amounts than their clients would desire, will not apply at all. Rickman (1999, p. 306) moreover states that contingent fees 'need not be dismissed for giving lawyers self-interested incentives: in some circumstances, this may be exactly what their clients need'. In a more intuitive study, backed by limited empirical research, Barendrecht and Weterings (2000) conclude that working exclusively on the basis of fixed fees has strong negative effects on the administration of justice.

Rickman (1999) shows that in a dynamic setting the argument that contingency fees lead to (too) early settlements does not apply. He argues that instead of considering one-shot models, one should take into account that there are several periods of bargaining and that contingency fees and litigation costs interact. In Rickman's model, lawyers can behave strategically if they have private information about the case and thereby have the opportunity to influence future periods of bargaining. By signalling to their opponents that they are confident in winning a case, this may result in a rejection of low settlement offers. Rickman calls this 'hard bargaining'. The final result is unclear, because bargaining costs produce strategic influences that work in opposite directions. Polinsky and Rubinfeld (2002) also cast doubt on the argument that lawyers would settle sooner and for lower amounts under a contingency fee system, but for different reasons. They show that it could well be that the argument does not apply because a lawyer working under QPL would spend an inadequate amount of time on a case, if it were to go to trial. This lowers the expected cost to the defendant if the case goes to trial and makes him less likely to accept any given settlement demand. Once that effect is taken into account, lawyers could have insufficient motives to settle, which is exactly the opposite from the commonly believed argument mentioned earlier.

Naturally, it is important also to take into account the degree of information asymmetry between lawyers and their clients.[11] If a client is well-informed and therefore less dependent on the assessment of his lawyer, the problem of a potential conflict of interests in the settlement phase is much less serious. After all, a client can refuse any settlement offers proposed by his lawyer. Stephen and Love (1999, pp. 1002–1003) argue that well-informed clients, such as organizations, are likely to prefer an hourly rate over a fixed fee. The authors refer in particular to Kritzer (1990), who reported that for a sample of tort and contract cases, 81 per cent of the fee contracts were on an hourly basis when the client was an organization, whereas 59 per cent of the fee contracts were on a contingency basis when the client was an individual.

All of this may lead us to conclude that the actual effects of the introduction of contingency fees are hard to predict. Rubinfeld and Scotchmer (1993) investigate how QPL can allow lawyers to signal the quality of their advice and clients to signal the quality of their cases. They argue – in line with the study by Kritzer mentioned above – that a client with a high-quality case is willing to pay a relatively high fixed fee and a relatively low contingency percentage. The opposite applies for a client with a low-quality case. High-quality lawyers, on the other hand, would signal their abilities by working for a relatively high contingency percentage. In the Rubinfeld-Scotchmer model the information asymmetry is hence of two types: not only might lawyers be better informed about their own abilities than prospective clients, also the clients themselves might be better informed about the facts of the case and the prospects for recovery. There are high-quality and low-quality cases, and there are high-quality lawyers and low-quality lawyers. The central question is then which type of information asymmetry is more important in practice. The authors conclude that abolishing or limiting NCNP and QPL 'could lead to a reduction in the number of low-quality cases filed as well as the number of cases taken by high quality attorneys' (Rubinfeld and Scotchmer 1993, p. 355).

A complicating factor is moral hazard. This particular principal–agent problem would occur in the market for legal services if a lawyer offers (additional) services that a client would not have bought if he would have had perfect information, or when he spends more hours on a case than would be considered necessary (efficient). Also a client could withhold information about a case (see, more generally, Philipsen 2007, pp. 114–115).

Summarizing this (predominantly theoretical) literature[12], it seems safe to conclude that one fee system is not by definition better than the other in giving the right incentives to both lawyers and clients. It all depends on the details of a particular case: how large is the information difference between lawyer and client; is it a high-quality case or a low-quality case; is there any risk of moral hazard on the side of the client; and is there any risk of moral hazard on the side of the lawyer?

3.2 Access to Justice and Claims Culture

An argument that has been used in the literature either in favour or against contingency fees is that they increase access to the judicial system. After all, a disadvantage of this increased access to justice might be that not only are liquidity constrained plaintiffs allowed to bring suit, but also that 'excessive' or 'frivolous' litigation is stimulated, because plaintiffs do not run any financial risks if a case is lost (apart from disbursements and litigation costs if these are excluded from the contingency fee agreement). When deciding whether to file a claim, financial matters then seem to be of no or at least less importance to these potential plaintiffs, although as noted this also depends on the question of whether additional experts will be hired to the case and whether any litigation costs have to be paid (which in turn depends on the existence or non-existence of a cost shifting rule). [13]

The risk of losing a case – and the corresponding financial losses – will under a contingency fee system be shifted, at least in part, from the client to the lawyer. Risk-averse and relatively poor persons, who have become the victim of a tort resulting in financial or bodily harm, would under an hourly fee system not (be able to) hire a lawyer, whereas under NCNP or QPL they would. In this respect it is generally assumed that lawyers are less risk-averse than clients, because they can diversify their business port-folio, whereas payoffs on individual cases are not correlated (except for class actions), and legal firms are typically organized as partnerships. This would make them better risk bearers (Gravelle 1998, p. 383).

Politicians, as has been the case in the Netherlands (see for example Faure, Hartlief and Philipsen 2006), often refer to the high volume of litigation in the US, arguing on that basis that contingency fees lead to a 'claims culture', without presenting any further explanation or analy-sis of this claim (see also Chapter 8 by Hensler in this book). Although some economic models have indeed supported this argument, many other economic models seem to suggest exactly the opposite (Stephen and Love 1999, p. 1003), or at least state that hard conclusions cannot be drawn (see also Helland and Tabarrok 2003, p. 518). Miceli and Segerson (1991) argue that there would be an increase in the number of suits filed as a consequence of result-based fees only if the number of accidents is held constant (and given the existence of equilibrium contingency fees), but state that it is also possible that the number of suits will decrease. This would happen if the increased incentives for accident victims to sue lead to an increase in the level of care taken by potential injurers. They conclude therefore that 'under either strict liability or negligence, once injurer incen-tives are considered, there appears to be little theoretical justification for the common claim that contingent fees lead to excessive litigation' (p. 398). Also Danzon (1983) and Rubinfeld and Scotchmer (1993) conclude on the basis of their respective economic models that the number of claims filed could either increase or decrease.

Gravelle and Waterson (1993, p. 1219) conclude that it is 'impossible to predict a priori whether there will be more or fewer trials' and what will be the welfare effects on the parties involved (plaintiffs, defendants, lawyer and society), in case of a move from an hourly rate system to contingency fees.[14] Dana and Spier (1993) show that result-based fees may reduce the proportion of frivolous lawsuits, under the (likely) condition that lawyers are better able than their clients to assess the quality[15] of a particular case. A client who cannot convince a lawyer to take his case on a QPL basis, receives a strong signal that his case has a low chance of success and will hence be deterred from filing a lawsuit. In contrast, under a fixed-fee system 'weak cases may be brought more frequently by unscrupulous attorneys who seek to profit from their client's ignorance' (p. 365).

It is important in this respect to point to the fact that lawyers operate as 'gatekeepers' in the civil justice system. Obviously, it is not only the plain-tiff's expected value of a case that needs to be positive; this also applies for the lawyer's expected value of that case. Lawyers who act in their economic self-interest will hence decline weak claims (Kritzer 1997, p. 29 and Miceli 1994, p. 212). Kritzer (1997) presents the results of a survey of 511 contingency fee lawyers in Wisconsin, USA, showing that these practitioners 'generally turn down at least as many cases as they accept, most often because potential clients do not have a basis for their case'.

Helland and Tabarrok (2003), along with many other authors, stress that one should not only consider the number of cases going to trial, but also the average quality of these cases. On the basis of two datasets – a time-series analysis of medical malpractice claims in Florida and a difference in differences test of data on a cross section of states in 1992 – the authors conclude that contingency fees discourage the filing of low-quality suits (hence increase legal quality) and decrease the time to settlement. Apart from a strong reputation constraint, lawyers paid under an hourly fee arrangements have few incentives to refuse a low-quality case, contrary to the situation under QPL. Nevertheless, many states in the US nowadays have restricted the use of QPL, for example in medical malpractice cases. According to Helland and Tabarrok, such restrictions on the freedom to contract have resulted in a decrease in the quality of cases.

From the above it appears that economic models do not generally support the often-heard claim that contingency fees lead to a claims culture and 'American practices'. On the contrary, several arguments supporting the opposite conclusion are coming exactly from the American literature. It is very well possible therefore that contingency fees reduce the number of trials. It seems important in this respect to do more empirical research, as only a few of the studies mentioned above were able to do so on the basis of concrete data, which are often hard to find.

4.   A COMPARATIVE OVERVIEW

In Faure, Fernhout and Philipsen (2009) regulations on lawyers' fees in several European countries and Hong Kong are compared with respect to contingency fees. These countries (Belgium, Denmark, England and Wales, France, Germany, Greece, Ireland, Hong Kong and the Netherlands) are similar in so far as:

– they instituted a profession with the exclusive right to represent parties in court by appearing at audiences and conducting litigation;
– this profession is only open to lawyers or to persons who have passed special exams (or both);
– these lawyers with the right of audience have a double duty (protect the interests of their clients and serve the interests of some kind of overriding

objective to enable courts to deal with cases justly) and therefore need a double independence;
- they have State-made or State-controlled regulations on fee agreements for these lawyers;
- these regulations on fee agreements are not extended to other professionals who give legal advice.[16]

A quick scan of the regulations on lawyers' fees in these countries reveals a number of interesting differences. In this section we will briefly present the regulations in each of these countries. It should be noted that the restrictions on lawyers' fees are sometimes restrained to contentious lawyering, that is representing clients in court procedures. This will be indicated in the text and will be summarized in Table 3.1.

4.1   Belgium

Article 446ter of the Belgian Judicial Code (*Gerechtelijk Wetboek*) orders solicitors to charge fees 'with modesty and not exceeding a just moderation'. The provision adds that any fee agreement relating lawyers' fees to the outcome of the dispute is forbidden, which is taken to mean that 'no cure no pay' is not allowed either (Demeulenaere 1988, p. 4; Stevens 1997, p. 532).

The ratio of this rule could not be traced but is undoubtedly based on the dignity of the profession. The rule goes back to the first half of the 19th century. A leading Dutch solicitor of those days (when Belgium and the Netherlands were still one country) expressed what being a lawyer implied: 'A barrister should always keep in mind that nothing as vile, base and despicable can be thought of as being seen by his fellow citizens as a robed bird of prey, whom is consulted only with fear and terror, being afraid that his thirst for gold will induce him to every form of injustice' (Van der Linden, 1824, p. 45). This is in line with a prohibition of contingency fees.

Nevertheless, success fees are allowed in Belgium (Smets 2005, p. 51), but rarely applied.[17] This can be explained by the fact that lawyers' fees in Belgium are considered to be low. This probably also accounts for the remarkable combination of limited expenses on free legal aid, the absence of claim agents, the absence (until recently)[18] of a cost-shifting rule and a low density of legal aid insurance policies (which could be summarized as the Belgian paradox). Consequently, no trace could be found of a public discussion on lifting the ban on contingency fees, even though the Ministry of Justice declared that 75 per cent of the population cannot afford to litigate without having access to alternative funding (Report of the working group '*Rechten van slachtoffers*' (Victims' rights), *Belgische Senaat* 2002–2003, 13 March 2003, 2–1275/1, p. 23).

4.2 Denmark

In Denmark lawyers' fees are limited by statute to what is reasonable (Article 126(2) Judicial Code (*Retsplejelov*)). Reasonableness depends on all aspects of the case, which is thus explained that charging only a straight hourly rate for the hours spent on a case is not allowed (Gomard 2000, p. 185).[19] Thus, in all cases the hours spent have to be justified taking into consideration all circumstances of client and case.

The Bar Association supplemented this statute by its own regulations. Article 3.3.1 *Advokatiske Regler* (Rules for Lawyers) stipulates: 'A lawyer should not enter into a fee agreement leading to payment of a part of the outcome of the dispute (pactum de quota litis)'. This is to be interpreted literally, which means that 'no cure no pay', success fees and a percentage deal *after* concluding the case are still allowed (Gomard 2000, p. 185). QPL-agreements beforehand are considered to be incompatible with a lawyer's independence.

Although success fees and NCNP are allowed, it appears that these modalities are rarely applied in practice (Faure, Fernhout and Philipsen 2009, p. 46). This can be explained from the fact that 95 per cent of the Danish population are covered by a legal aid insurance,[20] whereas free legal aid is available up to an income per annum of €50 000 for a family with two children (Faure, Fernhout and Philipsen 2009, p. 45).

4.3 Germany

Lawyers' fees in Germany are set by the Federal Lawyer Ordinance (*Bundesrechtsanwaltsordnung*, BRAO) and the Law on Lawyers' Fees (*Rechtsanwaltsvergütungsgesetz*, RVG). These statutes provide for a detailed system of obligatory fees, parting from a basic amount and a case-dependent factor. There is little room for freedom of contract.

Formerly, para 49b(1) BRAO contained a prohibition of almost all result-based fees: 'Agreements that make fees dependent on the outcome (*Erfolgshonorar*) or that entitle the lawyer to part of the result are void.' Reasons put forward for this prohibition are the lawyer's independence, the risk of lawyers pursuing illicit means and the consideration that commercial profits should not be a motive for lawyers (*Bundesgerichtshof* (Federal Supreme Court) 15 December 1980, *J. Z.* 1981, p. 204). There was just an exception for agreements on an increase of the statutory fee (para 49b s.1 BRAO), which made success fees acceptable.

These provisions were contested in a procedure before the German Constitutional Court, which ruled that they are incompatible with the constitutional right to free enterprise if there is no exception for special cases in which a contingency fee agreement would give access to justice (*Bundesverfassungsgericht* (Federal Constitutional Court) 12 December 2006, 1 BVR 2576/04). Consequently, the Law on Lawyers' Fees was changed as of 1 July 2008. A new para 4a RVG makes an exception for clients who would not have access to justice without entering into a contingency fee or any other result-based fee agreement. The agreement should mention the fee to be paid under a normal agreement and the reasons for which a contingency fee agreement has been concluded. If the case is won, the client should pay an uplift (success fee or otherwise). Other costs than lawyers' fees (like court fees) are to be excluded from the agreement.

4.4 England and Wales

For a long time champerty (the ancient English term for speculating on the outcome of a procedure by means of a fee agreement) and maintenance (the ancient English term for funding procedures in order to get a profit) were forbidden by statute (Statute of Westminster (1275), 3 Edw. c. 1). Excessive costs of funding free legal aid led to the green paper *Contingency fees*, which discussed several possibilities to use market mechanisms (free competition) to realize access to justice with no or few public expenses. Government and Parliament opted for what was dubbed 'conditional fee agreements' (CFAs): a combination of NCNP and a success fee in the form of an additional percentage based on the usual hourly rate or a flat fee.

The Courts and Legal Services Act 1990 (Article 58) lifted the ban on CFAs. The Conditional Fee Agreement Order 1995 allowed CFAs for personal injury cases, bankruptcy cases and human rights cases under the European Convention. The success fee was limited to a maximum of 100 per cent of what would have been agreed without NCNP. The Law Society advised to limit the success fee to a maximum of 25 per cent of the amount received by the client (Zander 2002, p. 266).

A 1997 survey showed no abuse (Yarrow 1997). Success fees were limited to 43 per cent on average of the normal hourly rate, whereas only 29 per cent on average was claimed. The total of lawyers' fees did not exceed the 25 per cent of the client's profit as advised by the Law Society (Yarrow 1997). After another consultation paper *Access to Justice with Conditional Fees*, CFAs were extended to almost all cases (Conditional Fee Agreements Order 1998). The right to legal aid was restricted to procedures that could not be funded under a CFA (Access to Justice Act 1999).

Since CFAs can be part of a cost order (Article 58A(6) Courts and Legal Services Act 1990), case law shows which uplifts are considered to be reasonable. Blackstone 2004, p. 53, mentions: 12.5 per cent for traffic accidents before trial; 20 per cent for medical negligence cases; 50 per cent for accidents in general (like tripping and slipping); 63 per cent for work-related accidents; 100 per cent for traffic accidents that go to trial, fatal work-related accidents and intellectual property cases.

A final remark must be made for a clear understanding. The prohibition of champerty and maintenance has always been strictly related to contentious lawyering. Outside of legal procedures, no restrictions are or have been in force. This distinction can be found in other countries as well.

4.5 France

In France fee regulations only see to contentious lawyering. Article 11 of the 1971 Law on the reform of certain legal professions (*Loi portant réforme de certaines professions judiciaires et juridiques*) forbids every agreement on fees as part of the judicial outcome, unless it is supplementary to the ordinary fee (success fee). In practice, this restricted kind of result-based fees (the 'Dutch agreements') are usually expressed as a percentage (10 per cent is mentioned on websites) of the outcome.[21]

Since success fees should always be combined with ordinary fees, these fees may not be such that the agreement should materially be qualified as NCNP (*Prés. Tribunal de Grande Instance de Dijon* (President of the Appeal Court of Dijon), ord., 15 February 1996, Gaz. Par. 1996, 2, 501). This is basically the same rule as is applied in the Netherlands.

Recently, the French Senate started a discussion to introduce CFAs based on the English model (*L'aide juridique, Étude de législation comparée* 137, July 2004). The Bar was opposed to the idea, claiming to fear the trust clients should have in their lawyers will be harmed (Conseil National des Barreaux, *Rapport d'étape de la Commission Accès au Droit et à la Justice,* 10 September 2005, p. 24 and p. 33). In the end, art. 37 of the Law on Legal Aid (*Law relative à l'aide juridique* (91–647)) was changed to allow lawyers to chose between legal aid and profiting of the costs order against the losing party.

Changes in the French system in the near future are unlikely. The Commission Darrois, installed in 2008 to advise inter alia on the question in which way legal aid should be organized, did not even mention the possibility of allowing outcome-related fees in its final report (Commission Darrois 2009).

4.6 Greece

Rather unexpectedly, Greece is the most liberal of the countries examined. Article 92(3) of the Solicitors Act (Κώδικας Δικηγόρων) allows contingency fees, only limiting them to a maximum of 20 per cent of the outcome and excluding disbursements. If a QPL-agreement regards labour income, it should be reported to the local Council of Lawyers (which seems to be a very wise provision).

Free legal aid is practically non-existent, since it is only available for the very poor (Article 194 Code of Civil Procedure). Nevertheless, claim agents do not operate on the Greek market. This corresponds with the fact that contingency fees are widely used (Kerameus & Kozyris 1993, p. 297).

4.7   Ireland

The Irish take a different view of the matter than their English counter-part. Whereas NCNP is part of the legal tradition (under the name of 'no foal no fee'), QPL (percentage charging) is considered to be unethical in contentious matters according to Article 68 of the Solicitors (Amendment) Act 1994. The same rule applies for barristers (Article 11 Code of Conduct for the Bar of Ireland). The idea is that costs should be covered by the losing party without any additional profit for the winning lawyer (Minister of Justice in Parliament, Seanad Éireann, Vol. 140, 6 July 1994, p. 2092). Although success fees are allowed, no instance could be found of lawyers actually charging them (Faure, Fernhout and Philipsen 2009, p. 76).

Ireland is the only country in which theory and practice seem to differ to a considerable degree. In Parliament, MPs complain that nothing is done to maintain the prohibition of champerty and maintenance, which has not been contradicted by the Minister of Justice (Dáil Éireann, Vol. 533, 3 April 2001, pp. 1618–1619). Some case law shows that this prohibition does not apply in all cases (*Fraser v. Buckle*, Supreme Court of Ireland, [1996] 1 IR 1). Moreover, a statistical analysis of personal injury cases tried in court has revealed that the actual height of lawyers' fees could only be explained by assuming that a flat fee plus a percentage of the outcome had been charged, in spite of the prohibition of contingency fees.[22] Nevertheless, the rules seem set to remain unaltered in the near future.

4.8   The Netherlands

According to Dutch fee regulations, result-based fees are very restricted. The regulations provide for a general prohibition except for bulk cases (debt collection) and the Dutch agreement (see above, Regulation on Outcome Related Fees of 26 June 2002, Dutch Official Journal 4 July 2002, p. 125 and p. 128). The latter was and is rarely used, partly because many lawyers are not acquainted with this possibility, which can only be found in the disciplinary court's case law (*Hof van Discipline* (Disciplinary

Court) 9 February 1998, No. 2472, *Advocatenblad* (Lawyers' Journal) 1999, p. 346; Hof van Discipline 13 July 1998, No. 2589, *Advocatenblad* 1999, p. 514).

Cuts on legal aid and the high costs of personal injury cases favoured the emergence of claim agents who proposed to fund these cases under a contingency fee agreement. For more or less selfish reasons – seeing half of their cases being taken away by these claim agents (Faure, Philipsen and Fernhout 2008) – the Dutch Bar Association (*Nederlandse Orde van Advocaten*) decided therefore on a five-year experiment, allowing contingency fees in personal injury and death cases if the client is not entitled to legal aid and liability is denied or difficulties in assessing the amount of damages or causation are foreseeable (Amendment of the Regulation on Outcome Related Fees of 25 March 2004, *Advocatenblad* 2004, pp. 313–316).

This experiment could never be put into practice, since the Minister of Justice vehemently opposed it. The regulation was first suspended (Royal Decree of 15 September 2004, *Stb.* 480) and then quashed (Royal Decree of 9 March 2005, *Stb.* 123). This was accompanied by a debate in and outside of Parliament on the reasons why contingency fees should be forbidden or allowed, which led the minister to appoint a commission to report on these (and other) matters.

In its report *Een maatschappelijke orde* (A Social Bar), published in 2006, this commission advised maintaining the prohibition of NCNP, but allowing CFAs, disregarding the fact that the Dutch agreement already permitted QPL-agreements and thus condemning them without realizing that they were already part of Dutch legal practice. The success fee should be limited to a 100 per cent uplift. The State Secretary of Justice followed the advice and asked the Dutch Bar Association to prepare an experiment under conditions more or less similar to those of the experiment quashed two years earlier (*Kamerstukken II* (Parliamentary Proceedings) 2007–2008, 31200 VI, nr. 93, letter of the State Secretary of Justice of 4 December 2007). This meant that CFAs should only be allowed in cases in which liability is denied or difficulties in assessing the amount of damages or causation are foreseeable. In this way the government intended to respect the wish of Parliament to take measures to guarantee the lawyers' independence and to prevent 'cherry picking' (*Handelingen II* (Acts of Parliament) 27 June 2007 and 3 July 2007 (Resolution Vroonhoven-Kok)).

Although one would expect that the Bar Association only had to copy the experimental regulation adopted earlier (but limiting it to a 100 per cent uplift above the ordinary hourly fee), it immediately announced that doing what the Ministry of Justice wanted would take some time. A survey was commissioned to one of the authors of this paper and Professor of

Civil Law, T. Hartlief, to advise on the economic and legal consequences of the experiment as proposed by the State Secretary. The outcome was crushing. Apart from some other criticisms, the main line of the advice was clear. If one forces lawyers only to take on difficult cases, thus limiting the average chance of winning to something below 50 per cent, you cannot ask them to restrict their success fees to 100 per cent. After all, basic calculations will show that they will always lose money in the end and therefore will refuse to take on cases on this basis.[23]

The advice made the Dutch Bar Association decide to stop the development of the experiment, which was announced to Parliament on 13 October 2008 (Appendix to Acts of Parliament II 2008–2009, p. 276). The Secretary of State promised to make a profound study of the matter. Nothing has been heard since.

4.9 Hong Kong

Although the countries studied above offer a wide variety of regulations, the picture emerging is that in many countries QPL-agreements are considered to be unethical or at least offer an ethical risk. The Special Administrative Region Hong Kong with its common law background is no exception. In contentious matters, litigating lawyers do not have the right to enter into contingency fee agreements or any other form of result-based fees (Article 4.16 Hong Kong Solictor's Guide to Professional Conduct; Article 124 Code of Conduct of the Hong Kong Bar Association).

However, litigating in Hong Kong is very expensive, especially in personal injury cases. An average procedure is estimated at HKD1 000 000 (approximately €100 000) on lawyers' fees alone (Faure, Fernhout and Philipsen 2009, p. 82), which is a huge sum compared to the €10 000 that one would have to spend in the Netherlands. Unfortunately, state-funded legal aid is only available for litigants with yearly incomes up to about €20 000, according to the Legal Aid Ordinance (LAO). From these figures it is clear that without contingency fees most personal injury victims cannot afford to go to court.

In Hong Kong this problem is resolved by introducing the Supplementary Legal Aid Scheme (SLAS, Article 5A LAO). According to this scheme, for some types of cases (such as personal injury cases and industrial accidents) the 'sandwich class' – those who do not qualify for legal aid but cannot afford the costs of civil proceedings – can apply for legal aid under SLAS if their yearly income is less than HKD 432 900 (Schedule 3 LAO). After a means and merits test the case is taken on by the Supplementary Legal Aid Fund (SLAF) on a contingency fee basis. The SLAF pays all costs (disbursements and lawyers' fees) and receives a percentage of the outcome if the case is won. The contracts with lawyers (solicitors and barristers) are concluded by the SLAF according to the existing rules on an hourly rate basis. Thus, the scheme benefits from the advantages of contingency fees without having to change lawyers' fee regulations.

This scheme turns out to function satisfactorily. The costs are covered by the small contributions paid by the applicants and the revenues of cases that are won.[24] Only the costs of the fund itself (housing, staff) are paid by the government. The applicants pay only a maximum of 12 per cent of the outcome of the case, which has been reduced to 5 per cent for settlements out of court and 10 per cent for all other cases in 2008 (Faure, Hartlief and Philipsen 2007, p. 84). This seems to justify the conclusion that the SLAS succeeds in profiting from the advantages of contingency fees (access to justice) while avoiding its disadvantages (effects on the legal assistance market) without paying the cost of a large sacrifice from the winning party.

The success of the SLAS inspired the Hong Kong Law Reform Commission to propose an extension of the scheme. The only cases to be excluded are criminal cases, family cases concerning children, defamation cases and cases in which no financial relief is sought. The contingency fee agreement with SLAF should be notified to the opposing party (see Faure, Hartlief and Philipsen 2007, p. 87).

5. EVALUATION

The findings of this quick scan can be summarized in a table (see Table 3.1). The abbreviations used in this table refer to, respectively, no cure no pay, success fees, quota pars litis, and conditional fee agreements. A Dutch agreement is defined as a combination of quota pars litis and a basic fee; Contingency fees are defined as a combination of quota pars litis and no cure no pay. The first sign in each cell stands for non-contentious matters, the second sign for contentious matters. The 'plus' means that the fee modality of that column is allowed, the 'minus' means that that fee modality is forbidden. If the sign is placed between brackets, the modality concerned is only conditionally allowed.

Table 3.1 shows that the rules vary enormously. There is no fee modality that is forbidden in all countries or is allowed in all countries in all circumstances (contentious or non-contentious matters). Only England and Ireland seem to have the same regulations, but in fact they differ in theory and in practice. Ireland for instance permits agreeing on a success fee, but in practice no lawyer ever uses this possibility.

These findings are in line with the unpredictability of the consequences of prohibiting or allowing result-based fees, as has been shown in the

Table 3.1   Results of quick scan

Country\Fee	NCNP	SF	QPL	CFA	Dutch agreement	Contingency fees
Belgium	–/–	+/+	–/–	–/–	–/–	–/–
Denmark	+/+	+/+	–/–	+/+	–/–	–/–
Germany	(+)/(+)	(+)/(+)	(+)/(+)	(+)/(+)	(+)/(+)	(+)/(+)
England/Wales	+/+	+/+	+/–	+/+	+/–	+/–
France	+/–	+/+	+/(+)	+/–	+/+	+/–
Greece	+/+	+/+	+/+	+/+	+/+	+/+
Ireland	+/+	+/+	+/–	+/+	+/–	+/–
Hong Kong	+/–	+/–	+/–	+/–	+/–	+/–
Netherlands	–/–	+/+	(+)/(+)	–/–	+/+	–/–

research in the field of law and economics. Indeed, Section 3 made clear that economic-theoretical literature has indicated that a potential conflict of interest can arise under NCNP systems, but that a conflict of interest, although in the opposite direction, may also arise under an hourly fee system. The economic literature therefore does not necessarily favour one fee system to the other. Empirical research was often concentrated on the claim that contingency fees lead to a claims culture, but that claim was not supported by the empirical research. It should hence not come as a surprise that the way in which result-based fees are regulated (and used) in practice also shows a great deal of variety. Given the uncertainties in (both theoretical and empirical) economic literature one can therefore also hardly conclude that one system is necessarily better than the other.

Nevertheless it can be concluded that contingency fees in relation to contentious lawyering are in most countries considered to be undesirable. Only Greece permits them in all circumstances, but in this case the percentage to be charged is limited to 20 per cent, disbursements cannot be included and some charges have to be paid anyway.

Even though it could be concluded that contingency fees in relation to contentious activities are often considered to be undesirable, the wide variety of fee regulations and unpredictability of their consequences might teach us that allowing contingency fees in order to secure access to justice, deserves a more than serious consideration. Germany recently 'made the first move', directly linking one with the other, and perhaps other countries will see that the risk is smaller than the benefits that could be obtained.

In many of the countries we examined the issue of result-based fees is in full evolution. Either recent changes took place or they are under discussion. A few countries recently allowed result-based compensation systems (Germany, England and France) although the reasons differ to some extent. In Germany, allowing contingency fees or any other result-based fee agreement is strongly related to providing access to justice to those clients who would otherwise not have access to a lawyer. Also in France allowing result-based fees was at the time strongly based on access to justice arguments. In England, on the other hand, CFAs were originally (in 1995) introduced on the basis of competition law arguments. Later the possibility of using CFAs was extended to almost all cases, again relating this directly to access to justice: the right to legal aid was restricted to procedures that could not be funded under a CFA. From an economic perspective especially the supplementary legal aid scheme from Hong Kong has the advantage that some of the potentially negative influences of NCNP and contingency fees on lawyers incentives are neutralized since lawyers are still paid according to the ordinary payment schemes. The SLAS can, however, make a specific result-based agreement with the client, which has the advantage that the legal system is not overburdened with cases that have no merit. However, in Hong Kong the lawyer has basically nothing to do with the fee agreement made between SLAS and the client and hence may not have any perverse incentive resulting from such a conditional fee agreement. Of course such a system can only work when there is a financial interest at stake (to pay for the lawyers fees) but may potentially have benefits for other legal systems as well.

6. CONCLUDING REMARKS

We started in our introduction by showing that in many legal systems the way in which lawyers are paid is apparently a hot issue that goes beyond the mere interests of the Bar itself: also politicians often intervene (for example prohibiting particular payment schemes) because they fear that when lawyers would have too great a stake in the outcome of the case this may negatively affect their incentives or have other negative effects for either the access to justice or the number of cases that would be brought to the judicial system. In the introduction we summarized the arguments in favour and against result-based compensation and noticed that many of these arguments are based predominantly on intuitive feelings, not backed by empirical research and sometimes even contradictory.

Since the confusion concerning result-based compensation for lawyers not only affects the argumentation in favour and against but also the terminology, we started in Section 2 by presenting a few definitions on how we use the various terms that express different modes of result-based compensation for lawyers.

It is important to stress these different definitions since they allow us to clarify that in fact some form of result-based compensation for lawyers is allowed in almost all legal systems. Whereas most legal systems (with the exception of Greece) have a negative attitude towards contingency fees in relation to contentious lawyering, they do often accept other forms of result-based compensation. The success fee especially is allowed in all European legal systems we examined. It is therefore noteworthy that many arguments that are often advanced against contingency fees or NCNP, would in fact also apply to success fees, which are allowed in most systems.

The widespread use of some form of result-based compensation for lawyers (even though the admitted modes vary substantially) also illustrates that the often-expressed fears that any form of result-based compensation for lawyers would lead to undesirable effects (perverse incentives to settle, increased number of cases, claims culture) are in fact ill-founded. In none of the countries examined, are result-based fees (to the extent that they are allowed) held responsible for whatever undesirable situation may occur. This is heavily underlined by the fact that none of the countries mentioned in this survey ever decided to come back on a decision to allow some form of result-based compensation.

Moreover, law and economics literature also substantially contributes to the debate. The empirical research provided by law and economic scholars may not provide clear indications in favour or against result-based compensation for lawyers (because a lot depends on the types of cases, clients and lawyers); theoretical law and economics research has rightly pointed at the fact that the hourly rate system (which is used in many countries) in fact generates substantial perverse effects for lawyers as well. Under that system lawyers have little incentives to settle and merely to produce as many billable hours as possible. This is an aspect that the critics of result-based compensation systems often seem largely to ignore.

It is, however, clear that many see an important advantage in result-based compensation systems as far as access to justice is concerned. It is argued that these types of compensation systems may more particularly be attractive for the so-called sandwich class. For them a result-based compensation system may, for example in a case of personal injury incident, substantially reduce the supposed risk and still allow access to justice. Moreover, in legal systems where result-based compensation systems are allowed it is often argued that these systems can increase access to justice and at the same time reduce the pressure on public budgets for legal aid.

One example of how on the one hand increased access to justice could be realized and on the other hand the potentially perverse effects of result-based compensation systems could be avoided originates from Hong Kong. Within the Hong Kong SLAS, lawyers are paid by the SLAS according to the common (hourly rate) payment system, but clients only contribute on a contingency basis, thus substantially reducing the risk for them. This is a model that may have benefits for legal systems in other continents as well and therefore surely deserves further attention.

NOTES

1. Subsequent reports expressed the same point of view. See the discussion in Europe, Philipsen 2007, pp. 122–125.
2. ECJ 19 February 2002, C-35/99 (Arduino and others); ECJ 19 February 2002, C-309/99 (*Wouters and others v. Algemene Raad van de Nederlandse Orde van Advocaten*).
3. Mainly to be found in Parliamentary Proceedings II 2004–2005, 29800 VI, nrs. 69, 109, 114, 132, and 159, and in the advice of the Counsel of State of 23 February 2005, W03.04.0633/I.
4. Especially the Dutch debate is polluted by incomprehensible terms. The terms are incomprehensible because English expressions are used, but with a most peculiar meaning. Thus in Dutch publications and discussions 'no win no fee' stands for CFAs (conditional fee agreements in the English sense; see below) and 'no cure no pay' stands for contingency fees (no cure no pay combined with percentage charging). In this chapter we use the meaning of the terms indicated in Section 2.
5. Variations are 'no foal no fee' (Ireland) and 'no win no fee' (UK).
6. Meaning literally 'a certain part of the case'. Also used is 'pars quota litis' or 'pactum de quota litis' (agreement about a certain part of the case).
7. Especially in an American legal context this is exactly what is meant by contingency fees.
8. This term is derived from the way it is defined in the United Kingdom.
9. There is no need to distinguish between these two, since no jurisdictions could be found in which one is allowed and the other is not.
10. The authors come to this conclusion on the basis of a theoretical model, adding that introducing NCNP does not only have an effect on decisions taken at the settlement stage, but at all stages of the litigation process, which further complicates the analysis. See also Rubinfeld and Scotchmer 1993, p. 344 for various references to papers that further analyse this problem, and Chapter 2 by Visscher and Schepens in this book.
11. See in this respect also the models in Rubinfeld and Scotchmer (1993) and Dana and Spier (1993). Information asymmetry here refers to knowledge about the law, legal procedures and favourable strategies.
12. In addition to the authors mentioned above, see also Danzon (1983), Miceli and Segerson (1991) and Helland and Tabarrok (2003) and references mentioned therein. This literature is also discussed in the next subsection.
13. This argument is also discussed by Stephen and Love 1999, p. 1003 and by Visscher and Schepens in Chapter 2 of this book.
14. In their model the concept of contingency fees also includes success fees (see Section 2 of this chapter for a definition). Gravelle and Waterson also take into account the level of care taken by potential defendants in order to prevent an accident. That is, their model considers more than the decision whether to go to trial or settle *ex post* (after the accident). The level of care is influenced by the type of contract between lawyer and client.
15. The authors use the word 'merits' instead of quality.
16. Here Greece is an exception. Article 92(5) Solicitors Act forbids everyone giving legal advice to enter into a contingency fee agreement unless he is a solicitor. Germany could be considered an exception as well, since legal advice may only be given by solicitors (*Rechtsberatungsgesetz*).

17. The Belgian Bar Association does not even mention the possibility on its website (<www.advocaat.be>, accessed 21 January 2009).
18. The cost-shifting rule was only introduced on 1 January 2008 (Article 1022 *Gerechtelijk Wetboek* (Judicial Code)). It provides for a scale of fixed amounts varying with the value of the case, with a lower and upper limit for special circumstances (Royal Decree of 26 October 2007 *tot vaststelling van het tarief van de rechtsplegingsvergoeding bedoeld in artikel 1022 van het Gerechtelijk Wetboek en tot vaststelling van de datum van inwerkingtreding van de artikelen 1 tot 13 van de wet van 21 april 2007 betreffende de verhaalbaarheid van de erelonen en de kosten verbonden aan de bijstand van de advocaat*).
19. It follows that no specification of hours worked is needed (Disciplinary Lawyer's Council (*Advokatennævn*), 4 July 2003, <www.advokatnaevnet.dk>, accessed 21 January 2009).
20. As stated by the Danish Bar Association on <www.advocom.dk>, accessed 21 January 2009.
21. This has expressly been allowed in *Cour de Cassation Civ. 1re* (First Civil Chamber of the Court of Cassation), 10 July 1995, JCP 1995, II, 22557.
22. €5,029 plus 15 per cent of the award for solicitors, €410 plus 2.3 per cent of the award for senior counsel. *Report of the Legal Costs Working Group*, Pn. A5/1816, Dublin: Stationery Office 2005, Appendix 2.
23. A similar discussion took place in the United Kingdom (Zander 2002, p. 266).
24. Hong Kong knows the 'costs indemnity rule', meaning that the losing party pays all costs (The Law Reform Commission of Hong Kong, Conditional Fees Sub-Committee, Consultation Paper, *Conditional Fees*, Hong Kong (September 2005, p. 7).

REFERENCES

Barendrecht, J. Maurits. and Wim C.T. Weterings (2000), 'Rechtshulp: Een Groot Goed met Schadelijke Bijwerkingen', *Advocatenblad*, **80**(12), 435–451.
Blackstone (2004), Plant, Charles (ed.), *Blackstone's Civil Practice*, Oxford: Oxford University Press.
Commission Darrois, *Rapport sur les Professions du Droit, Mission Confiée par le Président de la République,* 2009 (only published on the Internet, at www.justice. gouv.fr/art_pix/rap_com_darrois_20090408.pdf, accessed 27 July 2010.).
Dana, James D. Jr. and Kathryn E. Spier (1993), 'Expertise and Contingent Fees: The Role of Asymmetric Information in Attorney Compensation', *The Journal of Law, Economics, & Organization*, **9**(2), 349–367.
Danzon, Patricia M. (1983), 'Contingent Fees for Personal Injury Litigation', *The Bell Journal of Economics*, **14**(1), 213–224.
Demeulenaere, Bernadette (1988), 'Advocatenhonoraria, een consumentvriendelijk perspectief', *Tijdschrift voor Privaatrecht*, **25**(1), 1–29.
Faure, Michael G., Ton Hartlief and Niels J. Philipsen (2006), 'Funding of Personal Injury Litigation and Claims Culture: Evidence from the Netherlands', *Utrecht Law Review*, **2**(2), 1–21.
Faure, Michael G., Ton Hartlief and Niels J. Philipsen (2007), *Resultaatgerelateerde Beloningssystemen voor Advocaten: Een vergelijkende beschrijving van beloningssystemen voor advocaten in een aantal landen van de Europese Unie en Hong Kong*, Report for WODC/Dutch Ministry of Justice, Metro: Maastricht University.
Faure, Michael G., Niels J. Philipsen and Fokke J. Fernhout (2008), 'Het schaderegelingsproces vanuit rechtseconomisch perspectief' in Arno J. Akkermans,

Chris H. van Dijk and Siewert Lindenbergh (eds), *De kosten van het geschil*, 's-Gravenhage: SDU, pp. 65–92.

Faure, Michael G., Fokke J. Fernhout and Niels J. Philipsen (2009), *Resultaatgerelateerde Beloningssystemen voor Advocaten*, Den Haag: Boom Juridische Uitgevers.

Gomard, Bernhard (2000), *Civilprocessen*, Kopenhagen: Thomson.

Gravelle, Hugh (1998), 'Conditional Fees in Britain', in Peter Newman (ed.), *The New Palgrave Dictionary of Economics and the Law*, London: Macmillan, pp. 382–387.

Gravelle, Hugh and Michael Waterson (1993), 'No Win, No Fee: Some Economics of Contingent Legal Fees', *The Economic Journal*, **103**(420), 1205–1220.

Helland, Eric and Alexander Tabarrok (2003), 'Contingency Fees, Settlement Delay, and Low-Quality Litigation: Empirical Evidence From Two Datasets', *The Journal of Law, Economics, & Organization*, **19**(2), 517–542.

Kerameus, Konstantinos D. and Phaedon J. Kozyris (eds) (1993), *Introduction to Greek Law*, Deventer & Boston: Kluwer.

Kritzer, Herbert M. (1990), *The Justice Broker: Lawyers and Ordinary Litigation*, New York, US: Oxford University Press.

Kritzer, Herbert M. (1997), 'Contingency Fee Lawyers as Gatekeepers in the Civil Justice System', *Judicature*, **81**(1), 22–29.

Miceli, Thomas J. (1994), 'Do Contingent Fees Promote Excessive Litigation?', *Journal of Legal Studies*, **23**(1), 211–224.

Miceli, Thomas J. and Kathleen Segerson (1991), 'Contingent Fees for Lawyers: The Impact on Litigation and Accident Prevention', *Journal of Legal Studies*, **20**(2), 381–399.

Miller, Geoffrey P. (1987), 'Some Agency Problems in Settlement', *Journal of Legal Studies*, **16**, 189–215.

Philipsen, Niels J. (2007), 'The Law and Economics of Professional Regulation: What Does the Theory Teach China?', in Thomas Eger, Michael Faure and Naigen Zhang (eds), *Economic Analysis of Law in China*, Cheltenham, UK and Northampton, MA, US: Edward Elgar, pp. 112–150.

Polinsky, A. Mitchell and Daniel L. Rubinfeld (2002), 'A Note on Settlements Under the Contingency Fee Method of Compensating Lawyers', *International Review of Law and Economics*, **22**(2), 217–225.

Rickman, Neil (1999), 'Contingent Fees and Litigation Settlement', *International Review of Law and Economics*, **19**(3), 295–317.

Rubinfeld, Daniel L. and Suzanne Scotchmer (1993), 'Contingent Fees for Attorneys: An Economic Analysis', *The Rand Journal of Economics*, **24**(3), 343–356.

Smets, Dirk (2005), *Praktijkboek Marketing voor Advocaten*, Antwerpen: Kluwer.

Stephen, Frank H. and James H. Love (1999), 'Regulation of the Legal Profession', in Boudewijn Bouckaert and Gerrit De Geest (eds), *Encyclopedia of Law and Economics*, Cheltenham, UK and Northampton, MA, US: Edward Elgar, pp. 987–1017.

Stevens, Jo (1997), *Regels en gebruiken van de advocatuur te Antwerpen*, Antwerpen: Kluwer Rechtswetenschappen.

Van der Linden, Joannes van der (1824), *Redevoering over hetgeen de ondervinding van eene halve eeuw mij geleerd heeft, dat een advocaat voornamelijk behoort in acht te nemen, of te vermijden*, Amsterdam: P. den Hengst en Zoon.

Yarrow, Stella (1997), *The Price of Success: Lawyers, Clients and Conditional Fees*, London: Policy Studies Institute.
Zander, Michael (2002), 'Will the Revolution in the Funding of Civil Litigation in England Eventually Lead to Contingency Fees?', *DePaul Law Review* **52**(1), 259–297.

4. Financing and group litigation

**Sonja Keske, Andrea Renda and
Roger Van den Bergh**

1. INTRODUCTION

Group litigation is considered as having the potential to overcome the inefficiencies of private law enforcement by individual actions for damages, especially in cases where illegal conduct causes scattered damages for numerous victims, where the damage suffered by each individual victim may be small (Renda, Van den Bergh, Keske, Pardolesi et al. 2007, II.2.2). This is particularly true in fields such as antitrust, products liability, pollution, retail financial services, health services, and so on. In these and other fields, individual victims may lack information about law infringements and even about the damage suffered; and even if they do have enough information, they may still decide not to bring suit because of rational apathy, the risk of free-riding and the fear of having to bear huge upfront legal expenses (Renda, Van den Bergh, Keske, Pardolesi et al. 2007, II.2.2. See also Chapter 2 by Visscher and Schepens in this book), which greatly reduces the deterrence effect of actions for damages.

In group litigation, either an informed individual party or an association steps forward and initiates a proceeding. In this way, possible information deficiencies may be cured, the problems of rational apathy and free-riding may be mitigated, and costs may be shared by a group of plaintiffs, thus reaching economies of scale in litigation. For this reason, the need to ensure the availability of collective redress for consumers and businesses in some areas of law – most notably, private antitrust enforcement – has emerged as a hot topic in Europe in the past few years, with parallel initiatives being undertaken by the European Commission (DG Competition and DG Sanco) and a hectic debate taking place in some member states (Renda, Van den Bergh, Keske, Pardolesi et al. 2007, Section II.2).

However, a group action poses problems of its own. First, the party who takes the initiative to sue (a named plaintiff or an association) may pursue interests that are different from those of the victims as a whole (the so-called principal–agent problem, see Renda, Van den Bergh, Keske,

Pardolesi et al. 2007, Section II.2.2.2.1). Moreover, collective actions for damages may be initiated to inflict reputational loss on companies that may prefer early settlements instead of bearing the full cost of defending itself in court (so-called 'strategic' or 'abusive lawsuits'; see amongst others Rosenberg and Shavell 1985 and Bebchuk 1998). If the principal–agent problem and the risk of abusive suits cannot be overcome, the disadvantages of collective actions may well outweigh the benefits.

However, even if collective actions are socially desirable (as the net benefit is positive), victims may decide not to embark on such a challenging endeavour due to lack of funding or risk aversion. For this reason, appropriate funding and/or insurance mechanisms must be put in place to guarantee that socially desirable actions are initiated. On the one hand, to mitigate high risks a screening device which allows separating meritorious cases from unmeritorious cases is needed. Moreover, most plaintiffs will need a monetary incentive to initiate a proceeding. In the United States of America (US), contingency fees fulfil both functions. The lawyer selects the cases that are worth pursuing and bears the initial expenses (see also Chapter 8 by Hensler in this book). As a result, major obstacles to the decision of initiating a legal action are overcome.

The major problem with contingency fees is that they are not always allowed by the rules of the legal professions in many European countries. If states are not willing to change those rules, alternative screening devices and financing mechanisms must be developed to support the initiation of collective actions. Besides contingency fees as a way to fund group litigation, costs of collective actions may be borne by private insurance or public funds. Currently, common law countries offer the broadest spectrum of diverse financing options (see also Chapter 3 by Faure, Fernhout and Philipsen in this book).

On the other hand, in civil law countries an alternative way of financing collective actions is sought by giving standing to consumer associations. The latter approach comes close to public funding when membership fees are too low for financing the litigation costs and consumer associations rely mostly on funding by the government.

As neither collective nor representative actions are ways of financing group litigation in themselves, this chapter discusses four different ways to finance group actions: contingency fees (or conditional fees), private insurance, public funding and funding through representative actions by consumer associations. Particular attention is devoted to the impact of alternative funding mechanisms on the overall cost-benefit assessment of collective actions. Adequate funding should guarantee that legal action is taken when suing is in the social interest, so that problems of rational apathy and free-riding are overcome. At the same time, the funding mechanism should make sure that the interests of victims are properly protected and principal–agent problems are mitigated.

This chapter is structured as follows. Section 2 discusses the merits of collective actions. Representative actions are analysed in Section 3. Section 4 briefly introduces a general model of incentives to sue, which forms the basis for subsequent discussion of alternative ways of funding litigation when needed. Section 5 describes the impact of contingency and conditional fee arrangements in encouraging victims to file a damages action. Section 6 discusses private insurance mechanisms and comments on their current development in a number of jurisdictions. Section 7 comments on contingency-style public funds. Section 8 offers some concluding remarks.

2. COLLECTIVE ACTIONS

2.1 Advantages of Collective Actions

A major advantage of class or collective actions is the potential to overcome the problem of rational apathy, as argued in a seminal paper by Kalven and Rosenfield (1941). If individual damages are too small for plaintiffs to find it worthwhile to incur the costs of an independent legal claim, they will abstain from bringing a lawsuit. This advantage has meanwhile been acknowledged in a large number of papers (see, among others, Schäfer 2000, Micklitz and Stadler 2006). The increased willingness to bring suit is partially attributed to the cost-reduction effect for the plaintiffs who will be able to share the litigation costs, including the remuneration of lawyers and experts as well as the court fees (see for example Silver 2000, Rosenfield 1976). However, as will become clear in the following discussion, the problem of giving adequate incentives to individuals or lawyers to detect infringements and to initiate collective actions may still remain. Besides cost sharing, collective actions also allow risk spreading. If plaintiffs bundle their claims, the financial effects of losing the case are spread over all individuals participating in the collective action. Individual parties are better able to bear a small loss than a larger loss, so that the barriers to start a lawsuit are lowered. This will lead to more claims being filed and increase deterrence.

Empirical evidence in a study conducted by Eisenberg and Miller (2004) supports these insights. These authors found that costs of individual litigation and legal counselling decrease with an increasing number of participants in the class action. The argument is also supported in the field of American antitrust law by Duval (1976a and 1976b), who analysed class and non-class actions within a six-year period in the Northern District of

Illinois. The data suggest that class actions are a useful enforcement tool to enable cases that otherwise would not be brought due to the small size of the claims. There is also some evidence in Europe that the possibility of collective actions might overcome the rational apathy problem. According to a Eurobarometer survey conducted in 2004 and 2006, 67 or 74 per cent of European Union citizens, respectively, would be more willing to defend their rights before a court if they could join with other consumers who complain about the same issue (Eurobarometer 2004, Section 4, Eurobarometer 2006, p. 100). However, as the Eurobarometer is just a survey, it is risky to base policy conclusions on it since real life decisions (taken under budget constraints) may be different from hypothetical scenarios.

The overall impact of collective actions on the ability of overcoming rational apathy problems depends on the specific design of the collective actions. Collective actions may take different forms: they may be organized using an opt-in or opt-out mechanism. Compared to an opt-in mechanism (where harmed individuals have to explicitly express their wish to be represented in the collective action), an opt-out scheme (where harmed individuals will be represented, unless they express their wish to opt out) is superior in overcoming the rational apathy problem. Free-riding, in which a victim would wait for someone else to litigate first in order to use evidence or information gathered in the prior proceeding to save own litigation costs, could only be fully eliminated under a mandatory system, where no opt-out possibility is granted. Below, the three options (opt-in, opt-out, mandatory) are compared.

Even if an informed victim exists, who could act as lead plaintiff, she may still lack incentives to start collective actions, because opt-in collective actions will be initiated only if it is expected that a sufficient number of victims opt in after having been notified. On the one hand, victims who suffered a relatively large damage are likely to opt in, if the expected damage award is equal to or larger than the net damage award they could receive in individual litigation. On the other hand, victims who suffered small and widely dispersed damage may not have sufficient incentives to participate in an opt-in collective action. Consequently, incentives to sue may remain sub-optimal due to the remaining rational apathy of individual victims. Moreover, the prospect of having to share the risks and costs of the litigation (including defendants' costs under a loser-pays rule) may still impede decisions to opt in. Even though sharing of risks and litigation costs among those who opt in allows a decrease in these individual costs, one should keep in mind that the actual number of group members amongst whom the costs will be shared will be known only after the opt-in period has expired. Therefore, the potential named plaintiff may remain reluctant to initiate the proceeding, unless the risk associated with losing the claim is borne by another party, such as the attorney working on a contingency fee basis, an after-the-event insurance or a professional financier.

The level of deterrence may be increased by giving lawyers incentives to become actively involved in the detection of law infringements. This may be achieved if lawyers are paid on the basis of a contingency fee arrangement or receive a fee which increases with the total value of the claim. However, these benefits will not fully materialize in those EU jurisdictions that still prohibit contingency fees or limit advertising by lawyers. These anti-competitive restrictions will limit the lawyers' abilities to reach victims. Also, the free-rider problem will not be overcome in the case of an opt-in collective action. As only those members of the group that opt in are represented, free-riders may benefit from the collective action, if the judgment or settlement constitutes a prima facie case. Moreover, other victims who do not fit into the certified group may also free-ride on the outcome achieved in the collective action. Individual victims may thus delay the start of proceedings until they may free-ride on information revealed by the collective action.

Opt-out collective actions score better in terms of deterrence. First, the rational apathy problem will be much better overcome. Under opt-out, the group is larger from the outset and it seems reasonable to assume that opt-out rates will be low. Especially in cases of small damage amounts, victims are unlikely to opt out and start their own proceedings. Empirical studies in the US show that only few individuals make use of the opt-out option (Bertelsen et al. 1974, Willging et al. 1996, and Eisenberg and Miller, 2004). For example, Eisenberg and Miller (2004) found an average opt-out rate of less than one per cent. Hence, the number of individuals participating in the collective action will be larger than under an opt-in scheme. Given the larger group of victims, larger cost savings and better risk sharing will become possible. Secondly, individual parties who would like to free-ride on the decision must become active and make the effort of opting-out. Even though this formal requirement may have a negligible impact, a more important consideration is that victims who would not have joined an opt-in collective action (and would thus not have contributed to the costs of the trial) have incentives to stay in the group. In many cases of scattered losses, the individual losses of each victim are too small to make opting-out an attractive strategy. By staying in the group or class, the victim contributes to the costs of the lawsuit, but also has a higher chance of receiving compensation. By opting-out, the victim does not bear any costs, but given that her losses are only small, an individual suit is not worthwhile. Therefore, the possibility of free-riding does not appear to be a severe problem in cases of scattered losses.

If deterrence was the only goal, a strong case could also be made in favour of mandatory collective actions. As discussed above, opt-in collective actions have a limited potential to increase deterrence if only few victims decide to join. Under an opt-out scheme, the number of victims who decide to leave the group action may be low, but it is reasonable to assume that it will be those victims who expect a better outcome when pursuing individual litigation. As these may well be those plaintiffs with larger damages claims, their opting-out may have a negative effect on the overall benefits of the collective action. Deterrence will be negatively affected if the compensation claimed does not cover the entire societal damage, in particular the harm of those victims who suffered a large loss. The magnitude of the resulting inefficiencies will depend on a large variety of factors, including the individual values of the damages, the number of represented parties who remain within the group and the number of parties who opt out. A mandatory scheme avoids these inefficiencies and equally prevents free-riding. Under an opt-out scheme, the free-riding problem persists, in particular when individual parties expect higher damages in individual proceedings and opting-out is possible at a later stage of the collective action. An example is the Dutch system, under which victims can opt out after a contract regarding the compensation of harm between a foundation or association and the defendant has been declared binding by the court. Opting-out out can be done by free-riding victims who expect to receive a larger amount of compensation in an individual trial (Van den Bergh and Visscher 2008). Making collective actions mandatory would be an adequate remedy to both rational apathy and the remaining free-riding problem. However, this solution is usually regarded as contrary to the procedural rules of due process.

Beside the argument of increasing deterrence by facilitating private actions for damages, it is also argued that particular forms of group litigation bring benefits in terms of procedural efficiency. The litigation costs of collective actions are thought to be lower than the expenses that would be incurred if the same claims had to be tried in several individual proceedings. However, if we take a closer look at the procedural efficiency argument, it becomes clear that a more cautious analysis is required. The impact of collective actions on litigation costs has two sides.

On the one hand, the overall burden of litigation costs may largely be reduced as economies of scale can be exploited by filing a single law suit. It must be added that these cost savings are achieved only if several class members would otherwise have filed individual suits (Dam 1975). In reality, this will often not be the case since most small value claims would not have been brought in the absence of some form of group litigation. Another argument supporting the administrative efficiency of collective actions is the fact that these actions often lead to settlements. The large majority of US class actions are settled (Hensler and Rowe 2001, p. 138,

Bohn and Choi 1996, p.904). Similar experiences are reported from European countries. In Austria, most group actions (*Sammelklagen*)[1] settle (Pirker-Hörmann and Kolba 2006). In Sweden, six cases were brought under the Group Proceedings Act 2003 in the first three years and none resulted in a judgment. From a viewpoint of administrative efficiency, such a state of things may be desirable. Savings in litigation costs are one of the main motivations to settle. In cases of settlements, procedural requirements are lower and not all the merits of individual cases have to be evaluated and decided upon. However, as will be discussed below, early settlements may disadvantage individual parties and these losses may be larger than the savings in litigation costs. Optimal settlements should not only be cheaper but also provide parties the same expected net outcome as a trial. An economically ideal settlement avoids under-deterrence by keeping the amount of damages awards equal to what would have been obtained if the case had been pursued before the court. If this condition is met, settlements increase deterrence and save on overall and individual litigation costs.

On the other hand, it may be argued that collective actions are more expensive and time consuming than traditional individual litigation, since they demand additional legal controls that require a more active involvement of lawyers and judges (Miller 1998). Hence, the overall impact of collective actions on total litigation costs depends on whether the achieved economies of scale are sufficiently large to outweigh a more complex and potentially more expensive type of litigation. In addition, costs are incurred for the certification of the group and identification of group members. Compared to opt-in collective actions, opt-out schemes require an even more active involvement of lawyers and judges to manage the collective action. Litigation costs will be higher because the group will tend to be larger and the adequacy of representation will be even more difficult to assure, particularly when the victims are and may remain unidentified. Looking at the control mechanisms that have been developed in the US, the United Kingdom and Sweden[2], it may be assumed that a collective action will be more costly than an individual one-to-one litigation. In the US, Willging et al. (1996) provided evidence that class action proceedings take considerably longer than other trials and require more attention by the judge. Therefore, American commentators have proposed to introduce a cost-benefit analysis of class actions, to establish whether the costs of the trial would be justified (for an overview of this discussion, see Hensler et al. 2000, Chapter 15). These total cost increases have to be weighted against savings achieved by cost sharing and may also negatively influence the incentives for the named plaintiff to start a collective action when she is exposed to the financial risks involved.

2.2   Disadvantages of Collective Actions

It is clear from the above analysis that the potential efficiency savings from collective actions result from their ability to reduce rational apathy, but also information asymmetry and free-riding. To achieve these benefits, an individual victim should step forward and sue on behalf of an entire group of harmed parties. Since information gathering, preparing litigation and suing is a costly and risky business, some attractive financial award should be made available to compensate for the expenses made and the risks taken. Given such constraints, it is more likely that the initiative to bring a collective claim is taken by a law firm, which is better able to bear risks. From this perspective, it can be easily understood why class actions in the US are brought by attorney-entrepreneurs who hope to make a profit out of their risky investment. The person bringing the lawsuit can be seen as the agent who will act on behalf of the represented principal(s). This, however, implies that curing the noted inefficiencies (information asymmetry, rational apathy, free-riding) comes at a (potentially large) cost: the principal–agent problem.

Typical for principal–agent relationships is that the interests of the agent do not coincide with the interests of the principals. The resulting principal–agent problem is the consequence of the limited ability of the represented parties to monitor and control the conduct of the representing party. These problems become more serious as the number of represented parties increases and their interests are less homogeneous (see Coffee 1995, Macey and Miller 1991, Koniak 1995, Schäfer 2000). Compared to traditional litigation, the most significant feature of the US class action is that plaintiffs usually exercise virtually no control over the proceeding. Conflicts of interest already arise between the lead plaintiff and the (potentially numerous) passive group members, who may have different preferences. Even though US law requires that the named plaintiff is an adequate representative of the absent class members and his interest is typical of the entire class, 'the named plaintiff is nothing but a figurehead to begin with' (Miller 1998, p. 259). In reality, the case is controlled by an attorney acting as an entrepreneur, who makes a substantial investment hoping to obtain a generous fee in the event that a judgment is rendered or the case settles. The principal–agent problem is exacerbated if the attorney is the driving force, rather than the named plaintiff. Incentives of attorneys to litigate or settle can change dramatically in the context of aggregate litigation and control mechanisms are needed to align the interests of the class members with those of the attorney (see Miller 1987).

The principal–agent problem that arises in class actions is twofold. First, the lawyer may conspire with the defendant and deprive the plaintiffs of their full remedy through a collusive settlement between the wrongdoer and the attorney to share the proceeds among themselves (Harel and Stein 2001). Second, the lawyer may reduce his efforts below the appropriate level for securing the plaintiffs' rights. The principal–agent problem manifests itself in different ways depending on the lawyer's payment scheme (see Chapter 2 in this book and also Polinsky and Rubinfeld 2002). Under an hourly arrangement, the lawyer does not have a personal interest in maximizing the value of the judgment or the settlement, apart from reputation concerns. However, in markets characterized by serious information asymmetries (such as legal services) the principal–agent problem cannot be overcome by competitive pressure and reputation building (Schäfer 2000). Contingency fee arrangements may be seen as a valuable mechanism by which lawyers can reveal their quality to clients, thus reducing the seriousness of the principal–agent problem (see Chapter 2 as well as Chapter 3 in this book).

In the legal literature, concerns about inadequate representation seem to be corroborated by findings that most class actions lead to settlements. However, a large settlement rate is not necessarily a bad thing, as was explained above. However, settlements in class actions that resulted in gains to attorneys at the expense of the class members in US proceedings are found in studies by Rosenfield (1976) and by Hensler et al. (2000). A prominent example of the principal–agent problem is the discussion about coupon settlements in the US. These are cases where the class action settlement provides the victims with low-value coupons for price reductions on further purchases from the defendant instead of damage payments and the high attorney's fee is calculated on the basis of the total value of coupons (Bronsteen 2005). The perceived abuse of coupon settlements to the detriment of the class was one of the reasons for the Class Action Fairness Act 2005 (Roedder 2006).

The principal–agent problem in collective actions persists if there is no adequate monitoring. In individual cases where the plaintiff has an immediate interest in the case, she will spend some resources in monitoring the attorney, which limits the agency problems. In class actions not even the named plaintiff will have an incentive to monitor the attorney if her interest in winning the case is low. This will be even more true for the other members of the class and especially for the victims who do not even know that they will become a member of the class at a later stage (Silver 2000). If the class members' interests coincide with those of the lead plaintiff and the latter is able to monitor the attorney, the principal–agent problem could be reduced to a tolerable minimum. However, in US class actions attorneys act via a nominal client and pursue the case on behalf of silent plaintiffs. Moreover, the principal–agent problem is exacerbated by an opt-out scheme. Under an opt-in scheme a minimum of effort and interest by the represented parties is still guaranteed. Conversely, under an opt-out scheme, the group of silent plaintiffs is larger and more heterogeneous; many victims may not even be aware of the proceeding.

Collective actions also give rise to the concern that they may enhance the risk of unmeritorious cases, which are brought in order to extract an early settlement (for a formal model see Rosenberg and Shavell 1985). The risk of frivolous suits is substantiated as follows. Defendant firms may prefer an early settlement if this costs them less than the sum of the losses of handling the case in court. The latter losses consist of the attorney's fees (which in the US must be paid by the defendant irrespective of the outcome of the case), the harm to the company's reputation and the intra-company diversion costs (costs spent on the lawsuit that cannot be used for other purposes). The size of these losses creates scope for abuse if the suing attorney can easily pressure the defendant to pay damages (parts of which are paid to him under the contingency fee arrangement), because for the company the amount of this payment is lower than the costs of defending itself in court. Contingency fees may reduce the incentives to file unmeritorious suits, since trial costs will be high and expected fees should be lower.

Empirical research on the topic is not conclusive. Hensler et al. (2000) studied ten cases composed of consumer class actions and mass tort class actions, to find out whether the alleged disadvantages, such as frivolous suits, disproportional benefits for lawyers compared to plaintiffs and larger transaction costs than benefits to the class, had any merit. The results of the empirical studies were ambiguous, but hinted at some problems regarding the adequacy of representation. Willging et al. (1996) reported mixed findings when trying to assess the frequency of strike suits, but excluded cases with opt-in procedures. In the field of securities law, the concern about unmeritorious suits is corroborated by Bohn and Choi (1996), who found that most of the class actions analysed were frivolous in nature and targeted mainly at large firms. Similarly, Choi (2004) discussed three major problems concerning class actions in the field of securities litigation, namely frivolous suits, focus on large companies as targets and agency problems, using several studies conducted in that area and evaluating their results. He concludes that evidence suggests the presence of frivolous suits and that the introduction of the Private Securities Litigation Reform Act of 1995 in fact reduced the number of frivolous suits, as intended by the Congress, although also cases with merits may have been discouraged.

Different solutions have been suggested in the law and economics literature to mitigate the principal–agent and frivolous suit problems, which may materialize to different degrees in all forms of group litigation. A full discussion of these would be beyond the scope of this chapter, but the basic mechanisms should be mentioned here nevertheless.[3] These remedies can be divided into three broad categories: i) restoring control by class members, for example regulation on the choice of the lead plaintiff or strengthening the rights of class members, ii) judicial review of the merits of the case, the terms of the settlement and the amount of the contingency fee, and iii) auctions, either forwarding the full proprietary right in the action to the winning party and compensation of class members through the auction bid, or auctions determining the lawyer to represent the class, losing his fee when he fails to recover the amount promised in the auction.

Overall, though having the potential to reduce some obstacles of traditional litigation, the previous analysis shows that collective actions in themselves do not constitute a perfect solution to the problems connected to the financing of litigation. After discussing representative actions in the next section, this chapter will also analyse other possibilities for financing group litigation.

3. REPRESENTATIVE ACTIONS BY CONSUMER ASSOCIATIONS

Also representative actions can be seen as a method to overcome financial difficulties of individual victims by entrusting the group litigation to an association endowed with funds enabling it to bear the litigation costs. The European Commission promotes actions by associations as a promising alternative to US-style class actions. In the White Paper on Damages Actions for Breach of the EC antitrust rules (COM(2008) 165 final), the European Commission proposes: 'representative actions, which are brought by qualified entities, such as consumer associations, state bodies or trade associations, on behalf of identified or, in rather restricted cases, identifiable victims. These entities are either (i) officially designated in advance or (ii) certified on an ad hoc basis by a Member State for a particular antitrust infringement to bring an action on behalf of some or all of their members' (European Commission 2008, 165 final, p. 4). Representative actions brought by consumer associations may be considered also as an enforcement mechanism for violations of rules of consumer law. The need for an efficient collective redress mechanism in both areas of law is evident, since losses of victims are often widely spread and of too low a value to make individual claims worthwhile. However, if representative actions do not overcome the funding problem the efficiency benefits of group actions cannot be achieved.

The analysis of representative actions is largely similar to that of class actions, but differs in some respects. Representative actions may involve substantial costs and expose the consumer associations to high risks – potentially without corresponding gain. In Europe, the funding problem is exacerbated by the 'loser pays' rule (English Rule),[4] which forces the plaintiff to bear the defendant's costs in the event that the claim is unsuccessful. Hence, it is to be expected that lawsuits will not be brought if the costs of proving an infringement are high and the chances of success are low. Contingency fees may be a mechanism to guarantee the necessary screening of cases and make it possible to contain the risks of litigation. Attorneys can use their legal expertise for assessing the value of claims and invest effort in cases which offer the largest expected benefits for the victims of law infringements. They can also achieve risk-spreading by handling numerous lawsuits of unequal value. If bank financing is required, attorneys may get loans at better rates than their clients. Contingency fee arrangements thus permit attorneys to overcome liquidity problems that can make it impossible for individual consumers to pursue their rights (Issacharoff and Miller 2008, p. 19).

Merely from the perspective of funding, representative actions by consumer associations seem a less than optimal subsitute for American-style class actions. The hope is that consumer associations are better able to bear the costs and risks of legal proceedings than individual consumers. However, if consumer associations lack adequate funding they will refrain from bringing representative actions. There seem to be three different ways to solve or alleviate the funding problem: i) guaranteeing that the costs can be financed out of the consumer association's own budget, ii) reducing the costs of litigation if the plaintiff is a consumer association, or iii) allowing the consumer association to take a share of the expected recovery.

Even though consumer associations may have an own budget, it is doubtful that the financial means will suffice to generate an optimal amount of litigation activity. If the budget is financed out of membership fees paid in advance, enough funding will not be available if the members of the association prioritize other activities and are not willing to pay a higher fee to finance litigation expenditures. For (prospective) members the hope of an uncertain share in future damages recovery will seldom be a sufficient incentive to pay the additional costs. The membership fee can be seen as an insurance premium (Van den Bergh and Visscher 2008, p. 20) that low-risk consumers are not willing to pay. The more often the consumer association brings claims the higher the membership fee has to be in order to cover the costs of the proceedings and the fewer consumers may decide to become members. If claims for damages are financed out of membership fees, consumers may be deterred from becoming a member if they expect only a small loss, as is the case with scattered harm caused by price-fixing agreements or deceptive indications of quantity on food products.

If membership fees cannot generate a sufficiently large budget, the question arises of who will fund the consumer associations. Apart from donations received from private sponsors, an obvious candidate to provide funding is the government. If claims are brought on behalf of consumers at large, the argument in favour of using public funds is strong. Successful lawsuits also benefit non-members of the association who may take a free-ride on the association's efforts. Using taxpayers' money can be defended as a solution to the free-riding problem and a way to guarantee that cases are brought when this is in the interest of consumers as a whole. Germany offers an example of far-reaching public funding. The national consumer association (*Verbraucherzentrale Bundesverband*) is almost entirely financed by the federal government and regional consumer centres are financed by the state governments. Between 2000 and 2005, the former association brought, on average, no less than 450 actions for injunctions in areas of unfair competition law and standard contract terms. These are two fields of law where the number of individual lawsuits is likely to remain insufficient for reasons of lack of information, rational apathy and free-riding. Hence, government funding may go a long way in overcoming lack of financial incentives to initiate litigation.

However, government funding is not a miracle solution. To start with, governments also have limited budgets and consumer associations may not receive a part that is sufficiently large to become active in several fields of law (not only consumer law but also competition law) and cover all risks of litigation. Because of tight budgets, consumer associations may still refrain from bringing meritorious suits. In addition, financing by the government makes the consumer associations vulnerable to capture by politicians who may pursue an agenda that does not necessarily coincide with the economic interests of consumers. Politicians may also try to influence the association's behaviour by encouraging or discouraging particular lawsuits (Issacharoff and Miller 2008, p. 21). The resulting loss of independence may cause agency problems and lead to efficiency losses that outweigh potential benefits from curing the funding problem.

If the consumer association's budget is too small and sufficient government funding is not available, one can no longer avoid looking for other ways to reduce the costs of legal actions or making the initiation of proceedings financially more attractive. On the cost side, both court fees and the English Rule may impede the initiation of representative actions. In its White Paper on antitrust damages the Commission has suggested to 'set court fees in an appropriate manner so that they do not become a disproportionate disincentive to antitrust damages claims' (European Commission 2008, 165 final, p. 10). This, however, may be a too-conservative approach that will not effectively stimulate representative actions. The UK Office of Fair Trading has suggested that in representative actions it may be appropriate to cap the liability of 'specified bodies' (including designated consumer associations) for the defendant's cost at zero (OFT Discussion Paper 2007, at paras 8.11–8.18). One step further is to exempt consumer associations entirely from paying court fees and attorneys' fees and finance these costs out of the state budget, as is the case in Spain (Ashurst Study 2004, executive summary on Spain). The maintenance of the English Rule is usually seen as the biggest hurdle to overcome. Apart from the funding problem, the question arises of whether reducing costs and risks of litigation would be enough to induce consumers associations to bring more claims, or if further incentives are necessary.

It may be doubted that consumer associations' actions are motivated only by altruistic ideals and that pecuniary incentives are unnecessary. Reduction of court fees and moderation of the English Rule reduce the costs and risks of the litigation but do not make it financially attractive to bring lawsuits. Experiences in both France and Germany show that consumer associations do not use their rights to initiate legal proceedings in the interests of consumers as a whole if they get no financial benefit from their efforts (Ashurst Study 2004, country reports on France and Germany). To stimulate group litigation, national laws allowing claims for damages could include a rule entitling the association to receive a part of the damages award. Alternatively, states could prefer to give discretion to judges to decide which part of the damages award will flow to the association that brought the lawsuit. However, both options would be nothing else than a contingent fee by another name, even if its precise size would be subject to court approval in the latter scenario. At the end of the day, it would be wise for European jurisdictions to re-assess the strict prohibition on contingency fees (see Chapter 3 in this book).

Contingency fees also seem to score better as a device to overcome principal–agent problems than representative actions. Associations of consumers are expected to have a staff of dedicated people, who will more actively look into the behaviour of firms than individual consumers would be willing to do. It is generally believed that in deciding whether to bring a lawsuit, consumer associations may be less directly motivated by monetary profits, as these gains can generally only be used for achieving the purpose of the organization and not for private purposes. However, there are many reasons to doubt that representative actions are an easy escape route out of agency problems. The seriousness of the principal–agent problems will depend on i) the extent to which the members can control the consumer association, ii) the possibilities of the consumer association to control the lawyer acting on its behalf, and iii) the possible influence of third parties on the consumer association (Schäfer 2000, p. 198).

If membership fees have to be used for financing litigation, the cases to be pursued may be selected according to their potential to attract media attention, and subsequently new additional members. The choice of cases may thus be distorted by expected gains of the consumer association or its managers, who place personal benefits over the interests of the members. It must also be doubted whether European consumer associations will be able to avoid being captured by lawyers. If a consumer association collects members' claims on an ad hoc basis, the picture is not very different from the US class action, where the initiative to collect claims and prepare litigation is taken by an attorney. Agency problems become most serious if the association can sue on behalf of consumers at large. Particularly in cases of widespread losses, members have little control over the association, which may be influenced by political groups or groups with a moral concern. The interests of the latter groups may reflect ideological considerations that do not coincide with the economic interests of consumers. In conclusion, consumer associations may be well suited to bring a representative action if: i) the members control the association; ii) the association, in turn, is able to monitor the lawyer; and iii) the impact of political or ideological groups is negligible. Only if all these conditions are satisfied will consumer associations serve as perfect agents for their principals.

Hence, the question arises of how agency problems caused by representative actions brought by consumer associations can be contained. In the US, several remedies have been developed to mitigate agency problems in class actions (see also Chapter 8 in this book). They include auctions, regulatory measures and judicial control. The belief that representative actions pose fewer problems may divert the attention away from such remedies without providing effective alternative solutions. To guarantee that consumer associations are really representative, national laws contain a number of requirements regarding their credibility, reputability and commitment to acting in the collective interests of consumers. It may be doubted that such a light-hand control is sufficient. More emphasis should be put on the possibilities of members to actually control the decisions of the association (granting 'voice' to individual consumers). States should also create a competitive environment for consumer associations (granting individual consumers the possibility of 'exit'). In many states, consumer associations that are funded by the government enjoy a near-monopoly and dissatisfied consumers have no possibility of joining a rival association. Competition between consumer associations is an important instrument in reducing agency problems.

In conclusion, representative actions by consumer associations, unless organized in a way that provides adequate incentives and financing possibilities, seem less effective than collective actions financed by contingency fees. In the latter case financial incentives are given to initiate proceedings and agency problems may be mitigated in different ways. In the former case, the incentive to sue may remain suboptimal and agency problems cannot be easily solved.

4. A GENERAL MODEL OF LITIGATION INCENTIVES

In order to show the effects of different fee arrangements and fee shifting rules (which both have been discussed by Visscher and Schepens in Chapter 2 of this book), we will first introduce a basic model of litigation incentives. In the law and economics literature, a victim's decision to sue is normally framed as the result of an *ex ante* cost-benefit comparison (Landes 1971, Gould 1973, Posner 1973, Shavell 1982), or – according to more recent literature – as an investment decision (Cornell 1990). Accordingly, such a decision is the result of a rational initiative undertaken by individuals or companies seeking a positive payoff.

Assume that the prospective costs for a plaintiff are the opportunity cost of time spent in litigation (OC_t) or settlement (OC_s), costs of access to courts (AC) and – depending on the fee allocation rule chosen – legal costs for litigation (LC_t) and settlement (LC_s). Expected rewards are the damages claimed (D), times the probability of winning at trial (w), and the expected settlement amount (S), times the probability to settle the claim before trial $(1 - p)$.[5] The plaintiff will then sue whenever

$$p[wD - (OC_t + LC_t + AC)] + (1 - p)[S - (OC_s + LC_s)] > 0 \quad (4.1)$$

where $OC_s < OC_t$; $LC_s < LC_t$; and $S < D$.[6] In other words, the plaintiff's net expected reward from filing suit has two main components: the reward from settlement and the reward from trial. The relative weight of these two components, of course, depends on the (perceived) likelihood of settlement and trial. The plaintiff's decision to sue depends *in primis* on his subjective perception of p, w and S. With imperfect information, the plaintiff may overestimate the probability of winning at trial (w), or make a mistake in estimating the probability of settling the case $(1 - p)$. This can occur, for example, whenever the plaintiff expects the defendant to agree on the likelihood of plaintiff victory; whereas, in reality, the defendant expects a different outcome – that is, the parties are both optimistic about the trial outcome. Accordingly, the defendant's expected reaction is important for the plaintiff's decision. If the defendant signals his nature of 'tough negotiator', the plaintiff may overestimate p, and may refrain from suing in order to avoid a costly and lengthy litigation.

In this chapter, we look mostly at the impact of alternative ways of funding litigation – that is, we look at ways to reduce the $(LC_t + AC)$ component of formula (4.1) above. It must be explained, at the outset, that this component also heavily depends on the fee allocation scheme chosen (see Chapter 2, in this book). Based on the formula (4.1) above, it is easy to show that fee allocation schemes and funding schemes can exert a significant impact on the plaintiff's incentive to sue (see also Hughes and Snyder 1995, 1998, Shavell 1982, Braeutigam et al. 1984, Reinganum and Wilde 1986, Katz 1990, Cornell 1990, Kaplow 1993, Bebchuk 1996, Polinsky and Rubinfeld 1996, Spier 1997, Hylton 2002 and Wagener 2003).

For example:

- A one-way fee-shifting rule increases incentives to sue, as it reduces LC_t and AC in the equation. The claimant would indeed be exposed to these costs only if he loses, and losing would not mean having to pay also the opponent's legal expenses.
- All means of funding private litigation increase the probability that the plaintiff will sue, as they reduce or eliminate LC_t and AC.
- Contingency fees do not have a direct impact on LC_t and AC, but they reduce the overall distribution of LC_t: as a matter of fact, the victim will pay LC_t only if he wins at trial: the amount to be paid may be greater than under alternative fee arrangements in this case, but will drop to zero if the lawyer loses the case.

5. CONTINGENCY FEES, CONDITIONAL FEES AND FEE SHIFTING RULES

5.1 Contingency Fees

The merit of contingency fees has been extensively analysed in the literature, especially as a way to overcome the obstacles of financing the litigation when the liquidity of plaintiffs is constrained (see Schwartz and Mitchell 1970, Gravelle and Waterson 1993, Rubinfeld and Scotchmer 1998, Schäfer 2000 and Chapter 3 in this book). This occurs because the lawyer bears the initial expenses, and as a result the plaintiff can avoid paying legal expenses upfront – the latter being one of the major obstacles to the decision of initiating a legal action. More generally, the literature has analysed: (i) contingency fees as a way to share the risk between the client and the lawyer; (ii) the impact of contingency fees on litigation expenditure and lawyer's incentives to settle the case; and (iii) the impact of contingency fees on incentives to file strategic lawsuits.

As has been shown by Visscher and Schepens in Chapter 2 of this book, the literature is split as to the impact of contingency fees on the litigation expenditure, on the settlement rate and on the quality of the lawsuits filed by plaintiffs. On the one hand, most authors agree that contingency fees can significantly facilitate plaintiffs in initiating legal actions. As has been shown above, that is especially true in the case of collective actions. The named or lead plaintiff may hesitate to initiate a potentially more complex proceeding, if it is uncertain how many other victims may be involved and he is exposed to the financial risk or has to pre-finance the litigation. On the other hand, lawyers are likely to be more interested in contingency fees based on a larger total value of several claims, than in the contingency fee that may be earned in just one individual proceeding.

Despite the great attention that both fee allocation schemes and contingency fees have elicited among scholars, the interrelation between the two has been explored only to a very limited extent. As observed, amongst others, by Katz (2000), one obvious effect of a contingent fee agreement on the incentives to file suit, settle and litigate is the different management of risk under an English Rule. Such a loser-pays rule increases the risk associated with litigation, thus increasing the probability of early settlement if the litigating parties are risk-averse. If the parties can allocate part of the risk to their lawyers, two-way fee-shifting becomes less scary. In the most extreme case, a plaintiff may think that, if he loses the trial, he may be called to pay only the defendant's (reasonable) expenses, and not his own; whereas, if he wins, he would be indemnified from paying either expense. Of course, this finding completely changes the plaintiff's incentives during litigation, with an outcome similar to that of a one-way fee-shifting rule.

In other words, the main problem that arises under an English Rule – that is, that risk aversion of plaintiffs may be exacerbated, thus leading to scant incentives to file suit – may be mitigated by the use of a contingent fee system.

Dewees, Prichard and Trebilcock (1981) conclude that, especially in the case of class (collective) actions, rules that place the risk on lawyers are more suited to encourage litigation, especially under the English Rule. In addition, rules that are based on contingent fee agreements are more likely to encourage litigation: as a matter of fact, low-probability cases would not be taken on board by lawyers based on a fixed fee, unless such fee is particularly high. With a contingent percentage fee, especially in high-stakes, low-probability cases, lawyers may have an incentive to accept the case in view of a future reward, which may easily exceed the value of the time they spend in litigation or in settling the case. Farmer and Pecorino

(2004) warn that a combination of contingent fee agreements and (two-way) fee-shifting may lead to more negotiation failures at the settlement stage, in turn leading to more cases being litigated.

More generally, we can illustrate the effect of contingent percentage fee schemes on the plaintiff's incentive to file suit and settle. In addition to the model described above, we introduce another variable – the effort of the client's lawyer. If θ is the percentage of the final reward that accrues to the client's lawyer as a result of the contingent fee, our formula of the net expected plaintiff payoff from litigation becomes the following, under an 'each party bears her own costs' rule (American Rule):

$$p\,(wD - \theta D) + (1 - p)(1 - \theta)S > 0 \qquad (4.2)$$

In other words, the reward if the case is litigated (with probability p) depends on the probability of winning the case (w) and the size of the damage award (D), minus the percentage to be paid to the lawyer (θD).[7] If the case is settled (probability of $1 - p$), the settlement amount will be discounted by the lawyer's percentage payment.

Under the English Rule, the formula would become:

$$p\,(wD - (1 - w)\,\theta D) + (1 - p)(1 - \theta)S > 0 \qquad (4.3)$$

and the 'trial part' of the equation would be composed by the expected damages award at trial ($p \cdot w \cdot D$) minus the need to pay legal expenses for the other party's lawyer – here, for simplicity, considered as equal to the plaintiff's lawyer fees.

Finally, under one-way fee-shifting, the plaintiff files suit if:

$$pwD + (1 - p)(1 - \theta)S > 0 \qquad (4.4)$$

as in all cases the plaintiff would not have to pay his legal expenses – better, if the plaintiff wins, the damage recovery would cover legal expenses; if he loses, the contingent fee agreement with risk falling on the lawyer would lead to no payment.

Under these conditions, the plaintiff's expected payoff from trial will always be higher under the English Rule than under the American Rule, and will be highest with one-way fee-shifting.[8]

In addition,

- with the American Rule, the net expected reward from filing suit is greater under a contingent fee arrangement if the fixed legal expenses (X) are greater than θD;

- with the English Rule, the net expected reward from filing suit is greater under a contingent fee arrangement if the fixed legal expenses (X) are greater than half of θD, thus $X > \theta D/2$;
- with one-way fee-shifting, the net expected reward from filing suit is always greater under a contingent fee arrangement.[9]

In summary, under our very simple assumptions, fee-shifting rules tilt the balance in favour of contingent fee arrangements when seen from the perspective of plaintiffs. Under the English Rule, the cases in which the plaintiff will prefer a contingent percentage fee agreement are twice those under the American Rule. As appears obvious, with one-way fee-shifting, the plaintiff will always choose a contingent fee arrangement: if he wins, his lawyers will be paid on top of the damage award; if he loses, he will not have to pay his lawyers. In this respect, it can be easily seen that contingent fees mitigate the plaintiff's risk aversion, by allowing him to overcome his reluctance to sue in low-probability cases. If coupled with one-way fee-shifting, contingent fee arrangements can lead to 'full insurance' for the plaintiff, thus potentially encouraging frivolous and strategic suits. However, as pointed out by Miceli (1994) and Kritzer (1997), the lawyers themselves will act as gatekeeper in these cases, by turning down cases when the probability of winning is too low.

5.2 Contingent v. Conditional Fees

The main problem related to contingent fee agreements is the fact that such agreement are explicitly prohibited in virtually all member states, and *pactum quota litis* is not allowed by the ethical code of the European association of lawyers (see Chapter 3 in this book). However, some EU member states – starting with the UK already in the 1990s – have started allowing conditional fee agreements or 'no win, less fee' agreements, meaning agreements under which the plaintiff lawyer can obtain a success fee on top of the initial legal fee of up to 100 per cent if the client wins. The lawyer takes all the risk and, in case the client loses, the lawyer is responsible under the English Rule for both sides' costs.

A recent publication (Emons and Garoupa 2006) with two companion papers (Emons 2006 and 2007) provides an insightful comparison between contingent fees and conditional fees, with focus on the risk attitude of the plaintiff and the effort devoted to litigation by the plaintiff's lawyer. The underlying assumptions are that the probability of winning the case depends on the lawyer's effort in litigation (E) – which exhibits decreasing marginal returns – but such effort cannot be fully observed by the plaintiff. The papers address the issue of the plaintiff/lawyer relationship as a principal–agent setting. Emons and Garoupa (2006) conclude that under symmetric imperfect information contingent fees are more efficient than conditional fees if the lawyer is risk neutral and the plaintiff is risk-averse, as contingent fees will allocate the risk between the two actors more efficiently The different risk attitude of the parties may hold true when the plaintiff is a private individual, and be less likely when the plaintiff is a corporation.[10] The compromise between risk sharing and incentives offered by conditional fees suggests that conditional fees are superior also to flat fees in this case.

Emons (2009) compares conditional and contingent fees in a framework where lawyers are uninformed about the clients' cases, and once they learn about the case they can choose between a safe and a risky litigation strategy. He finds that under conditional fees lawyers are more geared towards safer strategies, whereas under contingent fees they tend to prefer the more risky ones. He also concludes that when legal costs are high, risk-averse plaintiffs prefer contingent over conditional fee agreements. Finally, he finds that, if there is asymmetric information about the merits of cases, in equilibrium attorneys will offer only conditional fees; whereas if there is asymmetric information about the risk of cases, only contingent fee contracts are offered in equilibrium.

In introducing conditional fee agreements, the UK government acknowledged that such agreements 'address the fundamental problem of the British legal system', as few people can afford to litigate unless they can get legal aid. In more detail, conditional fees were introduced to fill the gap between low-income citizens who could get legal aid, and high-income people who could afford a lawyer – for example they essentially targeted middle-income plaintiffs to improve their access to justice (Yarrow 2001a). Data reported by Yarrow (2001b) showed that by March 1999, about 60 000 conditional fee agreements had been signed, but only one in ten personal injury cases was funded by conditional fees, compared to 44 per cent funded by legal aid. He thus concludes that the impact of conditional fees on access to justice could be overstated. However, Fenn, Gray, Rickman and Mansur (2006) report that in 2002–2003 conditional fee agreements had become by far the predominant means of funding legal actions for personal injury cases, and suggest that the introduction of the Collective Conditional Fee Agreements (CCFA) may have exerted a significant impact on this observed trend. The impact of conditional fees on the litigation rate of cases seems to have been slightly positive, especially in the case of CCFAs. However, Peysner (2006, p. 99) warns that there is no evidence that conditional fee agreements are being frequently used in competition cases in England, due to the complexity of cases and their often unpredictable outcome. This evidence is consistent with the assumption that lawyers may behave in a rather risk-averse manner.

From a more theoretical perspective, it seems fair to conclude that conditional fees may improve access to justice for risk-averse plaintiffs, although not as much as contingency fees do. Risk-averse plaintiffs with limited financial resources also can find conditional fee agreements more advantageous than flat or hourly fees. At the same time, the limited empirical evidence available suggests that lawyers can also be significantly risk-averse, and may tend to drop low-stake, low-probability cases if the success fee does not justify the risk that they are 'buying'. Heavy capping of success fees can also discourage lawyers from accepting low-probability cases, although they could solve information asymmetries between the client and his lawyer, avoiding client's exploitation by the attorney, the uncontrolled increase of litigation costs and – under the English Rule – also the increase of defendant's costs in cases with a high probability of plaintiff verdict.

The assessment of conditional fee agreements also heavily depends on the fee allocation scheme chosen:

- Under an American Rule system, a conditional fee agreement effectively reduces the cost of access to justice for plaintiffs with low financial resources, but contingency fees – for the reason explained above – may appear even more efficient, depending on the client's and the lawyer's risk attitude.
- With two-way fee-shifting, a losing plaintiff would be bound to compensate the defendant's legal expenses, including at least the basic fee of the defendant's lawyer. This may stifle his incentives to take legal action compared to what occurs under the American Rule.
- Under one-way fee-shifting, however, the losing plaintiff will not be called to compensate the defendant's (reasonable) legal expenses, and will only bear his own lawyer's basic fee. This, in turn, provides him with greater incentives to sue.

These arguments seem to suggest that conditional fees improve access to justice when compared to hourly fees, but contingency fees can perform even better. The situation slightly changes after looking at the lawyers' behaviour and incentives.

For example, under the American Rule, a risk-averse lawyer will be more likely to accept cases under a conditional fee agreement, as even if the case is lost, he would still earn a basic fee. A simple example can help in understanding this point. Assume that the damage claim is €500 000, and that the parties' legal costs are equal. Then, assume that a contingency agreement implies a 30 per cent fee on the damage award (€150 000), whereas a conditional fee would imply a €50 000 basic fee plus a success fee of another €50 000.[11] Then, if the plaintiff's lawyer expects to have a 70 per cent probability to win, he will prefer a contingent fee, which would leave him with a total expected payoff of €105000. A conditional fee, on the other hand, would have an expected payoff of €85000. However, if the expected probability of winning the case is estimated at only 30 per cent, then the plaintiff's lawyer will prefer a conditional fee, as the expected payoff would be €65000, whereas with contingency fees the payoff would be €45000. This finding holds irrespective of the fee allocation scheme chosen.

From the perspective of the plaintiff, however, things are quite different. Under the same assumptions, if the probability of success is 70 per cent, then:

- Under the American Rule, the plaintiff will prefer to pay conditional fees, as his expected payoff would amount to €265000, whereas contingent fees would leave him with an expected €245000 stake.
- Under the English Rule, the plaintiff will face an expected payoff of €305000 irrespective of the fee agreement.
- Under one-way fee-shifting, the plaintiff will prefer to pay contingent fees, as his expected payoff would amount to €350000, whereas with conditional fees his expected payoff would be €335000.

On the other hand, if the probability of success is 30 per cent, then:

- Under the American Rule, the plaintiff will prefer to pay contingent fees, as his expected payoff would amount to €105000, whereas conditional fees would leave him with an expected €85000 stake.
- Under the English Rule, the plaintiff will face an expected payoff of €45000 irrespective of the fee agreement.
- Under one-way fee-shifting, the plaintiff will prefer to pay contingent fees, as his expected payoff would amount to €150000, whereas with conditional fees his expected payoff would be €115000.

As a result, there will be opposite preferences as regards the most appropriate fee agreement between client and lawyer in many cases. The English Rule is the only rule that makes the plaintiff indifferent about whether to use contingent or conditional fees, although such combination may lead more cases to be litigated when the parties have different beliefs and behave strategically in negotiating settlement. Otherwise:

- in high-probability cases a plaintiff prefers contingent fees under one-way fee-shifting, and conditional fees under the American Rule; the lawyer always prefers contingent fees;

New trends in financing civil litigation in Europe

- in low-probability cases a plaintiff always prefers contingent fees; the lawyer always prefers conditional fees.

Table 4.1 below shows the results of our exercise, for both a high-probability and a low-probability case, where *P* is the plaintiff and *PL* is the Plaintiff's Lawyer. We also show the payoffs of the Defendant (*D*) and

Table 4.1   Fee agreements, fee allocation and probability of success (amounts x 1000)

High prob			\multicolumn{4}{c}{Contingency fees}			
Each party bears her own cost			P	PL	D	DL
	70%	W	245	105	−350	0
	30%	L	0	0	−45	45
		Total	245	105	−395	45
Loser pays			P	PL	D	DL
	70%	W	350	105	−455	0
	30%	L	−45	0	0	45
		Total	305	105	−455	45
One-way fee shifting			P	PL	D	DL
	70%	W	350	105	−455	0
	30%	L	0	0	0	45
		Total	350	105	−455	45
Low prob			\multicolumn{4}{c}{Contingency fees}			
Each party bears her own cost			P	PL	D	DL
	30%	W	105	45	−150	0
	70%	L	0	0	−105	−105
		Total	105	45	−255	−105
Loser pays			P	PL	D	DL
	30%	W	150	45	−195	0
	70%	L	−105	0	0	105
		Total	45	45	−195	105
One-way fee shifting			P	PL	D	DL
	30%	W	150	45	−195	0
	70%	L	0	0	0	105
		Total	150	45	−195	105

of the Defendant's Lawyer (*DL*), under the simplifying assumption that contractual schemes and legal costs are identical.

5.3   Fee Allocation Schemes, Contingency Fees and Collective Actions

The combined impact of fee allocation schemes and contingent/conditional fee arrangements can also be appraised in light of collective litigation. As

Table 4.1   (continued)

High prob			Conditional fees			
Each party bears her own cost			P	PL	D	DL
	70%	W	280	70	−385	35
	30%	L	−15	15	−30	30
		Total	265	85	−415	65
Loser pays			P	PL	D	DL
	70%	W	350	70	−455	35
	30%	L	−45	15	0	30
		Total	305	85	−455	65
One-way fee shifting			P	PL	D	DL
	70%	W	350	70	−455	35
	30%	L	−15	15	−30	30
		Total	335	85	−485	65
Low prob			Conditional fees			
Each party bears her own cost			P	PL	D	DL
	30%	W	120	30	−165	15
	70%	L	−35	35	−70	70
		Total	85	65	−235	85
Loser pays			P	PL	D	DL
	30%	W	150	30	−195	15
	70%	L	−105	35	0	70
		Total	45	65	−195	85
One-way fee shifting			P	PL	D	DL
	30%	W	150	30	−195	15
	70%	L	−35	35	−70	70
		Total	115	65	−265	85

reported by Fenn (2006), the introduction of Collective Conditional Fee Arrangements in the UK seems to have positively influenced the litigation rate (also see Chapter 7 by Fenn and Rickman in this book). Overall, the impact of such schemes in combination with collective or representative actions can be summarized as follows:

- Contingency and conditional fees encourage collective litigation even more than individual litigation, as they shift the risk and responsibility of case selection to the lawyers, instead of leaving it to individual victims, who may be more likely to have a limited or distorted perception of the overall likelihood of winning at trial than a lawyer or association as repeat player.
- Contingency and conditional fees increase the lawyer's incentive to group as many cases as possible and settle before trial at favourable conditions, as his reward is based on the final damage award or settled amount.
- Contingency and conditional fees can also reduce the parties' risk aversion and rational apathy, depending on the type of collective action available.

As already mentioned, the introduction of mandatory one-way fee-shifting can encourage both victims and other plaintiffs wishing to file strategic or frivolous lawsuits to initiate litigation, absent certain safeguards such as rules aimed at sanctioning the unreasonable behaviour of the plaintiff. An alternative possibility is that some conditions are defined by law, under which the judge can order cost-shifting to protect the plaintiff from excessive cost exposure in case he loses at trial. However, *discretionary fee-shifting* rules – where all costs or only a portion is eventually shifted – introduce a discretionary element in the selection of the cost rule, which in turn can introduce also an element of uncertainty of the cost allocation that will emerge at trial. The impact of discretionary and/or partial cost-shifting depends highly on the way the rules are designed. Nevertheless, evidence from, among others, the US debate on Rule 68 of the Federal Rules of Civil Procedure and on the UK debate on cost-capping orders following *King v. Telegraph Road* reveals that to carefully and efficiently craft such rules is extraordinarily difficult (Sherman 1998).

6. PRIVATE FUNDING LINKED TO CONTINGENT/ CONDITIONAL FEE ARRANGEMENTS

Besides contingent or conditional fee agreements, in some jurisdictions private funding of litigation and other similar schemes have developed in the past years. These include private insurance products, such as 'before-the-event' (BTE) and 'after-the-event' (ATE) insurance and are discussed in detail by Van Boom in Chapter 5 of this book.

As one-way fee-shifting and especially contingency fees are normally introduced also with the aim of facilitating access to justice for low-income plaintiffs, such instruments may serve as useful complements or partial alternatives to solve the problem of access to justice also in the case of group litigation. Some authors, including Riley and Peysner (2006) and Peysner (2006) have suggested that some of the schemes could usefully contribute to the goal of facilitating access to justice by EU firms and consumers.

While conditional fees can reduce or eliminate a claimant's own lawyer's costs, it may not entirely cover a claimant's own outgoings or a successful (or partly successful) opponent's costs and outgoings. A solution to this problem, in some jurisdictions such as England and Wales, is ATE recoverable as an additional outgoing from a losing opponent.

The market for ATE products has developed essentially in England, where it is combined with conditional fee arrangements (CFAs). Under ATE agreements, 'the insurer will cover the contingent risk of both sides' costs if the case is lost, or, more commonly, the opponent's costs with 'own side' costs being covered by a CFA' (Peysner 2006, p. 99) In exchange, the insured party pays a premium.

However, there are doubts as to whether and to what extent ATE agreements can represent a suitable way to encourage litigation in highly uncertain and resource-intensive cases such as those often occurring in the domains of antitrust and products liability. As a matter of fact:

- The ATE instrument can develop mostly in countries that allow for conditional or contingent fee agreements. With CFAs, the basic fee due to the lawyer if the case is lost is known in advance, and the additional risk that the plaintiff faces can be more easily separated and subject to insurance. The same applies to contingency fees – the latter can indeed be seen as a form of CFA in which the basic fee is zero and the bonus fee is expressed as a percentage of the damage award.
- Because of the uncertainties in many areas of litigation, any ATE premium in this area would be so expensive as to be a huge burden

to buy at the start of litigation, especially when these costs are not necessarily recoverable.

7.   CONTINGENCY STYLE PUBLIC FUNDS

When litigation is very risky and uncertain, private insurance offers limited help to would-be plaintiffs. In these cases, legal aid or other forms of public funding of litigation may prove important in encouraging victims to sue. Beyond the typical and long-standing legal aid schemes for low-income victims, one interesting innovation to be assessed is the contingency legal aid fund (CLAF). CLAFs essentially operate as public, non-commercial, funds to support litigation. The operation of a CLAF is described by Faure, Fernhout and Philipsen in Chapter 3 of this book.

The success of these schemes, as well as the areas of litigation in which they have been applied, has varied noticeably in the past years. In Canada, the Quebec *Fonds* appear as a very successful experience (see Bogart, Kalaijdzic and Matthews 2007). This may be mostly attributable to the fact that: (i) the Fund is well-endowed, as it takes a levy on all settlements and judgments; (ii) this makes it relatively easy to accept applications and creates an incentive to apply; and (iii) it is used in most cases, as the funding is generous and the levy applies anyway.

On the other hand, the Ontario Class Proceedings Fund has been used by very few plaintiffs in the past years, also due to the rather high levy (10 per cent) on any judgment or settlement (Mulheron 2004, p. 475) but also to high transaction costs associated with preparing the application and the fact that it offers protection but not active litigation support – as a matter of fact, a lawyer willing to act on a contingency fee basis must still be found. Also in Australia, there have been few applicants to schemes such as the South Australia Litigation Assistance Fund and a low ratio of accepted applications on total requests: this is apparently due to the application of a fixed legal fee and a $1,000 application fee.

Comparing the two Canadian experiences, the striking difference in the success of the CLAFs schemes is not only attributable to the specific design of the scheme, but also to the application of the fee-shifting rule. While on the one hand the application of the English Rule is rather flexible and most often inexpensive for the parties, in Ontario the rule is applied very rigidly, and losing parties often lack adequate protection against onerous adverse cost orders. As stated by Riley and Peysner (2006, p. 9), 'it is unsurprising that in Ontario, whose attorneys are much more influenced by those to the south of the border, the fund with its levy is less attractive than the prospect of taking a contingency fee risk and sharing the spoils. The result is that the *Fonds* has been much more active'.

In summary, using public funds to encourage private litigation has shown to be potentially viable to solve the problem of access to justice for plaintiffs with limited financial resources, but mostly: (i) as a complement to other measures such as contingency fees; (ii) for areas in which litigation is not too uncertain and costly; (iii) in jurisdictions where the English Rule is not too strictly applied; and (iv) provided that the design of the system and its cost for claimants are such that it encourages the involvement of public funds. As a matter of fact, in many instances the use of CLAFs normally does not solve the problem of how the client's lawyer will be paid.[12]

8. CONCLUDING REMARKS

Group litigation promises much with regards to victim compensation and the deterrence of unlawful conduct. In this chapter, we have looked at ways to encourage litigation with regard to financing issues. The introduction of group litigation mechanisms (collective actions, representative actions) may help to reduce some of the problems faced by individual plaintiffs. However, other ways of financing, such as contingency fees, private and public insurance, cannot be replaced by these forms of group litigation. Our main conclusions are the following:

- Representative actions may not be a perfect substitute for collective actions backed by contingency fees. This is mostly due to problems that emerge within consumer associations (and also industry representations), as interests may not be homogeneous and managers may have a different agenda compared to their associates (principal–agent problem). In addition, limited resources often constitute an obstacle to effective and widespread representative actions. Finally, under-representation may lead to under-deterrence whenever tortfeasors face a lawsuit from a subset of the affected individuals.
- Private insurance appears viable only as a complement to other measures, most notably cost-capping and contingency fees. This is supported by evidence that the ATE instrument has developed mostly in countries that allow for conditional or contingent fee agreements. In addition, given the existing uncertainty in many areas of litigation and the relative difficulty of litigating in some areas of law (such as antitrust), any ATE premium would be so expensive that it would end up being costly to afford at the start of litigation.

- Public funding works only in combination with contingency fees. Using public funds to encourage private litigation has shown to be potentially viable to solve the problem of access to justice for plaintiffs with limited financial resources, but mostly: (i) as a complement to other measures such as contingency fees; (ii) for areas in which litigation is not too uncertain and costly; (iii) in jurisdictions where the English Rule is not too strictly applied; and (iv) provided that the design of the system and its cost for claimants are such that it encourages the involvement of public funds. As a matter of fact, in many instances the use of CLAFs does not solve the problem of how the client's lawyer will be paid.

Our findings suggest that Europe should act to promote contingent fee arrangements, coupled with measures aimed at disciplining lawyers' incentives to devote effort in litigation. This, in turn, would lead many private and public forms of insurance to flourish in only a few years. Absent any initiative in this respect, all other attempted measures are likely to prove hardly effective.

NOTES

1. For reasons of clarity, it should be added that these are not collective actions as defined in this chapter. Individual consumers must agree to transfer their claims to a consumer association, so that the *Sammelklage* resembles a joinder of claims.
2. Under the Swedish legislation the court shall replace the named plaintiff when she is no longer considered appropriate to represent the group. In a Group Litigation Order (GLO) in the UK, the judge becomes the case manager (Beuchler 2005, p. 891).
3. For a critical discussion of several such mechanisms and a proposed better solution, consisting of auctions combined with fee-forfeiture and a ban on inadequate settlements, see Harel and Stein 2001.
4. The British Rule (also called European Rule) as opposed to the American Rule, where generally each party bears its own costs. See Cabrillo and Fitzpatrick 2008, p 117; Polinsky and Rubinfeld 1998.
5. The expected reward can also be different from the damage award. For example, it could be a settlement that takes place at some time prior to the trial, or include an increase in the plaintiff's business reputation.
6. We assume that both the opportunity cost of litigation and the legal fees paid for litigating the case are greater than in the case of settlement. Consideration of time is also important, as the legal fees are to be paid upfront, whereas damages are awarded after the case has been adjudicated or settled.
7. For simplicity, here we do not take into account court fees and opportunity costs of time spent by the plaintiff's employees in litigation.
8. In algebraic terms, pwD is always greater than $p\,[wD - (1 - w)\theta D] = pwD - p(1 - w) \theta D$ and the latter will always be greater than $p\,(wD - \theta D) = pwD - p\theta D$. Hence, the net expected reward from trial is highest under one-way fee-shifting, and lowest with the 'each party bears her own cost' rule.
9. Indeed, $pwD > pwD - X$.

10. However, reputational effects and potential follow-on cases may lead to risk aversion of the plaintiff.
11. As contingency fee contracts are more risky, we assume that the maximum payoff with contingent fees is higher than with conditional fees.
12. Some schemes may pay the lawyer in any event (win or lose), with a higher rate in case of success, whereas some may only pay on success.

REFERENCES

Ashurst (2004), 'Study on the Conditions of Claims for Damages in Case of Infringement of EC Competition Rules – Comparative Report, National Reports', www.ec.europa.eu/competition/antitrust/actionsdamages/study.html

Bebchuk, Lucian Arye (1996), 'A New Theory Concerning the Credibility and Success of Threats to Sue', *Journal of Legal Studies*, **25**, 1–25.

Bebchuk, Lucian Arye (1998), 'Negative Expected Value Suits', *NBER Working Paper*, W6474, SSRN: http://papers.ssrn.com/sol3/papers.cfm?abstract_id=1534703, accessed 27 July 2010.

Bertelsen, Bruce, Mary Calfee and Gerald Connor (1974), 'The Rule 23 (b) (3) Class Action: An Empirical Study', *Georgetown Law Journal*, **62**, 1123–1172.

Beuchler, Holger (2005), 'Länderbericht Vereinigte Staaten', in Hans-W. Micklitz and Astrid Stadler (eds), *Das Verbandsklagerecht in der Informations- und Dienstleistungsgesellschaft*, Münster: Landwirtschaftsverlag, 1–181.

Bogart, William, Jasminka Kalajdic and Ian Matthews (2007), 'Class Actions in Canada: A National Procedure in a Multi-Jurisdictional Society?', www.law.stanford.edu/library/globalclassaction/PDF/Canada_National_Report.pdf, accessed 27 July 2010.

Braeutigam, Ronald, Bruce Owen and John Panzar (1984), 'An Economic Analysis of Alternative Fee Shifting Systems', *Law and Contemporary Problems*, **47**, 173–185.

Bohn, James and Stephen Choi (1996), 'Fraud In The New-Issues Market: Empirical Evidence On Securities Class Action', *University of Pennsylvania Law Review*, **144**(3), 903-982.

Bronsteen, John (2005), 'Class Action Settlements: An Opt-In Proposal', *University of Illinois Law Review*, **2005**(4), 903–928.

Cabrillo, Francisco and Sean Fitzpatrick (2008), *The Economics of Courts*, Cheltenham, UK: Northampton, MA: Edward Elgar.

Choi, Stephen (2004), 'The Evidence on Securities Class Actions', *Vanderbilt Law Review*, **57**(5), 1465–1526.

Coffee, John (1995), 'Class Wars: the Dilemma of the Mass Tort Class Action', *Columbia Law Review*, **95**(6), 1343–1465.

Cornell, Bradford (1990), 'The Incentive to Sue: An Option-Pricing Approach', *The Journal of Legal Studies*, **19**, 173–187.

Dam, Kenneth (1975), 'Class Actions: Efficiency, Compensation, Deterrence, and Conflict of Interest', *The Journal of Legal Studies*, **4**, 47–73.

Dewees, Donald, Robert Prichard and Michael Trebilcock (1981), 'An Economic Analysis of Cost and Fee Rules for Class Actions', *The Journal of Legal Studies*, **10**, 157–179.

Duval, Benjamin (1976a), 'The Class Action as an Antitrust Enforcement Device:

The Chicago Experience (I)', *American Bar Foundation Research Journal*, **1**(3), 1021–1106.

Duval, Benjamin (1976b), 'The Class Action as an Antitrust Enforcement Device: The Chicago Experience (II)', *American Bar Foundation Research Journal*, **1**(4), 1273–1358.

Eisenberg, Theodore and Geoffrey Miller (2004), 'The Role of Opt-Outs and Objectors in Class Action Litigation: Theoretical and Empirical Issues', *NYU Law and Economics Research Paper*, 04-004, SSRN: www.ssrn.com/abstract=528146.

Emons, Winand (2006), *Playing it Safe with Low Conditional Fees versus being Insured by High Contingent Fees*, American Law and Economic review, **8**(1), 20–32.

Emons, Winand (2007), *Conditional versus Contingent Fees*, Oxford Economic Papers, **59**(1), 89–101.

Emons, Winand and Nuno Garoupa (2006), 'US-Style Contingent Fees and UK-Style Conditional Fees: Agency Problems and the Supply of Legal Services', *Managerial and Decision Economics*, **27**, 379–385.

Eurobarometer (2004), *European Union Citizens and Access to Justice*, www.ec.europa.eu/consumers/redress/reports_studies/execsum_11-04_en.pdf, accessed 27 July 2010.

Eurobarometer (2006), *Consumer protection in the Internal Market*, www.ec.europa.eu/consumers/topics/eurobarometer_09-2006_en.pdf, accessed 27 July 2010.

European Commission (2008), *White Paper on Damages Actions for Breach of the EC Antitrust Rules*, COM 165 final, www.ec.europa.eu/competition/antitrust/actionsdamages/files_white_paper/whitepaper_en.pdf.

Farmer, Amy and Paul Pecorino (2004), 'Pretrial Signaling With Negative Expected Value Suits', *Southern Economic Journal*, **54**, 287–296.

Fenn, Paul, Alastair Gray, Neil Rickman and Yaseen Mansur (2006), 'The Funding of Personal Injury Litigation: Comparisons Over Time and Across Jurisdictions', *Report to the Department for Constitutional Affairs*, DCA Research Series September 2006, http://www.dca.gov.uk/research/2006/02_2006.pdf, accessed 27 July 2010.

Gould, John (1973), 'The Economics of Legal Conflicts', *The Journal of Legal Studies*, **2**, 279–300.

Gravelle, Hugh and Michael Waterson (1993), 'No Win, No Fee: Some Economics of Contingent Legal Fees', *The Economic Journal*, **103**, 1205–1220.

Harel, Alon and Alex Stein (2001), 'Law & Economics at the Animal Farm: Offering a New Solution to the Class Action Agency Problem', SSRN: www.ssrn.com/abstract=271431, accessed 27 July 2010.

Hensler, Deborah et al. (2000), *Class Action Dilemmas: Pursuing Public Goals for Private Gains*, Santa Monica: Rand Corporation.

Hensler, Deborah and Thomas Rowe Jr. (2001), 'Beyond "It just ain't worth it": Alternative Strategies for Damage Class Action Reform', *Law & Contemporary Problems*, **64**, 137–161.

Hughes, James and Edward Snyder (1995), 'Litigation and Settlement under the English and American Rules: Theory and Evidence', *Journal of Law and Economics*, **38**(1), 225–250.

Hughes, James and Edward Snyder (1998), 'Allocation of Litigation Costs: American and English Rules', in Peter Newman (ed.), *The New Palgrave Dictionary of Economics and the Law* 1, London: Macmillan, pp. 51–56.

Hylton, Keith (2002), 'An Asymmetric-Information Model of Litigation', *International Review of Law and Economics*, **22**, 153–175.

Issacharoff, Samuel and Geoffrey Miller (2008), 'Will Aggregate Litigation Come to Europe?', *NYU Law and Economics Research Paper 46*. SSRN: http://papers. ssrn.com/sol3/papers.cfm?abstract_id=1296843, accessed on 27 July 2010.

Kalven, Harry Jr and Maurice Rosenfield (1941), 'The Contemporary Function of the Class Suit, *University of Chicago Law Review*, **8**, 684–721.

Kaplow, Louis (1993), 'The Value of Accuracy in Adjudication', *The Journal of Legal Studies*, **23**, 307–401.

Katz, Avery (1990), 'The Effect of Frivolous Lawsuits on the Settlement of Litigation', *International Review of Law and Economics*, **10**, 3–27.

Katz, Avery (2000), 'Indemnity of Legal Fees', in Boudewijn Bouckaert and Gerrit De Geest (eds), *Encyclopedia of Law and Economics*, Cheltenham, UK and Northampton, MA, US: Edward Elgar, pp. 63–94.

Koniak, Susan (1995), 'Feasting While the Widow Weeps', *Cornell Law Review*, **80**(4), 1045–1158.

Kritzer, Herbert (1997), 'Contingency Lawyers as Gatekeepers in the Civil Justice System', *Judicature*, **81**, 22–29.

Landes, William (1971), 'An Economic Analysis of the Courts', *Journal of Law and Economics*, **14**, 61–107.

Macey, Jonathan and Geoffrey Miller (1991), 'The Plaintiffs' Attorney's Role in Class Action and Derivative Litigation: Economic Analysis and Recommendations for Reform', *The University of Chicago Law Review*, **58**(1), 1–118.

Miceli, Thomas (1994), 'Do Contingent Fees Promote Excessive Litigation?', *The Journal of Legal Studies,* **23**, 211–224.

Micklitz Hans and Astrid Stadler (2006), 'The Development of Collective Legal Actions in Europe, Especially in German Civil Procedure', *European Business Law Review*, **17**(5), 1473–1503.

Miller, Geoffrey (1987), 'Some Agency Problems in Settlement', *The Journal of Legal Studies*, **16**(1), 189–215.

Miller, Geoffrey (1998), 'Class Action', in Peter Newman (ed.), *The New Palgrave Dictionary of Economics and Law*, London: MacMillan Reference Limited, 257–262.

Mulheron, Rachael (2004), *The Class Action in Common Law Legal Systems*, Oxford: Hart Publishing.

Office of Fair Trading (2007), 'Private Actions in Competition Law: Effective Redress for Consumers and Business', www.oft.gov.uk/shared_oft/reports/comp_policy/oft916.pdf, accessed 27 July 2010.

Peysner, John (2006), 'Costs and Financing in Private Third Party Competition Damages Actions', *Competition Law Review*, **3**(1), 97–115.

Pirker-Hörmann, Beate and Peter Kolba (2006), 'Österreich: Von der Verbandsklage zur Sammelklage', in Bundesministerium für Ernährung, Landwirtschaft und Verbraucherschutz (ed.), *Kollektive Rechtsdurchsetzung – Chancen und Risiken*, Internationales Symposium Bamberg, 20–21 February 2006, 199–211.

Polinsky, A. Mitchell and Daniel Rubinfeld (1996), 'Optimal Awards and Penalties When the Probability of Prevailing Varies Among Plaintiffs', *The RAND Journal of Economics*, **27**(2), 269–280.

Polinsky, A. Mitchell and Daniel Rubinfeld (1998), 'The Deterrent Effects of Settlements and Trials', *International Review of Law and Economics*, **8**, 109–116.

Polinsky, A. Mitchell and Daniel Rubinfeld (2002), 'A Note on Settlements under the Contingent Fee Method of Compensating Lawyers', *International Review of Law and Economics*, **22**, 217–225.

Posner, Richard A. (1973), 'An Economic Approach to Legal Procedure and Judicial Administration', *The Journal of Legal Studies*, **2**, 399–458.

Reinganum, Jennifer and Louis Wilde (1986), 'Credibility and Law Enforcement', *Working Papers California Institute of Technology, Division of the Humanities and Social Sciences*, no. 604.

Renda, Andrea, Roger Van den Bergh, Sonja Keske, Roberto Pardolesi et al. (2007), *Making Antitrust Damages Actions more Effective in the EU*, Study for the European Commission DG COMP, http://ec.europa.eu/competition/antitrust/actionsdamages/files_white_paper/impact_study.pdf, accessed on 27 July 2010.

Riley, Alan and John Peysner (2006), 'Damages in EC Antitrust Actions: Who Pays the Piper?', *European Law Review*, **31**(5), 748–761.

Roedder, William C., Jr. (2006), 'An Introduction to the Class Action Fairness Act of 2005', *FDCC Quarterly*, **56**(4), 443–463.

Rosenberg, David and Steven Shavell (1985), 'A Model in Which Suits Are Brought for Their Nuisance Value', *International Review of Law and Economics*, **5**, 3–13.

Rosenfield, Andrew (1976), 'An Empirical Test of Class-Action Settlement', *The Journal of Legal Studies*, **5**, 113–20.

Rubinfeld, Daniel and Suzanne Scotchmer (1998), 'Contingent Fees', in Peter Newman (ed.), *The New Palgrave Dictionary of Economics and the Law*, London: Macmillian Reference Ltd., 415–420.

Schäfer, Hans-Bernd (2000), 'The Bundling of Similar Interests in Litigation. The Incentives for Class Action and Legal Actions taken by Associations', *European Journal of Law and Economics*, **9**(3), 183–213.

Schwartz, Murray and Daniel Mitchell (1970), 'An Economic Analysis of the Contingent Fee and Personal-Injury Litigation', *Stanford Law Review*, **22**, 1125–1162.

Silver, Charles (2000), 'Class Actions – Representative Proceedings', in Boudewijn Bouckaert and Gerrit De Geest (eds), *Encyclopedia of Law and Economics*. Cheltenham, UK and Northampton, MA, US: Edward Elgar, 194–240.

Shavell, Steven (1982), 'The Social versus the Private Incentive to Bring Suit in a Costly Legal System', *The Journal of Legal Studies*, **11**, 333–339.

Sherman, Edward (1998), 'From "Loser-pays" to Modified Offer of Judgment Rules: Reconciling Incentives to Settle with Access to Justice', *Texas Law Review*, **76**, 1863–1896.

Spier, Kathryn E. (1997), 'A note on the divergence between the private and social motive to settle under a negligence rule', *Journal of Legal Studies* **26**, 613–623.

Van den Bergh, Roger and Louis Visscher (2008), 'The Preventive Function of Collective Actions for Damages in Consumer Law', *Erasmus Law Review*, **1**, 5–30.

Wagener, William (2003), 'Modelling the Effect of One-Way Fee Shifting in Discovery Abuse for Private Antitrust Litigation', *New York Law Review*, **78**, 1887–1928.

Willging, Thomas, Laura Hopper and Robert Niemic (1996), 'Empirical Study of Class Actions in Four Federal District Courts: Final Report to the Advisory

Committee on Civil Rules', *Federal Judicial Center*, www.fjc.gov/public/pdf.nsf/lookup/rule23.pdf/$File/rule23.pdf, accessed 27 July 2010.

Yarrow, Stella (2001a), 'Conditional Fees', *Hume Papers on Public Policy*, **8**, 1–10.

Yarrow, Stella (2001b), 'Access to justice? Consumers and Conditional Fees', *Consumer Policy Review*, ed. 1 March 2001.

5. Financing civil litigation by the European insurance industry

Willem H. van Boom

1. INTRODUCTION

One of the ways in which legal services are financed, and indeed shaped, is through private insurance arrangement. Two contrasting types of legal expense insurance contracts (LEI) seem to dominate in Europe: before-the-event (BTE) and after-the-event (ATE) legal expense insurance. Notwithstanding institutional differences between different legal systems, BTE and ATE insurance arrangements may be instrumental if government policy is geared towards strengthening a market-oriented system of financing access to justice for individuals and business. At the same time, emphasizing the role of a private industry as a keeper of the gates to justice raises issues of accountability and transparency, not readily reconcilable with demands of competition. Moreover, multiple actors (clients, lawyers, courts, insurers) are involved, causing behavioural dynamics which are not easily predicted or influenced.

Against this background, this chapter looks into BTE and ATE arrangements by analysing the particularities of BTE and ATE arrangements currently available in some European jurisdictions and by painting a picture of their respective markets and legal contexts. This allows for some reflection on the performance of BTE and ATE providers as both financiers and keepers. What emerges from the analysis is that neither BTE nor ATE is perfect; the institutional settings in which they operate seem decisive for their success. There is, however, a specific problematic issue with the long-term sustainability of some ATE products.

2. FINANCING LITIGATION WITH INSURANCE ARRANGEMENTS

Fenn et al. (2006, p. 1) rightly note that 'the ways in which legal services are financed are fundamental to issues surrounding access to justice and the efficiency, quality and competitiveness of legal service delivery.' One of the ways in which legal services are financed, and indeed shaped, is through private insurance arrangement. In fact, in some European countries the insurance industry is crucial in financing the positions of both claimants and defendants in civil litigation and in smoothing out their settlement negotiations. Therefore, the insurance industry can be considered as one of the enablers and keepers of the gates to justice for both claimants and defendants. How do insurers perform their part as such?

To begin with, we need to distinguish liability insurance from legal expense insurance. *Liability insurance* contracts have a dual indemnity purpose, as they do not merely protect the policyholder against liability, but also contain elements of legal expense insurance as far as defending against claims is concerned.[1] Consequently, liability insurance is pivotal in defending against tort claims as it indemnifies the insured in capacity of alleged tortfeasor for legal costs and expenses incurred in defending claims made against the insured. Moreover, if the claimant prevails in court, the liability insurance policy may also cover the defendant's liability for the claimant's legal costs. Obviously, the extent to which such costs are actually shifted from the prevailing claimant to the defendant and his liability insurer depends on the applicable rules of civil procedure and the policy cover (see also Chapter 2 by Visscher and Schepens in this book).

This chapter does not focus on the role of liability insurers but rather on legal expense insurers. *Legal expense insurance* contracts (LEI)[2] may finance either side of the claim – although they incline towards the claiming rather than the defending side of the claim. Indeed, in some European countries LEI has matured into an extremely important branch of indemnity insurance offering a high level of service in kind, employing and educating professional panel lawyers or procuring contracts for legal services in bulk. By contrast, in other countries LEI has not (yet) gained much ground. Undeniably, institutional differences in markets for private insurance, lawyers and publicly funded legal aid are responsible for the differences in size and societal relevance of national LEI markets (see for example Kirstein and Rickman 2004, p.555 ff.). To name one of these differences: some countries are more reluctant than others to accept the concept of salaried in-house lawyers (cf. Schepens 2007, p.33). Institutional preconditions are also at the root of the advance in some countries of so-called *after-the-event legal expense insurance* (ATE LEI). This type of insurance is exactly what the name denotes: an insurance policy concluded after a dispute has arisen and litigation seems unavoidable. Unsurprisingly, ATE differs in many ways from regular LEI (also referred to as *before-the-event* (BTE) LEI).

In this chapter, I will look into BTE and ATE arrangements by painting a picture of their respective markets and legal contexts. This allows for some reflection on the performance of BTE and ATE providers as both financiers and keepers. Notwithstanding institutional differences between different legal systems, BTE and ATE insurance arrangements may be instrumental if government policy is geared towards strengthening a market-oriented system of financing access to justice for individuals and business. At the same time, emphasizing the role of a private industry as a keeper of the gates to justice raises issues of accountability and transparency, not necessarily reconcilable with the demands of competition. Moreover, multiple actors, ranging from clients, lawyers, courts, insurers (and possibly claims-managing intermediaries) are involved, causing behavioural dynamics which are not easily predicted or influenced. Against this background, I set out to analyse the particularities of BTE and ATE arrangements currently available in some European jurisdictions. By no means is this an exhaustive analysis, as this chapter merely concerns itself with some of the issues of insurer involvement in financing civil litigation.

3.   BEFORE-THE-EVENT LEGAL EXPENSE INSURANCE (BTE LEI)

3.1   Market Features

The role and relevance of BTE LEI varies among European countries. In Germany, BTE LEI is pervasive. The penetration rate of general household BTE LEI in Germany is some 50 per cent (Veith and Gräfe 2005, p. 978, Werner 1985, pp. 94–96, Flood and Whyte 2006, p. 92, Kilian 2003, p. 34, Faure, Hartlief and Philipsen 2006, p. 55, Jackson 2009, p. 564). By contrast, in England and Wales the demand for this type of BTE seems to be virtually absent. In yet other markets there is a trend towards multiple markets for BTE in which both middle-class households and small and medium enterprises display an increasing demand for BTE products.[3]

   Whether and how the BTE LEI markets in Europe will develop, depends on domestic institutional factors such as the extent of publicly funded legal aid and the intensity of regulation of legal services. For instance, one would expect a BTE market not to flourish in a country with comprehensive state-funded legal aid. And indeed, England and Wales spend a lot of taxpayers' money on legal aid[4] while German consumers spend less on taxation for legal aid but more on private BTE LEI.[5] As a result, the UK private insurance market may be the largest in Europe, but it is clearly surpassed by Germany with regard to LEI (Kilian 2003, p. 41, Rickman and Gray 1996, p. 312 ff.).

In some countries, BTE LEI has penetrated the consumer market preponderantly in the form of *add-on insurance*. In England and Wales, for instance, LEI is sold in a variety of ways (stand-alone, add-on) and through multiple channels (Jackson 2009, pp. 151–153. For a sketch of the BTE market in England and Wales, see Prais 1996, p. 433 ff., Rickman and Gray 1996, p. 312 ff., Rickman and Fenn 1998, p. 217 ff., Jackson 2009, p. 151 ff.). Unsurprisingly, cover provided by add-on LEI is fragmented, and sometimes duplicated (McDonald, Winters and Harmer 2007, p. 17). In fact, holders of certain policies (for example household insurance) may not even be aware that their insurance also covers certain legal expenses (McDonald, Winters and Harmer 2007, p. 53, Kilian 2003, p. 39). At first sight, the LEI coverage offered by household insurance (home insurance) and car insurance in England and Wales seems rather comprehensive, as it covers claims for personal injury, (most) employment and consumer disputes. On the other hand, the policy limits are not always very high (for example GBP 15 000–25 000). The penetration rate of comprehensive stand-alone covers remains low (Jackson 2009, p. 151 ff.).

One of the institutional settings that seem to be relevant in explaining differences in development of BTE markets pertains to the rules on cost shifting in civil procedure. Like providers of any type of insurance, BTE providers prefer *predictability*. Therefore, BTE LEI is more likely to thrive under cost regimes that generate a certain level of predictability (Dannemann 1996, p. 282 ff., Prais 1996, p. 440, Rickman and Gray 1996, p. 320, Walters and Peysner 1999, p. 6, Flood and Whyte 2006, p. 92, Kilian 2003, p. 42, Cabrillo and Fitzpatrick 2008, p. 143, Wagner 2009, p. 379 ff.). For instance, the German and Dutch costs rules (i.e., the loser pays according to fixed scales) are more beneficial to BTE LEI insurers looking for predictability than the current English cost shifting rules (Rickman and Fenn 1998, p. 210 ff. For German cost shifting rules, see in detail Wagner 2009, p. 367 ff.). Moreover, BTE insurers have every incentive to fix and control lawyers' remuneration and possibly even to employ in-house lawyers in order to accurately calculate (and cut) premiums (Dannemann 1996, p. 282 ff., Prais 1996, p. 440, Rickman and Gray 1996, p. 320, Walters and Peysner 1999, p. 6, Flood and Whyte 2006, p. 92, Kilian 2003, p. 42, Cabrillo and Fitzpatrick 2008, p. 143, Wagner 2009, p. 379 ff.).

Apart from institutional factors, which go a long way in explaining the development of the various markets, cultural factors such as the level of litigiousness may be relevant as well (Baarsma and Felsö 2005, p. 20).[6] It is sometimes said that Germans are more litigious by nature than, for example, the English (Dannemann 1996, p. 290). Whether this is true seems hard to verify – indeed, one may well conjecture that the level of litigiousness is dependent to some extent on the costs of getting access to justice, subjecting all cultures to seemingly universal laws of susceptibility to financial restraints.

3.2 Legal Context: the LEI Directive

At the European level, LEI is regulated to some extent under Directive 87/344 on the coordination of laws, regulations and administrative provisions relating to legal expense insurance.[7] The provisions of the LEI Directive are to be copied into the Solvability II Directive. No major overhaul of the regulatory framework for LEI is foreseen.

Three features of the LEI Directive are worth mentioning. Firstly, the Directive aims at neutralizing potential conflicts of interest between insured and insurer. Any conflicts of interest arising, in particular from the fact that the insurance undertaking is covering another person or is covering a person in respect of both legal expenses and any other class of insurance, should be precluded or resolved (European Commission 2008, Solvency II, COM(2008) 119 final, Recital 55). Secondly, specific conflicts between the LEI insurer and the insured persons on the issue of merit should be settled efficiently. Hence, the Directive obliges member states to implement some sort of arbitration or ADR procedure in order to settle the issue of merit swiftly (European Commission 2008, Solvency II, COM(2008) 119 final, Recital 56).

The third feature concerns free choice of lawyer. Article 4 (1) of the LEI Directive provides:[8]

Any contract of legal expense insurance shall expressly recognize that:

> (a) where recourse is had to a lawyer or other person appropriately qualified according to national law in order to defend, represent or serve the interests of the insured person in any inquiry or proceedings, that insured person shall be free to choose such lawyer or other person;
> (b) the insured person shall be free to choose a lawyer or, if he so prefers and to the extent that national law so permits, any other appropriately qualified person, to serve his interests whenever a conflict of interests arises.[9]

The free choice of lawyer embodied in article 4 is restricted in instances when legal representation by a lawyer (attorney, barrister, solicitor or whatever the official title of this representative may be) before an official court is compulsory by law. As we will see later on, the ideal of 'free choice of lawyer' does not sit easily with the business model of some BTE providers, causing a friction that leaves the question whether article 4 had better be abolished.

3.3 Changing Business Models in BTE

The institutional environment in which BTE LEI providers operate influences the interaction between insurers and independent providers of services on the market for legal services to a large extent. BTE insurers have an obvious interest in keeping the cost of litigation low (Kilian 2003, p. 35). This may not be easily achieved in markets in which lawyers have a statutory monopoly on giving legal advice, as is the case in Germany (Kilian 2003, p. 44).[10] Conversely, in countries where there is no such monopoly BTE insurers have every opportunity to develop their own in-house legal expertise by vertically integrating lawyers into their business. By doing so, they can achieve economies of scale and curtail agency problems inherent with outsourced legal services (cf. Rickman and Gray 1996, p. 311, Jackson 2009, p. 580). Moreover, they can be expected to attempt to broaden the scope of their product by adding easily available general legal advice to their services, in order to encourage self-help and deflect potential claims at an early stage.[11] For example, Dutch BTE insurers have thus far succeeded in keeping the number of files in which external lawyers were retained very low. Indeed, the Dutch BTE market is considered to be very much a market for 'in kind' policies in which services that are easy to access, such as advice by telephone, are as important as 'real' services, such as retaining a lawyer (Maas 2007, p. 127).[12]

As mentioned, by broadening the scope of their services and vertically integrating lawyers into their product, BTE LEI insurers may play an important role in bringing the cost of lawyers down.[13] The difference in incentive structure for law firms and BTE insurers goes a long way in explaining this phenomenon: law firms charge for services rendered whereas BTE insurers have already received their premium by the time they have to render a service. In contrast to a law firm working under an hourly fee arrangement, the insurer's efforts will be directed towards keeping out of court and settling swiftly at an acceptable level rather than maximizing the number of hours spent on a file.[14] Obviously, the BTE insurance arrangement in itself may pose information problems concerning quality of the service.

Generally speaking, the BTE business model of 'in kind service' seems successful in some jurisdictions and fills gaps that the German BTE model leaves. This model does, however, operate on the fringes of what is permitted in accordance with art. 4 (1) of the LEI Directive. BTE policies may well distinguish between lawyers appointed by the insurance company and lawyers selected by the policyholder, typically limiting the coverage with regard to the latter at a lower amount than with regard to the former. Under certain conditions this distinction may run counter to the ideal of free choice embodied in article 4.[15] In any jurisdiction that does not assign legal services (including advice) exclusively to lawyers, article 4 will create a tension between economical insurance practice and legal principles. This tension will not dissolve, because BTE insurers will still have a legitimate interest in testing the merits of the case and strategy. Therefore, a BTE insurer will typically want to stipulate that he will only cover legal expenses if:

- it is probable that the insured will prevail in litigation;
- the case has been approved as viable by an assigned panel lawyer and the insurer has agreed to the expense;
- the policyholder does not stop or settle a claim or withdraw instructions from the appointed lawyer without good reason.

Moreover, it is not uncommon for a policy to stipulate: 'We will choose an appointed representative to act for you. If you are not satisfied with the appointed representative we have chosen, you can choose another appointed representative' and 'We may choose not to accept an appointed representative of your choice but this will only be in exceptional circumstances.' By thus shaping the BTE LEI contract, the insurer remains in control of the choice of lawyer and minimizes control of the insured over the policy (Cf. Rickman and Gray 1996, pp. 311–312).

Unsurprisingly, the interests of the BTE LEI insurer do not necessarily converge with the interests of the policyholder with regard to both merits and free choice of counsel. As article 4 does not specifically oblige insurers to actively disclose the right of free choice of counsel to the policyholder, these rights are more or less obscured in the small print.[16] And even if insurers were to actively disclose this right to the policyholder in the claims process, there would still be the matter of *merit*. The Directive does not restrain the insurer from assessing merit before allowing the policyholder to litigate.[17] So, the policyholder does have a choice of counsel but he cannot force the insurer to fund unmeritorious claims. Moreover, there is the issue of interpretation of article 4. In England, for instance, article 4 is strictly interpreted as merely giving a right to choose counsel from the moment proceedings are issued, leaving the claimant in the hands of his BTE LEI panel solicitor prior to proceedings (See Wignall and Green 2008, p. 170, Prais 1996, p. 435).[18]

Although article 4 is undoubtedly founded on the fundamental principle that in civilized societies citizens should be given the right to choose their counsel, there is something to be said for the position that this principle should be considered less fundamental in private insurance contracts.[19] If consumers had the opportunity of informed choice between two types of LEI policies in civil litigation matters – one policy granting choice of counsel and another withholding that choice – why should the average consumer not have a right to choose? Possibly, explicitly introducing the power to waive the right acquired under article 4 before- or after-the-event could build up leverage for more competition in the market for legal services including BTE insurance (cf. Baarsma and Felsö 2005, p. 33). Moreover, the European legislature should reconsider article 4 anyway in light of the fact that insurance innovation (such as the upsurge of ATE) can easily render the article out of date.[20]

4.   AFTER-THE-EVENT (ATE) FUNDING AND INSURANCE

4.1   ATE Third Party Funding

After-the-event (ATE) funding and insurance arrangements reflect in some ways legal BTE LEI. The specific contract details, however, define the exact nature of the agreement. To appreciate what one is specifically dealing with one should read the exact contract terms. Some of these ATE contracts correspond with contingency fee arrangements, others approximate insurance contracts. What all have in common, however, is that ATE is exactly what the name suggests: an agreement entered into by the claimant (or his lawyer operating under some form of *conditional fee agreement*, in short: CFA) after the dispute has already arisen (Kilian 2003, p. 33, Jackson 2009, p. 156). It seems that there are at least two distinct versions of ATE arrangements currently available in Europe.[21] The first is ATE *funding* and is dealt with in this section. The second, ATE *insurance*, is a product which is especially popular on the English market; we will concern ourselves with this insurance in the next section.

In Germany and Austria the typical ATE funding product is the *Prozessfinanzierungsvertrag*.[22] It is offered both by companies with a track record in underwriting as well as companies with experience in capital investment.[23] In England and Wales, where this type of arrangement is advancing as well, it is usually referred to as *third party funding* (Jackson 2009, p. 160 ff).

In short, this type of contract typically entails the following:

● The ATE provider will typically offer to finance all costs involved in a money claim, against a 'premium' which is due only in case of success.[24]
● The provider diligently investigates the creditworthiness of the

defendant and the viability of the claim (with the help of legal opinion of the lawyer who analyses the case).

- If the claim is found valid, ATE will provide the upfront funding required.
- The success premium is both contingent on the disputed amount and staged (for example 20 per cent in case of pre-trial settlement, 30 per cent in case of success in court up to €500 000, 20 per cent of amounts over €500 000).[25]
- This ATE arrangement is typically available for (mainly commercial) claimants with high-value claims (for example €50 000–80 000 and upwards) with a high success probability (Veith and Gräfe 2005, pp. 975–976. Jackson 2009, p. 161).[26]

ATE funding operates in a segment of the market where there is little competition to be expected from BTE LEI. In any event, the economics applied in ATE funding are different from BTE insurance in the sense that the idea of pooling of risks may be a less prominent feature of ATE than it is in BTE (Peysner and Nurse 2008, p. 28). Instead, the selection criteria applied by the ATE provider assure a relatively comfortable chance of collecting high revenues. ATE providers typically favour contractual money claims over tort claims (which may turn out to be especially complicated if liability and causation are contested) and they assure themselves of the defendant's solvability (Coester and Nitzsche 2005, pp. 87–88). Since ATE providers take a monetary interest in the case contingent on the outcome, it seems doubtful if the contract they offer can be regarded as an insurance contract in the classical sense. Essentially, the 'premium' (a percentage of the recovered amount) is only due when the claimant prevails, and even then the claimant does not have to incur any out-of-pocket expense because the 'premium' is deducted from the proceeds. All in all, this type of ATE funding bears more resemblance to a contingency fee arrangement than to insurance (Cf. Jaskolla 2004, p. 35 ff.).[27] Unsurprisingly, the selection process applied by lawyers working under a US-style contingency fee arrangement is replicated (cf. Chapter 8 by Hensler and Chapter 2 by Visscher and Schepens in this book).

The benefits of this type of ATE to impecunious and/or risk-averse (commercial) claimants are self-evident, and in those jurisdictions that restrain lawyers admitted to the bar from charging their clients on any other basis than a (fixed) hourly fee the ATE arrangement has the potential of becoming a competitive product. It seems likely, moreover, that restrained lawyers would be tempted to associate themselves somehow with ATE providers. It is not difficult to imagine that in the near future legal systems will be faced with the question of whether lawyers would be allowed to accept commission for clients they refer to the provider.[28]

4.2 ATE as an Add-on Insurance with CFA

The institutional setting and practical operation of English ATE insurance is somewhat different from the ATE funding I described in the previous section. In England and Wales, under an ATE funding arrangement the success fee would typically be deducted from the award (as it typically is in Germany, Jackson 2009, pp. 163–164), whereas under specific conditions English costs rules allow for a specific CFA + ATE insurance arrangement. This typically English arrangement may be much more beneficial to the claimant. In essence, it works as follows.

For certain types of claims solicitors are permitted to offer their services under a CFA. CFA denotes a combination of *no-cure-no-pay* and a *success fee*, a mark-up success fee, either in the form of a flat fee or an upscale fee expressed as a percentage of the basic hourly fee, but not contingent on the amount of the sum successfully recovered. Under the CFA, if the claimant is defeated in court his solicitor will not claim any remuneration. There is, however, still the issue of the prevailing defendant's costs. English costs rules allow the claimant to take out ATE insurance covering these costs. If the claimant wins the case, he is allowed to shift the costs of both his lawyer's fee and the ATE insurance premium onto the defendant (Jackson 2009, p. 167). Unsurprisingly, the ATE + CFA arrangement has proved extremely popular with English claimants, leaving ATE funding little opportunity to germinate in those areas where ATE + CFA is allowed.[29]

As mentioned, ATE is taken out by clients to cover the residual risks associated with CFA. Under the ATE contract, the insurer undertakes to reimburse the insured for the costs incurred under the 'English Rule' (cf. McDonald, Winters and Harmer 2007, pp. 13–14). The defendant does not experience any specific financial consequences if he prevails. If he loses, however, he is forced to reimburse the claimant for the ATE insurance premium.[30] This is somewhat awkward in the sense that the losing opponent has to pay for the risk-aversion of the winning party. Moreover, the CFA gives the claimant's lawyer the right to a success fee (up to as much as 100 per cent of what he normally charges per hour), so the stakes are raised considerably: if the defendant loses, he will have to pay the normal hourly fee, the success fee and the ATE insurance premium, not to mention his own costs (Sime and French 2008, p. 89 (Ch. 6.2)).

ATE is available for cases with prospects of 65 per cent or more; the premium is some 20–30 per cent of the amount of cover required. Hence, while CFA takes away the risk of having to pay one's own solicitor, the ATE lifts the residual risk of losing the case and having to foot the opponent's bill. This puts both the ATE insurer and the lawyer in the position of risk assessor, as the claimant does not experience any financial consequences other than forfeiting the ATE premium if he loses the case.

In recent years, even the risk of paying the ATE premium has been lifted from specific claimants' shoulders. In the past, deferred payment and a rebate premium was commonly applied if the claimant failed in court, but in recent years English costs regulation has gone one step further by allowing the concept of 'self-insured deferred premium' to be applied. Incontestably, this concept has proved immensely popular with claimants. It is easy to see why: under a self-insured CFA + ATE arrangement the insured claimant does not have to pay premium upfront but only after-wards. If he wins the case, the full premium is shifted entirely onto the defendant and if the claim is unsuccessful in court no premium is charged at all.[31] As a result, a claimant who is secured by CFA + ATE does not run the financial risk of losing. So, if a solicitor and an ATE insurer are willing to financially underwrite a claim with a CFA + ATE 'quality mark', they signal great confidence in a victory to the defendant, even more so as the arrangement may expose the opponent to increased costs as compared to hourly fees. Hence, an opponent faced with a CFA + ATE may be more willing – rightly so or not – to settle than he otherwise might have been. He can also be expected to have an interest in knowing if the claimant has ATE and if so, what the exact premium build-up is. Currently, the insured must indeed inform both the court and defendant that he took out an ATE insurance, but in principle the level of premium does not have to be disclosed (See Sime and French 2008, pp. 85–86 (Ch. 5.11)). This puts defendants in the position of a participant in a rather uncomfortable *sunk cost auction*, which I will discuss later.

In theory, the reasonableness of the premium charged by the ATE is to be scrutinized by the cost judge[32] but because judges have little expert knowl-edge on the operation of insurance markets in general, let alone the rather intransparent market of ATE insurance (cf. Jackson 2009, pp. 479–480), chances are that insurance companies may have less than an optimal incen-tive to set their premiums at a competitive level (Wignall and Green 2008, p. 202).[33] Moreover, claimants – win or lose – have no interest in finding the cheapest ATE as they will not pay the premium. This is especially difficult with regard to the deferred 'premium' that is conditional on the stage of the procedure (staged or stepped) or even topped-up if the claimant wins the case. Restrictions on topped-up premiums seem indispensible because neither the claimant nor his lawyer has any interest in keeping the success premium down by searching for the cheapest success premium. Hence, the insurer can easily create negative externalities for losing opponents (Wignall and Green 2008, pp. 79–81).[34] Furthermore, it is the solicitor who offers the CFA + ATE arrangement to his client and who will recommend a certain ATE provider. This may in turn create an environment for unhealthy relationships between solicitors and ATE providers.

So, the upshot of all this is that a prevailing claimant can fully shift the costs of his solicitor and his ATE premium onto the defendant and a defeated claimant doesn't pay anything. The CFA + ATE industry justifies this on the basis that the policy is 'self-insured', which actually implies that the insurer pools all risks and funds all the unsuccessful cases from premiums charged to the defendant in successful cases (Wignall and Green 2008, p. 190, Jackson 2009, pp. 16–17, 30, 478).[35] So, what 'self-insured' really means is allowing claimants and insurers to design an aleatory contract through which the costs of both parties can be fully externalized on third parties. It is as awkward as a legal system that would allow fire insurers to recoup the aggregate costs of fires whatever their cause from convicted arsonists.

5. CONCLUSION

This chapter looked into BTE and ATE arrangements by analysing the particularities of BTE and ATE arrangements currently available in some European jurisdictions and by painting a picture of their respective markets and legal contexts. On balance, both BTE and ATE have much to commend them. What emerges from the analysis is neither BTE nor ATE is perfect; the institutional settings in which they operate seem decisive for their success. One of the inherent problems with BTE is assessing the quality of the services rendered by the insurer.

Especially worrying, however, is the issue with the long-term sustainability of some ATE products. First, we can conclude that as concerns the legal nature of ATE products we should be cautious in using the noun 'insurance'. It seems that the ATE *insurance* in England and Wales (as in CFA + ATE arrangements) bears more resemblance to insurance contracts[36] than the ATE *funding* arrangements that have entered the German and Austrian markets. The continental version of ATE is in fact much more a contingency fee arrangement offered by capital investors willing to invest in the legal costs in return for a cut of the expected proceeds. In fact, it seems doubtful this can truly be considered an insurance contract.

Secondly, as regards the utility of the CFA + ATE arrangement for keeping a fair balance between promoting access to justice for impecunious claimants and giving defendants the appropriate incentive for settling valid claims at reasonable costs, I have strong reservations. My impression (as an outsider) is that the current legal framework in England and Wales does little to stimulate the development of an ATE market functioning adequately. On balance, the English CFA + ATE practice is a far worse deal for defendants than the continental ATE practice. The English cost shifting rules in themselves may already incite a sunk cost auction: as the costs of losing are unpredictable, litigants may be tempted into investing just a little more with every procedural step the opposing party takes (Cf. Cabrillo and Fitzpatrick 2008, pp. 163–164, Bowles and Rickman 1998, p. 200. Beckner and Katz 1995, p. 206).[37] Obviously, not only the disputed amount itself is at stake but also the costs of the opposing litigant. On the other hand, uncertainty on these costs may constitute a countervailing psychological force: unpredictability may enhance willingness to settle at an early stage, even if contesting the claim in itself may seem reasonable.[38] The question is whether an undiluted English Rule, combined with the CFA + ATE leverage, sets the right level of willingness to issue or settle. Indeed, high stakes and a certain level of unpredictability of outcome may in fact cause an inefficient level of litigation by causing either too much settlement by risk-averse and too little settlement by risk-neutral litigants (cf. Fenn and Rickman 2001, p. 627).[39] I for one would expect English corporate defendants, faced with a claimant carrying CFA + ATE protection, to be far more willing to settle than under any other arrangement. One can only speculate if inefficiencies such as over deterrence are indeed involved. I personally would expect empirical evidence to show that the current English system enhances the nuisance value of relatively minor and straightforward claims, potentially causing overcompensation in that area.

NOTES

1. The Legal Expense Insurance (LEI) Directive (Directive 87/344/EEC of 22 June 1987 on the coordination of laws, regulations and administrative provisions relating to legal expense insurance, OJ L 1987/185, p. 77) excludes the LEI-aspect of liability insurance (that is, the activity pursued by the insurer providing civil liability cover for the purpose of defending or representing the insured person in any inquiry or proceedings if that activity is at the same time pursued in the insurer's own interest under such cover, art. 2 (2) Dir.).
2. Before-the-Event (BTE) LEI can be loosely defined as an undertaking, against the payment of a premium, to bear the costs of legal proceedings and to provide other services directly linked to insurance cover. Cf. art. 2 Directive 87/344/EEC of 22 June 1987 on the coordination of laws, regulations and administrative provisions relating to legal expense insurance, OJ L 1987/185, p. 77. Cf. art. 196 of the Solvency II Proposal (recent Commission Proposal for the overhaul of insurance directives (Solvency II), COM(2008) 119 final; EP resolution 22 April 2009. Note that the BTE element seems missing in this definition.
3. In the Netherlands, BTE LEI consists of two distinct markets, one for businesses (mainly SMEs) and one for households and traffic accidents. The number of BTE LEI policies taken out by SMEs in the Netherlands has almost doubled between 2000 and 2005 (meanwhile halving claim frequency). Generally, penetration of BTE LEI has increased from 14 per cent in 2000 to 19 per cent in 2004. See Maas 2007, p. 127 ff.

4. Notwithstanding the mid-1990s cut in expenditure (notably in civil cases) the overall legal aid bill for England and Wales remains one of the highest. See J Storer 'Legal aid bill "highest in world"' BBC News (London 24 September 2007) <http://news.bbc. co.uk/go/pr/fr/-/2/hi/uk_news/politics/7009686.stm> accessed September 2009.
5. See for example statistics on LEI premiums at www.cea.eu/statistics. Cf. Flood and Whyte 2006, p. 83 ff., Kilian 2003, p. 38 ff.
6. Cf. Marshall 2008, p. 525, who briefly touches on the issue of litigation culture. For a more elaborate socio-legal analysis of litigation culture, see Blankenburg 1994, p. 789 ff., Blankenburg 1998, p. 1 ff.
7. For a historical background, see Werner 1985, p. 249 ff.
8. Art. 199 Solvency II Directive has similar wording.
9. In England and Wales, art. 4 of the Directive was implemented with the Insurance Companies (Legal Expenses Insurance) Regulations 1990 (England and Wales), regulation 6, which adds that these rights 'shall be expressly recognized in the policy'.
10. See also Heinsen 1997, pp. 31–32, who is particularly critical of the German BTE market in this respect. See generally on lawyer regulation and LEI, e.g, Baarsma, Felsö and Janssen 2008, p. 1 ff.
11. Under the German model this integration of services is far less easy to achieve because of the lawyers' monopoly on legal advice. Cf. Kilian and Regan 2004, pp. 252–253.
12. Cf. on diversification of the BTE product Prais 1996, p. 435.
13. The insurance industry is said to play a pivotal role across the board in keeping legal costs of settlement and litigation low (see for example Kritzer 2006, p. 2053 ff. on shopping around behaviour by insurers for cost-efficient defence lawyering.)
14. Note that Dutch LEI policyholders are quite content with the legal services offered by their insurance companies. See *Rechtsverzekeringen in beeld* (Verbond van Verzekeraars, Den Haag 2008). Cf. Baarsma and Felsö 2005, p. 26.
15. Note that in its decision of 3 January 2005, the Dutch (formerly self-regulatory) supervisory council for the insurance industry (*Raad van Toezicht Verzekeringen*) declared this practice inconsistent with article 4 of the EC Directive (Raad van Toeizcht Verzekeringen nr. 2005/006, see http://www.kifid.nl/uploads//jurisprudentie/2005-006%20Rbs.pdf (last visited April 2009).
16. Solvency II does little to force insurers to disclose this right in any other manner than in the general contract terms, leaving every opportunity for de-emphasizing this right.
17. The policy should stipulate that, in case of dispute over merit, recourse can be had to some kind of arbitration procedure, art. 6 Directive 87/344(= art. 201 Solvency II).
18. A similar strict interpretation is to be found in the Netherlands, Baarsma and Felsö 2005, p. 58.
19. For criticism of art. 4, see Baarsma, Felsö and Janssen 2008, p. 125.
20. A case in point is the ECJ decision *Eschig vs. Uniqua Sachversicherung* (ECJ C-199/08, forbidding the LEI to reserve the right in case of a mass damage event to select itself the legal representative of all insured consumers concerned.
21. A rough idea of how the markets are currently developing can be gleaned from Wignall and Green 2008, p. 192 ff., Jaskolla 2004, p. 4 ff., Jackson 2009, p. 156 ff.
22. On these contracts, see for example Coester and Nitzsche 2005, p. 83 ff., Coester and Nitzsche 2005, p. 49 ff.
23. See for example Veith and Gräfe 2005, p. 973 ff., Peysner and Nurse 2008, p. 28. Allianz Litigation Funding, Claims Funding International, Foris and 80e are some of the providers active in Europe.
24. In England, percentages vary between 30 and 60, Jackson 2009, pp. 156–159.
25. Terms Allianz ProzessFinanz GmbH (Austria).
26. In Germany, ATE is also provided for smaller claims. See Coester and Nitzsche 2005, pp. 51–52, Coester and Nitzsche 2005, p. 88. However, given that the German consumer insurance market is saturated by BTE, high penetration rates of this form of ATE seem unlikely.
27. In the definition of 'legal expenses insurance' of art. 2 Directive 87/344/EEC, premium

is a precondition. Note, however, that the mere fact that the insured does not have to pay the premium in itself does not necessarily preclude the arrangement being an insurance contract. For instance, Clarke 2007, p. 22 and 347 ff. is very cautious in formulating an all-encompassing definition for English law. Under German law, the definition of an insurance contract specifically includes the duty of the policyholder to pay a premium (§1 (2) Versicherungsvertragsgesetz), which would lead to a tension under German law at least between the legal and the economic reality of CFA + ATE arrangements. Finally, note that under German law it has been argued that ATE third-party funding is in fact a contract of (silent) partnership; see Grünewald 2000, p. 729 ff., Jaskolla 2004, p. 72 ff., Coester and Nitzsche 2005, p. 95. Others argue that it is a contract 'sui generis'; cf. Eversberg, in: Veith and Gräfe 2005, pp. 962–963, Buschbell 2006, p. 829, Frechen and Kochheim 2004, p. 1214, Dethloff 2000, pp. 2226–2227.

28. In England, this problem already reared its head. See § 307 (d) Bar Code of Conduct, Bar Council Guidance on Conditional Fee Agreements, Part 1, nr. 8.
29. Note that CFA and ATE are not universally available for all claim types. See generally Wignall and Green 2008, p. 19 ff.
30. See fn. 32.
31. Jackson 2009, p. 479 refers to this arrangement as the 'magic bullet'. I think 'poison arrow' would be a more suitable name.
32. S. 29 Access to Justice Act 1999, Rule 44.5 CPR, par. 11.10 CPD. See Sime and French 2008, p. 85 (Ch. 5.10), Wignall and Green 2008, p. 73 ff.
33. Although ATE insurers deny this, they do admit that there is little experience with premium setting. See Jackson 2009, p. 159.
34. Note that this problem slightly resembles the practice of charging alternative tariffs for car rentals: one for common rentals and one (markedly higher) for replacement cars in case of accidents for which a third party is liable. Cf. the English 'credit hire industry' as described by Jackson 2009, p. 28.
35. Jackson (at p. 474) rightly notes that if cost shifting against claimants were to be abolished, the main purpose of ATE insurance premiums would disappear.
36. Cf. the definition of ATE insurance premium in CPR 43.2 (m): 'a sum of money paid or payable for insurance against the risk of incurring a costs liability in the proceedings, taken out after-the-event that is the subject matter of the claim'.
37. Marshall 2008, p. 526 seems to suggest that the auction-effect is exacerbated by the CFA + ATE arrangement. See also Cabrillo and Fitzpatrick 2008, pp. 222–223, who argue that policymakers should consider introducing scales in order to reduce the cost of litigation.
38. A feature that German costs law seems to lack, according to Wagner 2009, p. 382.
39. Cf. Beckner and Katz 1995, p. 215, who argue that cost-shifting rule is superior if care is irrelevant for liability and legal certainty is high.

REFERENCES

Baarsma, Barbara and Flóra Felsö (2005), *Het proces als domein – Over de effecten van het procesmonopolie van de advocatuur*, Amsterdam: SEO Economisch Onderzoek.

Baarsma, Barbara, Flóra Felsö and Kieja Janssen (2008), *Regulation of the Legal Profession and Access to Law – An Economic Perspective*, Amsterdam: SEO Economic Research.

Beckner, Clinton F. and Avery Katz (1995), 'The Incentive Effects of Litigation Fee Shifting When Legal Standards Are Uncertain', *International Review of Law and Economics,* **15**, 205–224.

Blankenburg, Erhard (1994), 'The Infrastructure for Avoiding Civil Litigation:

Comparing Cultures of Legal Behavior in the Netherlands and West Germany', *Law & Society Review,* **28,** 789–808.

Blankenburg, Erhard (1998), 'Patterns of Legal Culture: The Netherlands Compared to Neighboring Germany', *American Journal of Comparative Law,* **46,** 1–41.

Bowles, Roger and Neil Rickman (1998), 'Asyemmetric Information, Moral Hazard and the Insurance of Legal Expenses', *Geneva Papers on Risk & Insurance – Issues & Practice,* **23,** 196–209.

Buschbell, Hans (2006), 'Prozessfinanzierung als Instrument der Anspruchsverfolgung', *Anwaltsblatt,* **12,** 825–830.

Cabrillo, Francisco and Sean Fitzpatrick (2008), *The Economics of Courts and Litigation,* Cheltenham, UK and Northampton, MA, US: Edward Elgar.

Clarke, Malcolm (2007), *Policies and Perceptions of Insurance Law in the Twenty-First Century,* Oxford: Oxford University Press.

Coester, Michael and Dagobert Nitzsche (2005), 'Alternative Ways to Finance a Lawsuit in Germany', *Civil Justice Quarterly,* **24,** 83–102.

Dannemann, Gerhard (1996), 'Access to Justice: an Anglo-German Comparison', *European Public Law,* **2**(2), 271–292.

Dethloff, Nina (2000), 'Verträge zur Prozessfinanzierung gegen Erfolgsbeteiligung', *Neue Juristische Wochenschrift,* **31,** 2225–2230.

European Commission (2008), Directive on the taking-up and pursuit of the business of Insurance and Reinsurance (Solvency II), COM (2008) 119 final, http://eurlex.europa.eu/LexUriServ/LexUriServ.do?uri=COM:2008:0119:FIN:EN:PDF, accessed 27 July 2010.

Faure, Michael., Ton Hartlief and Niels Philipsen (2006), *Resultaatgerelateerde beloningssystemen voor advocaten – Een vergelijkende beschrijving van beloningssystemen voor advocaten in een aantal landen van de Europese Unie en Hong Kong (WODC rapport),* Den Haag: Wetenschappelijk Onderzoeks – en Documententatiecentrum Ministerie van Justitie.

Fenn, Paul, Alastair Gray and Neil Rickman (2006), *The Funding of Personal Injury Litigation: Comparisons Over Time and Across Jurisdictions,* London: Department for Constitutional Affairs.

Fenn, Paul and Neil Rickman (2001), 'Asymmetric Information and the Settlement of Insurance Claims', *Journal of Risk and Insurance,* **68,** 615–630.

Flood, John and Avis Whyte (2006), 'What's Wrong With Legal Aid? Lessons From Outside The UK', *Civil Justice Quarterly,* **25,** 80–98.

Frechen, Fabian and Martin L. Kochheim (2004), 'Fremdfinanzierung von Prozessen gegen Erfolgsbeteiligung', *Neue Juristische Wochenschrift,* **17,** 1213–1217.

Grünewald, Barbara (2000), 'Prozessfinanzierungsvertrag mit gewerbsmäßigem Prozessfinanzierer – ein Gesellschaftsvertrag', *Betriebsberater,* **55**(15), 729–733.

Heinsen, Andreas (1997), *Kundesorientiertes Schadenmanagement am Beispiel der Rechtsschutzversicherung,* Karlsruhe: VVW.

Jackson, Rupert (2009), *Review of Civil Litigation Costs – Preliminary Report,* London: Barlow Lyde and Gilbert LLP.

Jaskolla, Jürgen (2004), *Prozessfinanzierung gegen Erfolgsbeteiligung,* Karlsruhe: Verlag Versicherungswirtschaft.

Kilian, Matthias (2003), 'Alternatives to Public Provision: The Role of Legal Expenses Insurance in Broadening Access to Justice: The German Experience', *Journal of Law and Society,* **30**(1), 31–48.

Kilian, Matthias and Francis Regan (2004), 'Legal Expenses Insurance and Legal

Aid – Two Sides of the Same Coin? The experience from Germany and Sweden', *International Journal of the Legal Profession,* **11**(3), 233–255.

Kirstein, Roland and Neil Rickman (2004), '"Third Party Contingency" Contracts in Settlement and Litigation', *Journal of Institutional and Theoretical Economics,* **160**(4), 555–575.

Kritzer, Herbert M. (2006), 'The Commodification of Insurance Defence Practice', *Vanderbilt Law Review,* **59**(6), 2053–2094.

Maas, Gerard C. (2007), 'Kosten en financiering van rechtsbijstand', in: Judith G. van Erp, Bert E. Niemeijer, Marijke.J. ter Voert and Ronald F. Meijer (eds), *Geschilprocedures en rechtspraak in cijfers 2005*, Cahiers 2007/8, Den Haag: Wetenschappelijk Onderzoek- en Documentatiecentrum Ministerie van Justitie, pp. 117–130.

Marshall, Glen (2008), 'The Literature on the Loser Pays Rule: An Analysis of the Alternatives Within the Ambit of the CFA with the Effect on Settlement Strategies', *Civil Justice Quarterly,* **27**(4), 507–526.

McDonald, Oonagh, Ian Winters and Mike Harmer (2007), *The Market for 'BTE' Legal Expenses Insurance*, London: FWD thinking communications.

Peysner, John and Angus Nurse (2008), *Representative Actions and Restorative Justice – A Report for the Department for Business, Enterprise and Regulatory Reform (BERR)*, Lincoln, UK: Lincoln Law School.

Prais, Vivien (1996), 'Legal Expenses Insurance', in: Adrian A.S. Zuckerman and Ross Cranston (eds), *The Reform of Civil Procedure: Essays on 'Access to Justice'*, Oxford: Oxford University Press, pp. 431–446.

Rickman, Neil and Paul Fenn (1998), 'Insuring Litigation Risk: Some Recent Developments in England and Wales', *Geneva Papers on Risk & Insurance – Issues & Practice,* **23**, 210–223.

Rickman, Neil and Alastair Gray (1996), 'The Role of Legal Expenses Insurance in Securing Access to the Market for Legal Services', in: Adrian A.S. Zuckerman and Ross Cranston (eds) *The Reform of Civil Procedure: Essays on 'Access to Justice'*, Oxford: Oxford University Press, pp. 305–325.

Schepens, Tom (2007), 'Bridging the Funding Gap – The Economics of Cost Shifting, Fee Arrangements and Legal Expenses Insurance and their Prospects for Improving the Access to Civil Justice', *German Working Papers in Law and Economics*, paper 1. http://www.bepress.com/cgi/viewcontent. cgi?article=1196&context=gwp, accessed on 27 July 2010

Sime, Stuart and Derek French (eds) (2008), *Blackstone's Civil Practice 2009*, Oxford: Oxford University Press.

Veith, Jürgen and Jürgen Gräfe (eds) (2005), *Der Versicherungsprozess*, München: Beck.

Wagner, Gerhard (2009), 'Litigation Costs and their Recovery: the German Experience', *Civil Justice Quarterly,* **28**(3), 367–388.

Walters, Adrian and John Peysner (1999), 'Event-Triggered Financing of Civil Claims: Lawyers, Insurers and the Common Law', *Nottingham Law Journal,* **8** (1), 1–22.

Werner, Jürgen (1985), *Die Rechtsschutzversicherung in Europa – Eine Studie über die geschichtliche und wirtschaftliche Entwicklung sowie über die Versicherungsbedingungen der Rechtsschutzversicherungen in Europa*, Karlsruhe: VVW.

Wignall, Gordon and Steven Green (eds) (2008), *Conditional Fees – A Guide to CFAs and Litigation Funding*, London: The Law Society.

6. Financing civil litigation: the case for the assignment and securitization of liability claims

Andrea Pinna

1. INTRODUCTION

1.1 The Fundamental Value of the Right for Compensation and its Implementation

The right for an injured party of a tortious or contractual wrongdoing to receive compensation was granted the status of a fundamental value in Europe. The European Court of Human Rights has indeed decided that a credit for damages deriving from a wrongdoing, that is a liability credit or liability claim, is a good for the purpose of application of Protocol 1 of the European Convention of Human Rights.[1] However, in practice, the implementation of this fundamental right is far from being satisfactory. Several types of losses do not receive compensation because of the practical difficulties and the costs necessary to achieve it.

The traditional way for an injured party to seek compensation is to bring a claim directly and individually in court. In the last decades, legal systems have developed alternative mechanisms to grant compensation without exposing the injured party to the burdens of a lawsuit: compensation schemes have been implemented with regard to particular types of losses; the insurer is sometimes obliged to offer the injured party a compensation without having been sued or even having been requested to do so.[2] In other legal systems, the lawsuit has become an industry for lawyers who are entitled to exclusively finance the lawsuit and to be remunerated only in case of success on the proceeds of such action, even though this is not a common accepted rule for European legal systems (see Chapter 3 by Faure, Fernhout and Philipsen in this book). Nor is it possible for individuals to bring a claim also on behalf of a larger group of victims in a similar situation, the so-called class actions.

Where these alternatives do not exist, which is the most common situation, the creditor of the compensation is always obliged to finance the lawsuit whereas the public mechanisms aimed at granting access to justice are clearly insufficient and reserved either for specific lawsuits or individuals in particular financial distress.[3]

1.2   The Considerations for Deciding Whether to Bring a Claim or Not

As a consequence of this, the decision to bring a claim for compensation is taken in consideration of elements other than the mere meritorious character of the claim. Indeed, the plaintiff, winning a lawsuit, can only in few legal systems, such as England, be awarded a sum corresponding to the real costs spent on the litigation as additional damages. Whereas in many legal systems this is not considered to be a head of loss, in others, courts' practice has limited the compensation to a very low sum, incomparable with the effective price paid for having the plaintiff's rights enforced.[4] The observer therefore faces an unusual situation where the rights of the victims are nowadays particularly sophisticated, whereas the techniques for their protection have hardly evolved for several centuries.

1.3   The Example of the Compensation of the Losses Deriving from Breach of Competition Law[5]

The debate related to the recent initiative of the European Commission on Damages Actions for Breach of EC Antitrust Rules[6] has shown this paradox and incoherence of European legal systems: extremely protective of the victims in theory the system is profoundly inefficient in practice. The conviction of the three French mobile phones operators for the formation of an illegal cartel to a fine of several million euros[7] has shown the impossibility for the consumers – the direct victims of this illegal behavior – to be compensated for the loss they have suffered. In the absence of a class action-like mechanism to aggregate thousands of small individual claims, almost no individual claims were brought and French consumer associations could not provide a surrogate compensation mechanism since they cannot freely advertise to have consumers adhere to the claim they bring.[8] Nowadays, public enforcement of competition law is the only effective proceeding available and private enforcement is extremely limited in practice. The example of the mechanisms for private enforcement of competition law shows more broadly that each citizen is owner of a portfolio of credits in damages that he cannot, in practice, take advantage of, in the expectation that the prescription plays its inexorable role.

1.4　The Hypothesis of Assigning Damages Claims

From this remark and in the actual absence of efficient alternatives, one could explore the idea of making a more useful employment of these credits in damages by simply selling them to someone who is willing and able to make a more efficient use of them. Can unliquidated claims be assigned, just as traditional credits of a liquidated sum of money can be? Prima facie, this technique presents several advantages. If such a damages claim could be of interest for an investor, the original owner of the liability claim – the victim –, by assigning it, will not have to personally finance the lawsuit nor to bear the risk of losing the legal action. Moreover, the assignor will receive compensation for its loss faster than in the traditional course of action, that is by individually claiming damages.[9] Indeed, the price paid by the investor as consideration for the assignment would replace the compensation for the loss that would be judicially awarded. The price would be necessarily lower than the amount of the damages, but it would be paid in exchange for the absence of any cost and risk of the judicial procedure and would be given to the victim by anticipation. This anticipation seems to be susceptible of inciting the injured parties to assign their damages claims and the investor to speculate on the chronological difference between the investment and the expected gain from this investment. Therefore, the intrinsic worth of the assignment of liability claims appears to be real with comparison to the traditional mechanisms of compensation of a contractual or tortious loss.

1.5　The Comparison with Other Techniques for Seeking Compensation

Three main techniques for seeking compensation of a loss are offered by legal systems. Traditionally, the victim always has the right to individually claim for compensation in court, seeking an award for damages. Alternatively, in some cases, private or public compensation schemes are established in order to grant compensation without requiring a liability claim to be brought to court against the wrongdoer. Indeed, the main role of a compensation scheme is to grant compensation to an injured party even if no wrong was committed. However, practice has shown that compensation schemes also intervene when a wrongdoer can be identified and that after compensating the victim, the scheme is subrogated in the rights of the victim to sue the wrongdoer. The compensation scheme is only temporarily substituted to the liable party, but will run the risk of the lawsuit and of the wrongdoer's insolvency.

In some legal systems, in a case of mass injury that is a wrong that affects several individuals in the same or in a similar extent, specific procedures are available that, under various modalities, facilitate the aggregation of several individual claims in one single lawsuit. These collective actions – the US class actions being the most famous ones – allow injured parties to obtain compensation without taking an active part in the proceedings. They continue to bear the risk of losing the lawsuit, but in principle they do not have to contribute to its financing. Such collective actions are particularly efficient for minor losses that would not have, independently from their meritorious character, encouraged the victim to bring an individual claim. The aggregation of individual claims and the resulting economies of scale facilitate the access to justice.

These techniques for granting compensation present advantages and inconveniences on which it is not necessary to further discuss in the context of this chapter. What is important to stress is that, contrary to the assignment of liability claims, they all have in common that compensation for the victim is granted only once the merit of the claim is analysed in great detail. However, the assignment of liability claims is comparable to the system of a compensation scheme. Indeed, compensation schemes verify themselves that the conditions required are fulfilled and, in case they are not, refuse to award any sum to the victim. Alike, the assignment of liability claims shifts the risk of the unmeritorious character of a claim on to the assignee, who will naturally analyse it in great detail before accepting the assignment. In both cases, the victim will receive the consideration for the assignment without waiting for the outcome of the lawsuit and even before any action is brought to court.

The victim can find an advantage to have recourse to the assignment of liability claims in absence of compensation schemes for the injury he has suffered, showing that the private initiative can replace public solidarity, upon which compensation schemes are generally built.

At the end of the day, the assignment of liability claims produces the effects of a settlement for the assignor, which waives its right to bring an action against the liable party in exchange for a monetary advantage. However, the claim is not extinguished with respect to the liable party whose situation has not changed.

1.6   Issues at Stake

Financing civil litigation by way of assignment of liability claims has not been used in practice so far, at least not on a large scale. This naturally raises two main questions. The first one is to determine whether the assignment of liability claims for speculation purposes is legally admissible or contrary to public policy. In Part 2, the comparison between English and French law regarding the legality of an assignment of liability claims indicates that European legal systems are divided on the issue.

In Part 3, the second question of whether *de lege lata* or *de lege ferenda*, the assignment of liability claims, is a technique economically viable and desirable will be addressed. In this part, it will be submitted that this is the case, especially as a solution to the absence of other techniques, such as mandatory damage insurance, compensation schemes or class actions, which already aim to find an alternative to the traditional way of seeking compensation for an injured party that is to individually claim for it in court. Finally, in Part 4, one of the advantages of the assignment of liability claims over other techniques will be highlighted, that is to technically enable the recourse to financial markets by the securitization of such claims. This facilitates the raising of capital for financing civil litigation and allows the transfer of the risk related to liability claims at low transaction costs. Naturally, the inconveniences of this technique of financing civil litigation and of the securitization of claims should not be underestimated.

2. THE LEGALITY OF THE ASSIGNMENT OF LIABILITY CLAIMS

European legal systems are divided on the issue of whether assignments of liability claims are legally acceptable. Some consider that public policy considerations prohibit the commodification of unliquidated liability claims and their transfer for pure speculation purposes. The analysis of English and French law shows this difference of approach. However, it seems that one of the tendencies is now to admit this technique of financing civil litigation since the general prohibition of champerty is fading away.

2.1   The General Prohibition of Assignability of Rights of Action in English Law

England is probably the European country where the costs of legal proceedings are the highest. For financing civil litigation, several methods have been developed such as after-the-event insurance, which is the insurance policy subscribed after the loss is suffered, in order to guarantee the risk of losing the lawsuit and to be obliged to reimburse the legal costs incurred by the winning party (see Chapter 5 by Van Boom in this book). The Access to Justice Act 1999 has further encouraged the recourse to this mechanism by allowing the policy subscriber to be awarded, as damages, the price paid for contracting the insurance.[10]

However, a pure speculative assignment of liability claims is still prohibited in English law. It is true that the Criminal Law Act 1967 has abolished the criminal and tortious liability for maintenance and champerty, but the same act provides that this decriminalization 'shall not affect any rule of law as to the cases in which a contract is to be treated as contrary to public policy or otherwise illegal'.[11] As a consequence of this, the traditional prohibition of assignment of 'mere rights of action' remains the rule. Posterior case law has indeed maintained the solution and, even if the scope of the prohibition was restricted, it remained for speculative assignment.

2.2   Assignment of Claims in Tort

Legal doctrine synthesizing case law distinguishes between claims in contract and claims in tort (see Peel 2007, para. 15–058 ff.). For the latter, it is impossible for the injured party to sell his right to sue the tortfeasor and there are no other exceptions than the right for the insurance company to be subrogated in the rights to sue the tortfeasor after the compensation of the victim who is the insured party. Lord Denning at an earlier stage of the *Trendex Trading Corporation* case explained the reasons behind the prohibition of assignment of liability claims in tort by stating that: 'as far as personal torts are concerned, like damages for libel or slander, or for assault, or for personal injury, the judges have often said that they cannot be assigned. This, I think, still holds good. There are good reasons of public policy for not allowing an assignment: because of the danger that the assignee may buy up the claim at a small figure and use it to get a big profit for himself. In short, all the evils which our fore fathers saw in champerty'.[12]

What is admissible instead is the possibility of agreeing with an investor to assign the proceeds of the action that could be recovered in exchange for the financing of the lawsuit.[13] A clear distinction has therefore to be made between the assignment of the liability claim and the assignment of (part of) the proceeds of the liability claim. The situation is different because the control over the claim is transferred to the assignee in the first case, but not in the latter, and because in the first situation the price is immediately paid and in the second one the consideration for the assignment of part of the proceeds of the action is only the funding of the litigation.

2.3   Assignment of Claims in Contract

As regards contractual claims, the prohibition of assignment of mere right of action is discussed in practice and the House of Lords has adopted an intermediate solution in the leading case *Trendex Trading Corporation v. Crédit Suisse*.[14] Until recently, funding of litigation by third parties was prevented by the rules of champerty and maintenance. These rules made it illegal to financially assist a party to litigation without lawful justification.[15]

In 1982 the position began to change in England when the House of Lords decided that a bank that had financed a sale of cement by one of its customers could validly take the assignment from the customer of his claim for damages for wrongful failure to pay for the cement. However, the essential condition required for the validity of the assignment was that the assignee had a 'genuine commercial interest' in accepting the assignment and enforcing it for its own benefit. The assignment in the case at hand was held to be champertous and invalid because it was expressed to have been taken for the purpose of enabling the bank to resell the customer's right of action to a third party.[16] For the House of Lords, the fundamental condition for the validity of an assignment of liability claims is that the assignee does not contemplate a further sale of the right of action.

By this condition of genuine commercial interest, the House of Lords' main concern was to prevent trafficking in litigation where large profits may be available to parties whose primary interest is in speculation as opposed to seeing justice done. By retaining the legitimate interest requirement, the courts are limiting trade of liability claims to persons with a connection to the litigant (that is the bank that financed him), preventing a speculative market of liability claims from developing. Treitel seems to have a different interpretation of the 'genuine commercial interest' requirement restricting illegal assignments to operations that allow or involve further resale of the claims, and considering lawful assignments where the assignee intends to enforce the right of action by himself (Peel 2007, para. 15–065). However, this liberal interpretation does not seem to be in line with the intention of the House of Lords, which was to prevent the speculation on liability claims.

The 'genuine commercial interest' seems to be an interest separate from the benefit that the assignee would seek to gain from supporting the litigation, such as making a profit. In the model of assignment of claim described in this chapter, it seems that the existence of a genuine commercial or financial interest for the assignee is generally not characterized. Indeed, the interest in the action should exist prior to the assignment. However, considering the advantages of the assignment of a liability claim in terms of the shifting of the risk of losing the lawsuit and the anticipation of payment, one should wish that subsequent case law will consider that the interest required by *Trendex Trading Corporation* is met.

2.4 The General Permission of Assignability of Liability Claims in French Law

French law prohibits the transfer of the right of action in damages independently from the credit for damages. It has, for example, been decided that a capital contribution to a company cannot be the sole right of action without credit for damages and therefore the possibility for the company as assignee to receive the ownership of the proceed in case of successful legal action.[17]

Article 1597 of the French Civil Code prohibits judges, attorneys and other legal professions to acquire lawsuits, rights and credits of action which are of the jurisdiction of the tribunal where they exercise their profession.[18] This article of the Civil Code, which provision has not changed since 1804, has been enacted officially for the purpose of preventing speculation.[19] However, had this provision been enacted in fear of speculation over liability claims, the prohibition should not have only concerned some specific professions, but everyone striving for investing in liability claims. The real reason for this prohibition is the protection of the image of the justice in the society. Therefore, nothing prevents interpreting Article 1597 of the French Civil Code *a contrario* and admitting in principle the legality of the assignment of a liability claims.

Case law has not had the chance to rule on the issue, but the most eminent authors seem to admit the legality of assignment of liability claims without trouble (see essentially Terré, Simler and Lequette 2005, no. 882). However, it shall be acknowledged that, only after a complex analysis, one can conclude the legality of their assignment.[20]

In addition, in case the liability claim is assigned after a legal action is brought to court, the Civil Code contains specific rules allowing the debtor to extinguish the claim by refunding the assignee the price paid for acquiring it from the assignor, the so-called *'retrait litigieux'*.[21] This provision considerably limits the interest of the speculation, since when an assignee has made a good bargain by acquiring a liability claim, he will be exposed to the *retrait litigieux* from the liable party.

However, this provision does not apply when the liability claim is assigned before any action is brought to court.[22] The question arises then to know whether the assignment of a liability claim prior to any legal action is practicable. Indeed, article 1693 of the French Civil Code, applicable to the traditional assignment of monetary liquidated credits, provides that the initial creditor (the assignor) is obliged to guarantee the assignee of the existence of the credit at the moment of the transfer. Since the damages credit only exists if it is subsequently recognized by a final ruling awarding damages, in case of loss of the lawsuit the assignee could argue for the rescission of the assignment for breach of the guarantee. However, legal doctrine and rare case law consider that the provision of article 1693 is not mandatory and that contracting parties to an assignment can deviate from it, stipulating that the assignment is concluded at the assignee's own risk.[23]

These considerations lead to the conclusion of the legality of the assignment of liability claims at least in one legal system . . . but legality does not necessarily mean desirability.

3. THE DESIRABILITY OF THE ASSIGNMENT OF LIABILITY CLAIMS

3.1 Economic Interest in the Speculation

The assignment of liability claims has not yet become common practice. What is on the contrary common practice is what is referred to as 'litigation funding', especially in countries where access to justice is difficult and expensive and the materialization of the risks of losing the case leads to bearing substantial legal costs. The activity of financing a legal claim in exchange for a part of the proceeds of the litigation, in case of success, was considered to be champerty and was even considered in some jurisdictions as a criminal offence (Martin 1992, p.485, Abraham 1992, p.1297). The recent evolution of the legislation is more and more favorable to this kind of litigation funding especially in the United States (Simon, Jr 1989, p.10, Martin 1999–2000, p.57). Some have also clearly expressed the wish of having pure speculative assignment of claim legally admitted.[24]

If the assignment of a claim can be used for 'access to justice' purposes, its function is much broader than only funding the costs of litigation. Its advantages are not only to shift the risk of having to pay litigation costs to a third party, but all the risks of the litigation, including all the consequences of losing the case and being deprived of any compensation. For this reason, the assignment of liability claim can do more than what an after-the-event insurance or litigation funding in general can do.[25] Indeed, insurers will hardly offer after-the-event insurance policies when the victim has too few chances to obtain compensation in a subsequent litigation. Speculative investors, including insurers, would on the contrary accept to bear such a risk only if they could get a rather important share of the damages awarded. This stresses the difference between insurance policies and assignment of liability claims. In the first case, the insured party pays a premium for shifting a risk to a third party, while in the latter, the injured party receives payments in exchange for the potential total proceeds of a successful future legal action.

The existence of benefits for all interested parties will demonstrate that the assignment of liability claims is grounded on incentives to enter into the bargain and that there is an economic interest in this type of speculation.[26]

3.2   Advantages for the Injured Party in Assigning its Liability Claims

The main advantages for an injured party in assigning his liability claim to a professional investor are of two kinds. First of all, the victim can be awarded compensation even if the outcome of the subsequent litigation is negative. Since it is a speculative bargain, the risk of losing the case is shifted to the assignor that will bear alone the risk of losing its investment and, on the contrary, will alone have the chance to make profits. The victim will receive as a consideration a lump sum on which he will have definitive ownership.

Secondly, by assigning a liability claim, the injured party receives compensation before the claim is brought to court instead of waiting for the outcome of the litigation. This advantage is primarily an economic one. People are often in need of rapid payment after they have suffered injury and the traditional litigation techniques generally do not offer them such a possibility. There are of course exceptions already discussed above, but as a rule one will receive compensation when courts definitively rule on the case.

For example, the problem of immediate loss of income by the injured party due to a breach of contract or a tort is not always properly addressed by legal systems. The assignment of the claim can avoid this problem by putting the victim in the position to receive immediate compensation in the form of a price for the definitive sale of its rights and claims against the liable party to an investor that is in a better position to wait for an even longer period before receiving compensation for the damage suffered by the injured party. Moreover, one should not underestimate the psychological aspect of the assignment of claim. Indeed, for some victims it is important to get the compensation fast and not be concerned anymore with the issue. The economic satisfaction often has also psychological benefits for the victims and can reduce stress, emotion and depression.

3.3   Advantages for the Investor in Acquiring Liability Claims

The main feature of the system is that the injured party receives compensation before a ruling on the liability and the measure of damages has been made. The assignee therefore makes a risky bargain because he is not sure that he will receive sufficient money to cover his investment. This is, however, a sound system because the assignee, before accepting the assignment and determining its consideration, will assess the chances the assignor has to win and will measure the damages he could reasonably claim in courts. Of course the consideration – the price – of the assignment will be lower than this valuation because the risk of losing the case is taken into account. Moreover, the cost of the litigation and a reasonable surplus shall be necessarily deducted from the value of the injury. Added to this, the price will include an additional discount corresponding to the advantage for the assignor of receiving immediate compensation instead of waiting for the conclusion of the litigation. Indeed, a monetary amount of 100 is more valuable today than in ten years time, not only because of inflation, but above all because of the mere availability of it. This last point has to be stressed because one of the most important features of the assignment of claim technique consists in awarding the victim with a fast 'compensation' for its injury, instead of waiting for the outcome of the action.

Being a speculative investment, the assignment can generate benefits for the investor. The benefits correspond to the difference in value between the expected damages awarded by court and the price paid to the injured party for the transfer of the claim. It is important to stress that the importance of the investor surplus depends not only on this difference in value, but also on the difference in time elapsed between the date of the assignment and the date damages will be awarded. The annualized rate of return on investment is determined by the difference in value divided by the number of years the investor shall wait for the gain from investment.[27]

An example can better show how the investor could calculate its return on investment. Considering a claim where an investor can reasonably expect an award of damages equal to 250 after five years from the assignment, if the claim is assigned for a price of 140, to which it is necessary to add 20 for the costs of the proceedings, the return on investment will be 11.25 per cent per year over five years: a sound investment, which will probably be also acceptable for the injured party.

3.4 Advantages with Regards to Small Claims for Mass Wrongdoings and Comparison with US Class Actions

The system can give better access to justice especially in cases of small claims, where an individual action would probably not be brought. In this perspective, the assignment of a claim is an alternative to class actions. It has the same advantage of class actions compared to individual litigation, but additionally has further advantages. The technique of assignment of a claim can be used to promote collective claims. This happens when the assignee can benefit from several assignments in relation to the same cause of action from more than one injured party. The technique is therefore comparable to class actions.

Added to the main advantages stressed above which are the compensation of the injured party before the start of the litigation and even if the case is eventually lost, other advantages can be indicated. First of all, the assignment of liability claims is a good alternative to class actions in legal systems that do not permit this mass litigation mechanism. Indeed, nothing in theory prevents investors from openly asking the public for the assignment of their claim against a possible liable party. An offer to contract can legally be made to the public in general and in some legal systems even binding if the essential elements of the future contract are present in the offer, which in this case correspond with the individualization of the rights to be transferred and the determination of the price of transfer.

This mechanism can provide easier access to justice with regard to small claims where an individual victim would not bring an action because of the importance of legal costs and the time required to deal with the litigation. The aggregation of the individual small claims to massive assignment by injured parties and the economies of scale resulting from it make the technique a possible sound investment. Here the valuation of the claims could be lower for putative assignors and higher for putative assignees, which make the bargain possible. Assignors can sometimes even evaluate their claim to zero since they would never consider bringing a legal action. This means that they would be interested in assigning their rights towards the liable party for a very small amount. The chances for mass assignments of small claims, such as the one of the example given in the introduction of breach of antitrust rules, are therefore very high.

Even in legal systems where class actions can be brought, the assignment of liability claims can present advantages over class actions. Not only are injured parties compensated immediately and even in case of negative outcome of the future litigation, but, contrary to class actions, the control of the claim is given to others than attorneys and this can provide more transparency than a class action does with respect to the financing of the litigation. Important criticism was expressed in the United States as regards the behavior of lawyers and the indirect financing of the claim.[28] On the contrary, when the claim is assigned to a professional investor it could be easier to track the source of financing.

Contrary to the usual class actions procedures, an assignment of liability claim can be promoted and financed by public organizations or non-profit associations. As a consequence of this injured parties could receive higher compensation than in class actions, since the assignment would include no surplus for the assignee and the system of contingent fees could be excluded. Thus, one can suggest that the assignment of a claim would often provide the injured parties with a higher compensation than they could expect in case of success in class action: for example the contingency fees of attorneys in class action procedures can be higher than the surplus of the investor in case of assignment of liability claims.

Moreover, the technique of assignment of liability claims allows competition between the investors as regards the price for assignment, which class action mechanisms cannot in principle provide. The existence of several operators offering the same services on the market can reduce their surplus to the benefit of injured parties and the judge is not required, like in class actions proceedings, to scrutinize and decide on the method of compensating the attorney representing the class.

Having the US class actions model in mind, the last, but not the least advantage is related to the complex and strict conditions that must generally be fulfilled to grant the certification of a class action. As a principle, class actions cannot be brought where the members of a putative class are not in an almost identical situation. Requirements of homogeneity are set in Rule 23 (a)(2) and (3) of the Federal Rules on civil procedure that require for the certification the commonality and the typicality. The commonality is the fact that the legal and factual questions of the litigation are common to all members of the class.[29] This typicality refers to the fact that the allegations and legal motions asked to the court are common to all members of the class. Added to this, in case of '(b)(3) class action', the one that mainly concerns mass liability cases, it is also necessary that these common questions predominate over individual questions of the members of the class. The elements that could determine the judge's decision are listed: one of these is the manageability of the procedure. According to this, the judge could refuse certification in case it considers that the class action is difficult to manage. This has happened often when the assessment of damages cannot be made collectively, but requires individual measure.[30] Some courts circumvented this problem by certifying class actions only as regards the question of the principle of liability, leaving the award of damages to the members of the class to posterior individual claims.[31]

On the contrary, the assignment of claims more easily accepts the diversity in 'class' members' situation, especially when the damage suffered is of diverse importance and when the law applicable to the different injured parties having assigned their claim can vary. Moreover, since there is no certification procedure, the admissibility of the claim is not dependent on the decision of the judge and the procedure strategy is left to the assignee. The risk of refusal of certification does not exist in cases of assignment of claims, where the investor can bring all the claims that have been assigned to him. In cases of lack of homogeneity of the group of assignors, it is up to the investor to determine whether to aggregate the different claims that have been transferred to him or to bring more than one action to court. Bringing more legal actions can also be seen as a diversification method of the risk of the investment considering that different solutions (as regards the principle of the liability, but also of its consequences in terms of monetary damages) can be held by courts. The diversification of the risk strategy can include *forum shopping*, where the investor because of the particular situation of their different assignors is in the position to claim in different courts or jurisdictions.

The main disadvantage of the assignment of liability claims compared to certain class action models is that the former can only be made voluntarily, that is by individualized consent of the assignors. Contrary to class actions an opt-out 'assignment' is in principle incompatible with the system. In some legal systems, a plaintiff can be included in the certified class actions by failing to opt-out after having received notification.[32] Even if an opt-in procedure is not incompatible with a class action procedure, opt-out is one of the keys to its success in the United States.[33] The attorneys representing the plaintiff class do not have to ask all putative members to give their agreement to be part to the litigation and therefore to be bound by its preclusive effect.

There is, however, a very important difference in cases of assignment of claims that makes the opt-in requirement less burdensome than for class actions. The opt-in in class actions, when it exists, is posterior to the certification of the class because it is first necessary to determine precisely the boundaries of the class before proceeding with the notice in order to gather the agreement of the individuals to be part of the procedure. In case of assignment of claim, the decision to assign the claim is always the first step. It is therefore much easier for the investor to inform by way of advertising in the press, on the radio, television and even the Internet its proposal to acquire legal claims of a certain type for a proposed price. The investment to acquire more claims of the same nature against the same defendant would become profitable only after a certain number of assignments because of considerations of economies of scale or even risk diversification. If such is the case, the investor can subject the assignment to the condition precedent of the existence of a certain number of acceptances by injured parties.

These are some of the elements that could be put forward to underline the desirability of the assignment of liability claims. A further step in the analysis is to explore the possibility and the consequences of creating a financial market where liability claims could be traded.

4.   THE SECURITIZATION OF LIABILITY CLAIMS

4.1   The Consequences of the Creation of a Market for Liability Claims

If the assignment of liability claims develops, a market can be created. This has to be understood not only as a new professional activity, but also as a market in the common sense of the word, a place where the claims are bought and sold. Once the injured party has transferred his rights, they become an economic and speculative value. There are no barriers as for it to become a negotiable instrument. Like more traditional securities, the claim could be further traded also on financial markets. The securitization can be made through normal succession of assignments. However, the securitization can also be the consequence of the setting up of an ad hoc structure (special purpose investment vehicle), that is a juridical person to which the claim is initially assigned and whose only asset is the potential future credit against the defendant. The transfer or partial transfer of the rights in the claim can subsequently be realized by share purchase agreements. This has the advantage of allowing syndication of a claim where more than one investor takes part to the investment and also to permit, if necessary, trading the shares of the company on a regular stock market.

One can therefore be assigned with a claim and not bring it to court straight away, but transfer it again to a new assignee for a higher price. This speculation can be interesting for investors because the value of the claim can change between the moment it was first transferred and the date of a final ruling on the issue. Not only could 'natural' causes modify the value of the claim, but also legal causes, like the modification of a line of case law or a practice of a court in measuring damages, or a lower court decision held in the lawsuit in which rights for action have been assigned. If the likelihood that the claim will be successful is higher than initially expected, the investor could resell it and realize an anticipated gain for investment. The opposite could also incite the investor to sell, especially if he wishes to limit its risks, in favor of an investor willing to make very risky investments. In such a case, the resale price would be lower than the initial assignment consideration.

In other words, this could facilitate the raising of capital for financing civil litigation and allows the transfer of the risk related to liability claims at low transaction costs.

4.2 The Barriers to the Securitization of Liability Claims

The main barrier to the negotiation of a claim is its prescription. The claim has to be brought to court before it is time barred. However, prescription is not necessarily an issue since the liability claim can be traded even once the legal action is brought.[34]

Another possible barrier to the securitization of liability claims needs to be addressed. At first glance an assignee has an interest in a fast outcome of the legal action and therefore has incentives to bring a claim fast, which would prevent the negotiability of the right to bring a liability claim.

Indeed, the longer is the period between the investment and the date of the gain from investment the worse the investment can be. If the investor waits for 10 years after the investment before getting its proceeds, the proceeds need to be larger in order to be profitable, than if he obtains a return on investment after 1 year only. This seems to be an incentive for the investor to bring a claim immediately after the assignment.

However, all depends on the date at which damages are assessed. Two different solutions can be found in European legal systems. The first one, which corresponds to the French solution, is that damages both in contract and in tort are to be assessed at the date of the judgment awarding them and not at the date of the harm.[35] When such a solution is being followed, the date of assessment of damages becomes an element of speculation in itself. The second solution, based on the same logic of the victim's obligation to mitigate the loss, is followed notably by English law where damages are in principle assessed at the date of the breach and the exceptions are quite limited (Chen-Wishart 2008, p. 557, Peel 2007, para. 20–063 ff. and the case law quoted), and even if exceptions to this rule exist, damages may in any case be reduced 'if the claimant unreasonably drags his heels through the courts'.[36] Such a solution is the consequence, especially in breach of contract matters, of the duty to mitigate that obliges the injured party to seek for a replacement rapidly.[37] This does not mean that the possibility of securitization of legal claims is limited when the law applicable to the claim in damages requires the injured party to mitigate its loss. Indeed, if the mitigation only consists in having to resort to a substitute transaction to the one promised by the assigned party, nothing prevents the injured party from mitigating and assigning the claim at the same time. The assignment could also help the injured party in financing the mitigation. The duty to mitigate does not necessarily oblige the injured party or the assignee of the liability claim to bring an action in compensation rapidly. This means that after the assignment and the mitigation, the assignee can decide to bring a claim at its discretion within the prescription period.

4.3 An Example of the Practicability of the Securitization of Liability Claims

The above discussion shows that the legal preconditions for the existence of a market of liability claims are at least fulfilled in some countries. However, the observer notices the absence of development of the assignment of liability claims and the sole attempt that could be recorded in Europe is the so-called *Begaclaim*. This is a public company established in 1997 which has as its sole asset a liability claim against the Dutch government for damage to the reputation of a businessman who as a consequence of long proceedings was eventually declared not guilty of an insider trading accusation. If the claim for damages was partially successful before the first instance court,[38] it was reversed on appeal.[39] The trials and tribulations of the proceedings continued and the Dutch Supreme Court partially, although on minor points, quashed the decision and decided that partial retrial was necessary by the Court of Appeal of Amsterdam.[40] It goes without saying that as a consequence of the different decisions the market value of the company has considerably changed.

4.4   The Effects of a Market for Liability Claims

The existence of a liability claim market can bring about important advantages. One of them is the circulation of the information following the market theories developed by Eugene Fama. A market is a place where operators meet and where the information is not only exchanged, but created by the aggregation of the different pieces of information exchanged. As a consequence of this, one can notice that the evaluation of the claim by the market is a synthesis of the information available. This diffusion of information on the market helps the operators on the market. Indeed, the evaluation is an indication of the merit of a claim to be brought to court. The analysis of the prices on the market is an element of decision and shows the consideration of the operators as regards the meritorious character of a claim. It is true that the different claims are in principle individualized, but regrouping them on the market allows standardization.

In theory, the creation of a market for liability claims can provide better knowledge of the law, better evaluation of the chances of a claim to be successful and better knowledge of the amount of damages that could be awarded on a typology of claim. The market will therefore work as a concentrator of information and will automatically provide to the systematization of the law. In doing this, the market will take the role of legal doctrine.[41] The market will particularly be of help in developing a system of precise assessment and measure of damages in case of injury. Legal systems know general rules in this area, but the practical application of these rules leads to divergences according to the court settling the case. This divergence can be lowered if a general market is created. However, a too-high uncertainty on the result expected by the application of the principles of measure of damages could prevent the system from working in the first place.[42] Indeed, investors could be in a position of being unable to assess the risk they run with sufficient precision. The higher the certainty is, the better the risk can be assessed, but at the same time, this certainty will result in a reduction in the risk itself. The progressive lowering of the uncertainty will necessarily lead to easier assessment of which cases are meritorious or not. At the extreme opposite, the certainty about the future outcome of the case and its consequences would be the negation of the risk, making the assignment of claim a low-risk investment because it is similar to a money lending activity making profits only on the difference of time between the payment and the reimbursement. The credit so given is, however, not secured since it depends on the solvency of the liable party.

5. CONCLUDING REMARKS

As a general conclusive consideration, and I admit we are slowly entering into legal science fiction, it is possible to imagine that the information gathered and systemized by the market can be of help not only to the operators, but also the judge. Indeed, the knowledge of the value of a claim can give the judge indications on the meritorious character of a claim. As a consequence of this, the market could influence the decision of the judge, whereas the normal situation would be the opposite, that is the expected decision of the judge giving indications of the value of the claim.

More seriously, it is clear that the possible effects of a market of liability claims on the Justice have not been explored yet and the dangers involved shall require further and attentive assessment.

NOTES

1. ECourtHR 20 November 1995, *Pressos Compania Naviera v. Belgium, RTD civ.* 1996, 1019, J.-P. Marguenaud, for tortious matters; ECourtHR 9 November 1994, *Raffineries grecques Stranis Stratis Andreabis v. Greece, RTD civ.* 1995, 652, F. Zenati, for damages claims deriving from breach of contract. The right for compensation has Constitutional value in France, *Conseil Constitutionnel* 9 November 1999, no. 99-419 DC, *JCP* 1999, II, 20173 with annotation G. Viney.
2. See for example Article L. 211-9 al. 2 of the French Insurances Code, which provides that the insurer in case of traffic accident has to address to the victim an offer of compensation within eight months as of the accident.
3. Such is for example the case in England, where small businesses are not entitled to the state's legal aid. For this argument, see Lord Hoffmann in *Circuit Systems Ltd (In Liquidation) V. Zuken-Redac (UK) Ltd,* and in *Norglen Ltd and Others (A.P) (In Liquidation) v. Reeds Rains Prudential Ltd and Others,* [1997] *UKHL* 51; [1997] 3 *WLR* 1177: 'The cost of obtaining justice in England, only too often prohibitive, is a current social problem which goes to the roots of civil society. The provision of a system of justice to resolve disputes between citizens is one of the most ancient and important duties of the state. But the cost of litigation is today so high that the majority of people are in practice unable to seek redress for the wrongs they have suffered. This applies not only to individuals but also to companies with modest resources.'
4. For example in France the judge has discretionary power to assess the compensation for the cost of litigation pursuant to Article 700 of the Code of Civil Procedure and this

sum is not calculated as damages normally are, Cass. Civ. 2, 8 July 2004, Bull. civ. II no. 365.
5. On the possible approaches to compensate losses deriving from breach of competition law, see Chapter 4 by Keske, Renda and Van den Bergh in this book.
6. Green Book of 19 December 2005, COM(2005) 672 final; White Book of 2 April 2008, COM(2008) 165 final.
7. Judgments partially confirmed by the *Cour de Cassation*, Cass. Com. 29 June 2007, Bull. civ. IV no. 181.
8. See Trib. Com. Paris, 6 December 2007, RG no. 2006057440.
9. In some cases, interim measures can be granted by courts awarding provisional indemnification in the expectation of a final ruling on the merits.
10. Section 29 of the Access to Justice Act 1999. The House of Lords has ruled that the possibility for receiving the reimbursement of the premium is subject to the reasonableness of the amount of the insurance premium, *Callery v. Gray* [2001] *Lloyd's Rep* IR 765.
11. Section 14(2) of the Criminal Law Act 1967.
12. See *Trendex Trading Corporation v. Crédit Suisse* [1980] 1 QB 629, at 656 (CA).
13. The mere agreement to participate in the proceeds of an action does not constitute champerty, see *Glegg v. Bromley* [1912] 3 K.B. 474 (CA): The plaintiff in this case, Mrs. Glegg brought an action against another lady for damages for slander. She needed money to pay for her solicitor's costs in the action so she assigned to her husband any amount to which she would become entitled if the action settled or was successful. It did not matter that the action was for a personal tort because only the fruits of the action were being assigned. It was critical to the Court of Appeal that such an assignment did not give the assignee any right to interfere in the proceedings in the action. Hence it was decided that the assignment was not against public policy. For the more recent restatement of this solution, *Trendex Trading Corporation v. Crédit Suisse* [1982] AC 679, at 702 (HL).
14. [1982] AC 679 (HL).
15. On the history of the champerty, see M. Radin (1935), 'Maintenance by Champerty', *California Law Review*, **24**, 48. See more recently Y.L. Tan (1990), 'Champertous Contracts and Assignments', *The Law Quarterly Review*, **106**, 656.
16. This is exactly what happened in this case since the bank acquired the claim for damages for $ 800 000, resold it for $ 1 100 000 to a third party, who settled for $ 8 000 000.
17. Cass. Com. 31 May 2005, *Bull. civ.* IV, no. 124; *D.* 2005, 1699, with note A. Lienhard; *Rev. soc.* 2006, 114, with note B. Dondero; *Bull. Joly* 2006, 77, with note P. Scholer.
18. 'Les juges, leurs suppléants, les magistrats remplissant le ministère public, les greffiers, huissiers, avocats, défenseurs officieux et notaires, ne peuvent devenir cessionnaires des procès, droits et actions litigieux qui sont de la compétence du tribunal dans le ressort duquel ils exercent leurs fonctions, à peine de nullité, et des dépens, dommages et intérêts.'
19. See Portalis, 'Exposé des motifs devant le corps législatif', séance du 7 Ventôse an XII, *Recueil Rondonneau*, t. VII, p. 15; 'Discussion au Conseil d'État', séance du 9 nivôse an XII, in : Fenet, *Recueil complet des travaux préparatoires du Code civil*, t. XIV, p. 44 ff. This idea was already expressed by Pothier (Œuvres de Pothier, par M. Dupin, Béchet Aîné, 1824, t. 2, *Traité du contrat de vente*, p. 264) who talks of '*odieux acheteurs de procès*'.
20. See Andrea Pinna, 'La mobilisation de la créance indemnitaire', *RTD civ.* 2008, 229 and in particular pp. 233–240 for a detailed explanation of the issue of legality of the assignment of liability claims in French law.
21. Article 1699 of the French Civil Code.
22. Consistent line of case law as of Cass. Civ. 5 July 1819, *S.* 1820, 1, 53.
23. Req. 17 November 1875, *S.* 1876, 1, 33; Req. 4 July 1905, *D.P.* 1910, 1, 222.
24. See the discussion *de lege ferenda* of Peter Charles Choharis (1995), 'A Comprehensive Market Strategy for Tort Reform', *Yale Journal on Regulation*, **12**, 435.
25. As in the UK *Trendex Trading Corporation* case mentioned above, in

Charlotte-Mecklenburg Hosp. Auth. v. First of Georgia Ins. Co., 455 S.E.2d 655, 657 (N.C. 1995), the Supreme Court of North Carolina noted the difference between the assignment of a claim whereby the assignee acquires control over litigation, and assignment of the proceeds of a claim whereby the real party in interest retains control over the litigation, and held that the former was champertous and thus void on public policy grounds.

26. For a law and economics analysis of 'litigation funding' in general, see Ari Dobner (1995–1996), 'Litigation for Sale', *University of Pennsylvania Law Review*, **144**, 1530. See also Robert D. Cooter (1989), 'Towards a Market in Unmatured Tort Claims', *Virginia Law Review*, **75**, 2.

27. The annualized rate of return on investment formula is easy to establish:
Annualized ROR = [(damages expected – price of the assignment – non refundable costs of the litigation)* 100 / (price of the assignment + non refundable costs of the litigation)] / difference in years between the assignment and the compensation

28. See for example P.B. Wilson (1994), 'Attorney Investment in Class Action Litigation: The *Agent Orange* Example', *Case Western Reserve Law Review*, **45**, 291, who explores the ethical and practical issues involved in financing class action litigation by speculative attorney investment. See the contributions of Hensler and Keske, Renda and Van den Bergh in this book.

29. See for example *In re Rhône-Poulenc Rorer Incorporated*, 51 F.3d 1293 (7th Cir. 1995), decertification of a class action against a pharmaceutical laboratory by a group of hemophiliacs that contracted aids by blood transfusion because of the novelty of the legal issue and the diversity of law applicable.

30. One recent example of this is the decertification of a tobacco class action claim for the reason that the injured parties were in a different position as regards causation and measure of damages, *Howard A. Engle M.D. et al. v. Liggett Group Inc. et al.*, (Fla. SC, 6 July 2006, n° SC03-1856), decertifying the class action and reversing an award of 145 millions dollars in punitive damages. Refusal of certification is also frequent in case of difference in law applicable to the different victims: see for example *Smith v. Brown & Williamson Tobacco Corp.*, 174 F.R.D. 90, 94 (W.D. Mo. 1997); *Castano v. American Tobacco*, 84 F.3d 734 (5th Circ. 1996): 'In a multi-state class action, variations in state law may swamp any common issues and defeat predominance'; In re *Ford Motor Co. Ignition Switch Prods. Liab. Litig.*, 174 F.R.D. 332, 340 (1997); In re *Bridgestone/Firestone Inc., Tires Products Liability Litigation*, 288 F.3d 1012 (7th Circ. 2002).

31. See for example *Olden v. LaFarge Corp.*, 383 F.3d 495 (6th Cir. 2004), at 509, according to which a court can 'bifurcate the issue of liability from the issue of damages, and if liability is found, the issue of damages can be decided by a special master or by another method'; *Carnegie v. Household Int'l, Inc.*, 379 F.3d 656 (7th Cir. 2004), at 661: 'Rule 23 allows district courts to devise imaginative solutions to problems created by the presence in a class action litigation of individual damages issues'. Section 3:305a of the Dutch Civil Code allows collective actions only for the purpose of declaration of liability.

32. Such is the case according to Section 23(b)(3) of the Federal Rules on Civil Procedure.

33. It has also been suggested by the Scottish Law Commission, Multy-Party Actions (Report 1996), §§ 4.51, 4.54 and 4.55 for the discussion and recommendations 13 et 14.

34. In some legal systems, however, the defendant has then the right to buy the claim back at the price of its assignment (see the French *retrait litigieux*). As explained above, this situation can be prevented by including the claim in an autonomous juridical person and then trading the shares of that legal person, owing the claim, instead of the claim itself.

35. In tort, Cass Civ. 15 July 1943, *D.A.* 1943, 81; *J.C.P.* 1943.II.2500, with note Hubrecht; in contract, Cass. Com. 16 February 1954, *Bull. civ.* no. 56 ; D. 1954, 534 with note R. Rodière; *J.C.P.* 1954.II.8062 with note J.G.B (constant line of case law). On this question and the nuances of the solution, see Andrea Pinna (2007), *La Mesure du Préjudice Contractuel*, LGDJ, Paris, pp. 294–319.

36. See, *Malhotra v. Choudhury* [1980] Ch 52.
37. *McGregor on Damages* (1997), London: Sweet & Maxwell, 16ᵗʰ ed., §§ 308–312, and the case law there quoted. The duty to mitigate however does not apply so strictly in tort, since it is considered that the injured party does not necessarily have sufficient money to finance the mitigation. A similar argument is put forward when the contracting party has already paid the price, *McGregor on Damages*, § 312.
38. Rb. den Haag, 4 April 2001, LJN: AB0850. On this question, see S.C.J.J. Kortmann, N.E.D. Faber (2003), 'Aansprakelijkheid van de Staat voor het optreden van politie en justitie (de Begaclaim)', in C.J.M. Klaassen, R.J.N. Schlössels, G. van Solinge, L. Timmerman (eds), *Aansprakelijkheid in beroep, bedrijf of ambt*, Deventer: Kluwer, p. 547–570.
39. Hof Den Haag, 14 October 2004, *JOR* 2004, 318, with note B.P.M. van Ravels.
40. Hoge Raad, 13 October 2006, LJN: AV6956; *NJ* 2007, 432 with note J.B.M. Vranken.
41. Legal doctrine's main task is to systematize the legal solution also deriving from case law. On this role of legal doctrine even in civil law countries, see, for example F. Terré (2006), *Introduction Générale au Droit*, Paris: Dalloz, 7ᵗʰ ed., no. 199.
42. See for example it is generally considered that the mechanisms of measuring damages of French law is particularly underdeveloped, B. Nicholas (1992), *The French Law of Contract*, Wotton-under-Edge: Clarendon Press, p. 225; H. Beale, A. Hartkamp, H. Kötz, D. Tallon (eds) (2002), *Cases, Materials and Text on Contract Law*, Oxford: Hart Publishing, p. 812.

REFERENCES

Abraham, Donald L. (1992), 'Investor-Financed Lawsuits: A Proposal to Remove Two Barriers to an Alternative Form of Litigation Financing', *Syracuse Law Review*, **43**, 1297–1320.

Beale, Hugh, Arthur Hartkamp, Hein Kötz and Denis Tallon (eds) (2002), *Cases, Materials and Text on Contract Law*, Oxford: Hart Publishing.

Chen-Wishart, Mindy (2008), *Contract Law*, Oxford: Oxford University Press.

Choharis, Peter C. (1995), 'A Comprehensive Market Strategy for Tort Reform', *Yale Journal on Regulation*, **12**, 435–526.

Cooter, Robert D. (1989), 'Towards a Market in Unmatured Tort Claims', *Virginia Law Review*, **75**(2), 383–412.

Dobner, Ari (1995–1996), 'Litigation for Sale', *University of Pennsylvania Law Review*, **144**, 1529–1592.

Kortmann, Sebastiaan C.J.J. and N.E. Dennis Faber (2003), 'Aansprakelijkheid van de Staat voor het optreden van politie en justitie (de Begaclaim)', in Carla J.M. Klaassen, Raymond J.N. Schlössels, Gerard van Solinge, Levinus Timmerman (eds), *Aansprakelijkheid in beroep, bedrijf of ambt*, Deventer: Kluwer, pp. 547–570.

Martin, Susan L. (1992), 'Syndicated Lawsuits: Illegal Champerty or New Business Opportunity?', *American Business Law Journal*, **30**(3), 485–511.

Martin, Susan L. (1999–2000), 'Financing Plaintiffs' Lawsuits: An Increasingly Popular (and Legal) Business', *University of Michigan Journal of Law Reform*, **33**, 57–86.

McGregor, Harvey (1997), *McGregor on Damages*, London: Sweet & Maxwell.

Nicholas, Barry (1992), *The French Law of Contract*, Wotton-under-Edge: Clarendon Press.

Peel, Edwin (2007), *Treitel on the Law of Contract*, London: Sweet & Maxwell.

Pinna, Andrea (2007), *La mesure du préjudice contractuel*, Diss. LGDJ, Paris
Pinna, Andrea (2008), 'La mobilisation de la créance indemnitaire', *Revue trimestrielle de droit civil*, 229–248.
Pothier, Robert-Joseph (1824), *Œuvres, t. 2, Traité du contrat de vente*, Paris: Béchet Aîné.
Radin, Max (1935), 'Maintenance by Champerty', *Caifornia Law Review*, **24**, 48–78.
Simon, Roy D. Jr. (1989), 'Lawsuit Syndication: Buying Stock in Justice', *Business & Society Review*, **69**, 10–14.
Tan, Y.L. (1990), 'Champertous Contracts and Assignments', *The Law Quarterly Review*, **106**, 656–679.
Terré, François, Philippe Simler and Yves Lequette (2005), *Droit Civil, Les Obligations*, Paris: Dalloz, 9th ed.
Terré, François (2006), *Introduction Générale au Droit*, Paris: Dalloz, 7th ed.
Wilson, Paula Batt (1994), 'Attorney Investment in Class Action Litigation: The *Agent Orange* Example', *Case Western Reserve Law Review*, **45**, 291–350.

7. The empirical analysis of litigation funding

Paul Fenn and Neil Rickman

1. INTRODUCTION

Litigation raises a number of significant difficulties for the participating parties. In particular, it is regularly claimed to be costly and risky and, because of the asymmetric information problem between lawyer and client, to raise principal–agent incentive problems. Problems can be exacerbated by procedural rules: perhaps the most obvious being the one in many jurisdictions where the losers pay winners' costs.

Such problems may compromise the twin aims of any system of litigation: efficiency (in terms of deterrence through the bringing of meritorious claims) and equity (through the compensation of those who have suffered genuine harm). The contracts between lawyers and clients – hence 'litigation funding' – can be seen as market and regulatory responses to such concerns. In some jurisdictions, clients bear all the litigation risk through 'out-of-pocket' hourly fee contracts; elsewhere lawyers take on this role through contingency payment, while insurance may also be provided by state-sponsored legal aid or by the insurance industry itself.[1] Clearly, these examples suggest that a potentially complex set of agency relationships (between lawyers, clients and third-party funders) surround issues relating to fees, incentives and information asymmetries in litigation.

Of course, the choice of funding mechanisms is of theoretical interest but only has practical consequences if it can be shown to affect key outcomes of the litigation process; in particular, ones related to the objectives set out above. This requires empirical analysis, which is the scope of this chapter. Our aim is to explain briefly why funding may influence litigation, then to indicate some of the main papers and results that have sought to test and quantify these relationships. Space constraints prevent a comprehensive coverage, though we are also mindful of Helland and Tabarrok's (2003) observation that 'very few empirical studies of contingency fees have been conducted' (p. 522): perhaps for some of the reasons raised in Section 3, studies of litigation funding are not especially common. Of course, many things influence the decision to bring a legal claim, and its subsequent outcome and many of these are linked to the financial aspects of this process. In particular, procedural rules affect the cost of litigation and specific legal rules affect who might ultimately meet these costs. Thus, a preliminary task is to define the scope of the chapter. Two points are relevant. First, for the purposes of this chapter, we take 'litigation funding' to be separate from such procedural concerns: instead, we define it to mean the contracts that lawyers, clients and (possibly) third parties enter into in order to fund litigation.[2] Second, to the extent that procedural rules differ across jurisdictions, it is possible that their empirical effects in one setting may not be replicated in others. This raises the standard (but nonetheless important) difficulty of how to interpret such results in a general sense. We acknowledge this issue but its resolution is beyond the scope of this chapter; in particular, we believe that it would need a more careful marriage of theoretical predictions from models making different jurisdictional assumptions and empirical results to address this effectively.

This chapter is structured as follows. We begin with a simple model of litigation that is intended to indicate the potential effects of litigation funding, thereby justifying the issues that empirical research has focused on: the filing of cases, and their outcomes (drop, settle, trial, settlement amounts and conflicts between lawyer and client). We then note briefly some basic issues in the data requirements for empirical work in this area before turning to several examples of the available research in this area. Our focus is on econometric studies: Kritzer (2002) provides other, complementary, perspectives on the issue.

2.   LITIGATION FUNDING IN THEORY

We follow the model popularised by Gravelle and Waterson (1993), itself a version of Bebchuk's (1984) one-shot model of litigation with asymmetric information. Our purpose is to indicate some of the effects that funding may have on litigation.[3] The model is convenient because it is simple enough to be tractable yet detailed enough to illustrate several effects that subsequent empirical studies have considered. There are, of course, many other models of litigation and not all of them produce the qualitative results set out below.[4]

An accident may take place with probability p which, in turn, is dependent on a (potential) defendant's care level x. We assume that more care reduces the accident probability at a decreasing rate: mathematically, we have $p'(x) < 0$; $p''(x) > 0$. Accidents cause damage L but only the plaintiff (P) knows the true value of L; the defendant (D) knows its distribution – that is there is asymmetric information. To capture D's uncertainty here, we model the distribution of possible damage levels using a draw from the cumulative distribution $Q(L)$, and associated density $q(L)$ on $[L_0, L_1]$.[5] The defendant can make a single settlement offer (S) to P, who then decides whether to accept this or reject it in favour of trial, where his probability of winning is w (which is exogenous and, so, independent of efforts at trial and commonly known). He takes legal advice on this though, for simplicity, we assume this advice to be unbiased.[6] Settlement costs P's lawyer c_0 while trial costs him c_1. In return, P pays the lawyer a fee of f^s if the case settles, f^w if the case wins at trial and f^0 if the case loses at trial. The defendant pays her lawyer f^D at trial. All parties are risk neutral.[7]

Consider the offers that P would accept. A well-informed P would accept the settlement offer S if and only if

$$S - f^s \geq w(L - f^w) - (1 - w)f^0 + t \qquad (7.1)$$

where $t = k[wf^w - (1 - w)f^D]$ is the expected cost transfer from D to P at trial: this accommodates the UK cost rule ($k = 1$) and the US one $k = 0$ and intermediate ones ($0 < k < 1$). Equation (7.1) says that P's net return from settling (the expression on the left-hand side) must be at least as large as his expected return from trial (on the right-hand side) for S to be acceptable. Rearrangement of the above defines an acceptance threshold for P such that anyone with damages less than $l(S, \cdot)$ will accept an offer of S:

$$l(S, \cdot) \equiv [S - f^s + wf^w + (1 - w)f^0 - t]/t \qquad (7.2)$$

The defendant chooses a settlement offer to minimize her expected post-accident costs. These are made up of the expected costs of settlement (that is, the probability of P having $L \leq l(S, \cdot)$) and the expected costs of trial (the expected damages in the event of losing and the expected costs transfer). We denote D's expected costs by H:

$$H = Q(l)S + [1 - Q(L)](f^D + t) + w\int_l^{L_1} L dQ \qquad (7.3)$$

To solve D's problem, we take the first derivative of H and set it equal to zero (hence we solve the first-order condition defining the optimal settlement offer (S^*)):

$$\frac{dH}{dS} = Q(l) + \frac{q(l)}{w}[S^* - wl - f^D - t] = 0 \qquad (7.4)$$

This balances the marginal benefit to D from increasing the offer (the higher probability of acceptance) with the marginal cost (the additional sum to be paid out). Rearranging equation (7.4), the settlement offer becomes:

$$S^* = wl + f^D + t - w\frac{Q(l)}{q(l)}$$

$$= f^D + t + wl\left[1 - \frac{1}{\eta(l)}\right] \tag{7.5}$$

where $\eta(l) \equiv q(l)l/Q(l)$ is the elasticity of settlement probability with respect to P's acceptance level. As might be expected, this optimal offer is influenced by the likelihood of success at trial (w), costs, fees and damages (t, f^D and l) and P's flexibility in reacting to slight changes in the offer (η) – the less reactive is P, the less benefit there is for D in increasing the offer.[8]

It is immediately clear from (7.2) and (7.5) that the nature of P's litigation finance (that is f^S; f^w; f^0) will affect the settlement offer and the probability of settlement. In fact, we can also show that these arrangements affect the volume of litigation as well. The defendant chooses her care expenditure x to maximize her *ex ante* welfare, which is given by:

$$W_D = [1 - p(x)](y_D - x) + p(x)(y_D - x - H^*) \tag{7.6}$$

for $H^* \equiv H(S^*)$ and an initial wealth level for D of y_D. This combines the expected cost of not causing an accident (that is, wealth net of care expenditure) with the expected cost of causing one (which we have been examining above). As with S^* above, we solve for D's optimal care using the first-order condition. Thus, assuming her optimal care x^* is positive, it satisfies

$$-1 - p'(x^*)H^* = 0 \tag{7.7}$$

and is obviously increasing in H^*. Since we know that H itself is a function of the fees for the case, it is clear that the type of financing involved will affect D's choice of x.

We can amend the model in a number of ways. For example, litigation finance clearly affects whether a claim will actually be filed. If $l(S^*, \cdot) < L_0$ then P will not bring a claim.[9] Similarly, a dynamic version of the model can be used to demonstrate that fees may affect the timing of settlement as well as just its probability.[10]

More concrete results are difficult without two things: a specification of the fees themselves and a way out of the non-linearity generated by η in (7.5). A simple solution to the latter, which is convenient for illustrative purposes, is to assume that $Q(L)$ is uniform on $[L_0, L_1]$. It is then readily shown that

$$S^* = f^D + t + wL_0 \tag{7.8}$$

$$l = L_0 + \frac{f^D + wf^w + (1 - w)f^0 - f^S}{w} \tag{7.9}$$

We can now consider a variety of fee schemes. For example:

Legal Aid: P's costs are covered by the opponent or the state: $f^S = f^w = f^0 = 0$.

Hourly fees: P pays all the lawyer's costs: $f^S = c_0, f^w = f^0 = c_0 + c_1$.

Contingency fees: P pays a fraction (α) of any positive recovery (S or court award), and nothing otherwise: $f^S = \alpha S^*, f^w = \alpha L_{L>j}, f^0 = 0$.

Conditional fee agreement: P pays the lawyer's costs plus a pre-specified fraction (m) if the case is successful, and nothing otherwise: $f^S = (1 + m)c_0, f^w = (1 + m)(c_0 + c_1); f^0 = 0.$[11]

Gravelle and Waterson (1993) show that many of the results now depend on the values of m and α, which they endogenize via a competitive market mechanism. To avoid these difficulties, let us compare the effects of legal aid (LA) and hourly fees (HF). We have

$$S_{LA}^* = f^D + wL_0 < f^D + k(c_0 + c_1) + wL_0 = S_{HF}^* \tag{7.10}$$

$$l_{LA} = L_0 + \frac{f^D}{w} < L_0 + \frac{f^D + c_1}{w} = l_{HF}$$

Thus, the model predicts higher settlement offers under hourly fees (since D wishes to avoid the payment of 'loser' costs at trial) and faster settlement. This loosely supports the results in Fenn and Rickman (1999) where legal aid was found to reduce the cost pressure on the parties and, as such, lessen the incentives to settle.

We have established the potential for litigation funding to affect litigation itself, and have identified some key variables that might especially be involved: the probability and timing of settlement, the size of the settlement outcome, the likelihood of a claim being filed and probability of an accident (and hence the volume of litigation) itself. We now turn attention to empirical analysis of the links between litigation funding and these key variables, pausing first to say a few words about data requirements.

3. DATA REQUIREMENTS

In order to examine the effects of litigation funding on some of the key variables identified above, it is necessary to have data on claim outcomes (settle/drop/trial) and settlement amounts (if relevant), and on the types of funding that the plaintiff used. It is also necessary to have information on relevant control variables (those in the above model), perhaps most importantly, the likelihood of success at trial (w) and costs. These requirements seem obvious but they raise a number of diffculties, some of which are relevant to most empirical work on litigation but others are peculiar to litigation funding.

To begin, one needs variation in funding methods in order to be able to make comparisons across them. This, of course, is restricted by the availability of such methods within a given jurisdiction. For example, a substantial fraction of personal injury litigation in the US is funded on a contingency fee basis. In this case, variation has to be sought within this particular kind of fee itself: variations across states in (say) allowable contingency percentages, or variations over time as these rules are changed by tort reform. Another example occurs where one fee is introduced to replace another (as was broadly the case with the introduction of conditional fees as substitutes for Legal Aid in England and Wales in 1999).

It is often difficult in litigation to gain access to sufficiently detailed data in order to support high-quality empirical work. Participant surveys can be expensive and are reliant on participant recollections (and it is not clear that plaintiffs will always recall the detail of the fee schemes they used), while claim files themselves are difficult to access (for reasons of confidentiality) and expensive to sample in statistically useful numbers (though they are extremely valuable sources of data). Another potentially valuable source of data is the largescale databases held by insurers (in particular). While being difficult to access (for sound commercial reasons), these have the benefit of collecting reasonable case-level data in very large numbers. Yet problems may still arise. Plaintiff insurer claims may well have been funded by one mechanism – insurance – thereby depriving the data of sufficient variation. On the defendant insurer side, problems may arise because the insurer may not be aware of the funding contract between the plaintiff and her lawyer. As such, crucial information may be missing. Other sources of data, such as court records will only record claims at a fairly advanced stage in their life-cycle.

These problems are not insurmountable (as we shall see below) but they limit the prospects for empirical research on litigation funding.[12] This is especially true for some questions, a good example being the effects of funding on the volume of litigation. The reason is in two parts. The first is familiar: litigated claims are the 'tip of the claims iceberg' and only by knowing how many potential claims never happened can one really gain insight into what affects the volume of claims. Second, however, once a subset of claims is identified from this 'iceberg', the effects of funding can only be identified if the variations and controls mentioned above are present. For a low-probability event like pursuing a legal claim, this means that a very large sample needs to be questioned in the first place, something that research resources do not always allow.

4.   EMPIRICAL STUDIES

A review of empirical studies of litigation finance can be structured in a number of ways. One possibility is to group studies according to funding methods; another could group them according to the effects of funding on particular stages of the litigation process. In the current review, we prefer to groups studies according to their jurisdiction. This avoids the need to add regular caveats about the interjurisdictional procedures which, arguably, can prevent a clear picture of the effects of different fees from emerging in the first place.

4.1   The Use of Fees over Time

A useful place to start when considering how legal fees affect litigation is with the use made of different fees themselves. This is interesting because the use of different fees relates to individual preferences or regulatory constraints: evolutions in the fee landscape may therefore tell us something about the market for funding mechanisms. Fenn et al. (1999) explore the effects of plaintiff finance in two datasets: one containing data on 3749 closed claims brought against a UK health authority; the other containing 309 closed road traffic accident (RTA) claims (as of January 1999) collected from an insurer's claim files. Immediately, there are some interesting distinctions between the two datasets. Claims involving higher cost and assessed as being less strong were funded largely by legal aid (60 per cent of claims where the source of funding was known.) Understandably, given the availability of legal aid, private funding accounted for 10 per cent of the cases and trade unions for 7 per cent. By contrast, the bulk of RTA claims (57 per cent) were funded by before-the-event legal expense insurance, with legal aid meeting the costs of 24 per cent of claims, private funding accounting for just over 11 per cent of cases and trade unions and conditional fees making up about 4–5 per cent each.

Over the next few years, the legal landscape began to alter and conditional fees increasingly replaced legal aid as a significant source of 'high street' funding. Fenn et al. (2002) survey all members of the Law Society's 1100 personal injury panel firms about fee use. The results from 109 useable responses are given in Table 7.1. The table indicates a clear decline

Table 7.1   Number of closed, commenced and outstanding conditional fee, hourly fee and legal aid cases in 109 firms between July 1999 and June 2000

Type of case	Mean number
CFA cases closed 7/99–7/2000	25
Hourly fee cases closed 7/99–7/2000	31
Legal aid cases closed 7/99–7/2000	34
Total cases closed 7/99–7/2000	90
CFA cases commenced 7/99–7/2000	33
Hourly fee cases commenced 7/99–7/2000	30
Legal aid cases commenced 7/99–7/2000	25
Total cases commenced 7/99–7/2000	88
CFA cases outstanding 7/2000	48
Hourly fee cases outstanding 9/2000	41
Legal aid cases outstanding 9/2000	36
Total cases outstanding 9/2000	125

Source: Fenn et al. (2002).

in the use of legal aid funding, in favour of funding by conditional fee agreements (CFAs) when comparing those cases closed between July 1999 and June 2000, and those cases either commenced between those dates or which were outstanding in October 2000.[13] This reflects the removal of legal aid for most personal injury claims in 1999 and the growth in take-up of the new CFA alternative.

To examine whether the landscape had changed further as CFAs became more widely available, Fenn et al. (2006) conducted an equivalent survey (on cases closed, current and opened between September 2002 and October 2003). This time, there were 101 useable responses. By this stage, it was apparent that the nature of the route by which the client was referred to a lawyer (the 'referral route') was important to the funding decision and this needed to be accounted for in the survey. For non-medical negligence claims, results indicated a large monopoly of CFAs (89 per cent of closed claims and 91 per cent of current and opened claims). Legal aid had all but dried up and the remaining funding mechanisms were split between hourly fees paid out of pocket and paid by BTE insurers. Accident Management Companies referred about 20 per cent of the closed claims but 26 per cent of the CFA ones. Trade Unions referred 32 per cent of closed claims, virtually all of them on CFAs. BTE insurers were responsible for about 8 per cent of closed claims.

Two trends are evident as we move between these studies: first, as legal aid disappears (as a result of policy), it is replaced by the private risk-sharing arrangements present in CFAs (in non-medical negligence cases). One interpretation of this is that potential plaintiffs are unable to bear significant risks of litigation so, if the State withdraws from doing so, private market solutions can be expected to emerge. Of course, these were also regulated (for example, American-style contingency fees were not allowed but the market was able to offer an alternative in the form of a contingency arrangement contained within CFAs). Second, bulk purchasers began to appear in the market, spurred by the need to pool risk on contingency-style payments schemes and after-the-event policies.

4.2 Conditional Fees, Hourly Fees and Legal Expense Insurance: Evidence from England and Wales

Fenn et al. (1999)[14] collect data from claims records held by insurers and hospitals; they cover medical negligence, public liability and RTA – all chosen to give important differences in perspective on litigation. In particular, they allow analysis of the role played by liability in settings where this is likely to differ: in RTA cases, the defendant is reasonably confident of being liable for damages, whereas in medical negligence ones, the defendant's views will differ from case to case, and are likely to evolve over time. Of course, a wider set of case-types allows wider coverage of plaintiff finance: legal aid, legal expense insurance, trade union finance and private finance.

The authors use econometric methods to examine several issues (each highlighted by the theory in Section 2). The first relates to case screening (an issue related to access to justice and the efficiency of the legal system). They find that legal aid appears to focus crucially on the severity of an injury, whereas other sources of finance also take account of liability. A particularly interesting comparison is between legal aid and trade unions, both of which are third-party funders but the latter appears statistically more likely to take account of liability. Arguably, facing a market (as opposed to an administrative) budget constraint may sharpen trade unions' incentives to screen cases more carefully. In addition, privately financed cases were also likely to be associated with high levels of defendant (perceived) liability, which is consistent with clients' self-screening given that their own finance is at stake.

The timing of settlement (or, the duration of claims) is clearly an important issue for efficiency. The authors use survival analysis to examine the role of fees here and find statistically significant differences when comparing the effects of plaintiff finance. In both data sets, legally aided cases were associated with longer delay to case closure than alternatives (legal expense insurance, trade unions and private funding). They argue that this result is consistent with the incentives for monitoring inherent within the funding methods they review.

How does finance affect the way a case progresses? One approach to this is to examine the relationship between funding and key litigation events. The authors' data on medical negligence cover data on the use of explanatory letters by the defendant, the issue of a writ, use of expert witnesses, and payments into court. Perhaps the most interesting story here concerns the role of private finance: such cases tend to receive a higher number of explanatory letters than third-party funded cases and to issue far fewer writs (as a result, private finance is associated with less use of experts and fewer payments into court). One interpretation is that, in medical negligence cases, an explanatory letter is helpful in screening plaintiffs and reducing their propensity to embark on formal proceedings.

Of course, these results are positive rather than normative. Thus, despite the apparent concerns they raise about legal aid (and the apparent support they give to the reforms adopted in England and Wales), they also hint at some potential welfare loss. This is especially the case in medical negligence: legal aid remains available here and it is clearly an important weapon against the cost and uncertainty of such claims – thereby helping to generate claims and high settlements. Whether this is desirable is unclear, but the existence of such a trade-off should be recognized.

Fenn et al. (2002) update the previous study, recognizing the developments that had taken place in funding during the preceding period (in particular, the growth of CFAs and the virtual disappearance of legal aid for non-medical personal injury claims). Once again, the focus is on the types of claims brought by litigants and their outcomes.

Hourly fee cases (with a private client) were characterized by defendants who admitted a much higher proportion of liability – they were 'less risky' cases than those run under CFAs. The same was true to an even greater degree with referral agent cases, but legal aid cases and third-party payer cases did not differ significantly from CFA cases with respect to liability risk.

An important question for contingent payment methods (not only CFAs) is whether the fee reflects the risk inherent in the case. The authors examine this by correlating percentage uplifts with the lawyers' recorded beliefs about liability: as expected, there was some evidence of lawyers applying higher uplifts to cases which tended towards greater risks on average, though the variability in estimated liability was greater than that in uplifts towards the 100 per cent level – perhaps suggesting a degree of risk-pooling on the part of the lawyers.[15]

In relation to litigation outcomes, the authors focused on the net return to the client from pursuing the case. By comparison with 'traditional' cases financed either through standard hourly fees by the client, or through legal aid, CFAs appeared to produce higher payouts from defendants, both in relation to settlement awards agreed and costs recovered. The additional costs recovered from defendants may have reflected the combined effect of insurance premiums and insurance monitoring costs, but they did not appear to reflect any differences in the duration of cases. However, for the majority of the cases the lawyer's success fees were recovered from the client rather than the defendant, and so the overall effect on the plaintiff's net award was negative by comparison with hourly fees and legal aid. This presumably reflected the intended shifting of risk to lawyers that under-lies the introduction of CFAs. Of course, it is hard to draw clear welfare conclusions from such results: for instance, we need to know whether plaintiffs were willing *ex ante* to trade off lower sums if successful, with reduced costs if not.

For referral agents (who act as intermediaries between prospective plaintiffs and lawyers, referring the former to the latter for a fee), the picture in relation to outcomes was substantially different. By comparison with CFAs these cases obtained around 27 per cent lower damages for their clients. The additional removal of a referral fee *ex post*, inevitably meant that they compared badly in terms of the amounts paid to clients: they paid around 40 per cent less to clients than CFAs, after controlling for case characteristics. Third-party payers, by contrast, had a very similar set of outcomes to CFAs in terms of recovered costs and damages. The main difference was that third-party payers did not deduct a fee from the client's settlement award, but instead funded their litigation expenses from premiums or subscriptions paid by the client in advance.

The authors conclude that CFAs appear to be providing access to legal services for the kind of cases previously funded through legal aid: hence the merit test as applied by CFA lawyers seemed to be broadly compa-rable with that applied by legal aid lawyers. This risk-acceptance on the part of CFA lawyers was inevitably at some cost to both defendants and plaintiffs, given the arrangements by which costs were recovered from each during the period of the survey. Moreover, because plaintiffs were on the whole bearing the cost of the CFA uplift, and because this uplift was not normally applied on a case-by-case basis, there was substantial cross-subsidization amongst CFA clients. An unanswered issue is whether or not CFA costs jointly borne by defendants and plaintiffs are greater or smaller than the costs of administering the legal aid scheme, or other forms of third-party payment such as legal expense insurance plans.

Finally, Fenn at al. (2006) continue the theme of examining the effects of fee reform in England and Wales. As we have seen, they pay special attention to the referral route by which a lawyer and client are matched. They also study a variant on the CFA whereby largescale buyers of legal services (such as trade unions) negotiate a 'collective' CFA with their lawyers: this typically involves a common hourly rate and success fee and economizes on the transactions costs of individual fee negotiation at the start of each case – the lawyers benefit from the assured supply of cases. These were known as 'collective CFAs' (CCFA). A number of findings are of interest. First, in relation to the type of case funded under each arrangement, CCFA and BTE funding were associated with 'softer' cases (that is, where the defendant's liability was clearer), especially in relation to CFA claims. In relation to the likelihood of legal proceedings, CCFA cases were nearly 10 per cent more likely to be litigated than other types of claim funding after controlling for measures of case complexity. Settlement delay was lowest under BTE claims by comparison with all other forms of case funding, including CFAs. Finally, in relation to costs, after controlling for case value and delay, BTE cases were estimated to incur similarly base costs to CFAs but lower total costs (about 20 per cent lower (as a consequence of the success fees and ATE premiums)). By contrast CCFA cases were significantly lower than BTE cases in terms of base costs, but, after adding in success fees and ATE premiums, their costs were indistinguishable statistically.

The authors also consider a very different type of personal injury claim: medical negligence cases. Now CFA funding was associated with relatively high-value but relatively low-risk claims. After controlling for this selection effect, CFA cases tended to settle later than cases funded by other means (typically legal aid in this context).

4.3   US Studies

We now consider US studies, where the principal interest has been (unsurprisingly) on the effects of contingency fees. Helland and Tabarrok (2003) remark 'that very few empirical studies of contingency fees have been conducted' (p. 522), citing Danzon and Lillard (1983) and Thomason (1991), with their own adding a further contribution. We cover these studies but also note the considerable body of work by Kritzer and colleagues over the last twenty years or so, upon which we also dwell (see also Rosenfield 1976).

Danzon and Lillard (1983) provide one of the earliest empirical analyses of litigation. Their regressions seek to explain settlement awards and rates, and the incidence of drops but, by using medical negligence data covering a number of states with different limits on contingency fee percentages, the authors can make use of this variation to consider the effects of litigation funding. The data cover 1974–1976 so law changes within this period can also be used to similar effect. The results suggest that states with fewer fee controls have 5 per cent higher drops, 1.5 per cent more settlements and 9 per cent higher settlement amounts.

Helland and Tabarrok take Danzon and Lillard's analysis further in terms of the techniques they employ. Again, they examine cross sectional and time series data to look at the effects of different state fee regulations and the effects of law changes (in Florida) over time. They consider the effects of these on 'case quality' and on the timing of settlement. The former is proxied by the probability of the case being dropped: it is argued that more drops means poorer case screening at the beginning so these are a proxy for lawyer monitoring strength. This seems a loose proxy in the sense that greater drops could equally imply that lawyers take their monitoring role seriously once the case is in motion and information is produced.[16] A difficulty is the variety of fee regulations across the sixteen states in the study, and across the types of case covered, which the authors seek to overcome by computing an implicit 'tax rate' for contingency fee claims – that is the extent to which states 'tax' their lawyers by constraining allowable contingency percentages below the typical market rate. This is calculated for each state as $S^A (\alpha^m - \alpha^r)/\alpha^r$, where α^m is the standard 33.3 per cent contingency percentage (the 'market rate'), α^r is the maximum regulated rate and S^A is the average contingency fee award. Hence, states with stricter regulation have higher implicit tax rates (on lawyers). As mentioned, the authors estimate regressions for the drop incidence and time to settlement across states, and across time in one state (Florida), following a change in contingency fee regulations. Taking drops first, the evidence from state courts suggests a statistically insignificant 7 percentage point increase in drops as the tax rate moves from 0 per cent to its maximum value (62 per cent). The preferred result is for the dummy on fee limits, which yields a 13 percentage point increase when limits are present. The Florida data indicate a 15 per cent increase in the drop rate immediately after the introduction of contingency fee limits. Moving to duration, the authors run Tobit estimates and show a 21 per cent increase in settlement duration when fee limits are present. The Florida data exhibit an 11.1 per cent increase in time to settlement in the thirteen months following the fee change, when compared with the ten months before it.

Helland and Tabarrok interpret their findings as being consistent with contingency fee limits reducing the lawyers' incentives to monitor cases carefully: weaker ones are started and those that do not drop take longer to settle. Apparently, regulations designed to protect clients may have had unintended consequences. It is notable that the results on drops run counter to those in Danzon and Lillard's earlier study (which is consistent with the alternative interpretation of drops sketched above). Other authors have suggested that contingency fees encourage lawyers to perform a gate-keeping role (for example see Kritzer 1997) and neither of the above papers is inconsistent with this because they do not benchmark against non-contingency fees. Nonetheless, the conflicting results suggest that this gate-keeping role may be a little more complicated than Helland and Tabarrok's interpretation.

Another pair of studies is interested in the relative payoffs to plaintiffs under contingency fees in comparison to other forms of payment: that is, in the presence of conflict between lawyer and client under different fees. First, there is Kritzer's (1990) study of 'ordinary litigation'. This is an in-depth study of 1600 cases across five US federal judicial districts, and includes a section on the effects of fees on litigation outcomes (the focus of our discussion here).[17] He seeks to study the effects of contingency fees on 'plaintiff success' (PS), measured as:

$$PS = (\text{Recovery} - \text{Legal Fees and Expenses})/$$
$$\text{Plaintiff's Highest Stakes Estimate}$$

that is how much of the case's potential was realized for the plaintiff. Kritzer estimates various multivariate equations that seek to explain PS by, *inter alia*, a dummy for the presence of contingency fees. In each of the models, the effect is significant and negative, suggesting that the contingency fee lowers the plaintiff's net success. Of course, there are issues to bear in mind. Kritzer himself acknowledges that his measure of output (PS) is narrow, and we might add the potential for selection effects amongst claimants when choosing their fee scheme.

Thomason (1991) employs a different approach to finding variation in payoffs under fee types. He employs data from workers' compensation claims in New York for the period 1971–1977 when a mixture of fees were in operation: in particular, cases with lump-sum payment attracted a flat fee (typically 10 per cent of the award), while other claims involved a contingency percentage depending on compensation and stage reached. In addition, of course, workers' compensation claims often attract litigants in person (and no legal fee) – another source of variation. Thomason's results suggest that contingency fee cases tend to settle earlier and for less than their counterparts. In a result that echoes Fenn et al. (2006) (see above) and Kritzer's, he also finds that the removal of the contingency percentage leaves the return to legal representation *negative*. Helland and Tabarrok note, however, that self-selection could play a role here, with weaker cases being taken to lawyers – a measure of underlying case quality is required. They also note that it is impossible to distinguish the effects of representation from fees in the results. Thus, although there is evidence of some level of conflict, the jury is still out on its extent and significance.

5. CONCLUSIONS

This survey has established a prima facie role for litigation funding in the outcomes of litigation and, therefore, in the achievement of the dual objectives of equity and efficiency. Broadly, the empirical work we have covered confirms the presence of such influence. In particular, evidence from both sides of the Atlantic suggests that lawyers who bear some risk (through contingent payment) are likely to screen cases more carefully than those who do not, while the removal of the contingent payment in successful cases appears to reduce net payoffs to plaintiffs. In addition, lawyers bearing contingent risk appear to settle their cases sooner, *ceteris paribus*.

Of course, a normative interpretation of these results needs to take great care. For example, it is striking in the English data that a variety of fees appear to be used – suggesting that different clients or circumstances may call for different funding mechanisms – while, when especially high risk is involved (as in medical negligence), lawyers and insurers are either less experienced at valuing risk or less able to offer attractive prices, and claimants are keen to pass risk onto the State (through legal aid). Thus, the monetary outcomes and results that we observe may not reflect the utilities enjoyed by the parties when they evaluate these factors: a risk-averse litigant may be pleased to share risk with a lawyer while settling for less, sooner. Perhaps the ultimate lesson for policy is that, because fees have different effects, they may suit different preferences and circumstances, so a reasonably liberal approach to the fees that are allowed (albeit with some regulation) may be a sensible strategy.

Where will the literature go next? Clearly, there is always a call for good data and, to the extent that these can be found or collected, newer versions of the work we have reviewed can be expected. At the same time, we have seen that fee innovations are often emerging and an interesting one (especially in Australia, the US and the UK) involves third-party litigation funding. To the extent that some third-party mechanisms are focused on the corporate market this raises an obvious gap in the foregoing studies: the role of funding in corporate litigation. Finally, one might hope for more European research in this area. As activity becomes more global, legal services do as well and it will be important to have this European space in the funding research addressed.

NOTES

1. Of course, there are many variants on these broad themes. For instance, contingent payment can be via a share of damages, as in the US, or a mark-up on hourly fees, as with the conditional fees used in England and Wales (see Chapter 3 by Faure, Fernhout and Philipsen in this book). Similarly, legal expense insurance can be purchased 'before the event', as in much of Europe, or 'after-the-event' as in conjunction with a conditional fee policy. (Such insurance is discussed in more detail by Van Boom in Chapter 5 of this book.)
2. Inevitably, this distinction is somewhat artificial, and a principal justification is one of tractability for present purposes. For example, tort reform that uses damage caps immediately affects the contingency fee that is paid in a successful case, yet we ignore the wider aspects of tort reform because it does not affect the structure of the contract in question. Similarly, our definition also rules out methods of defraying costs such as class actions: members of the class will enter into a contract that will govern their financial relationships with their lawyer(s) (see Rosenfield's study (1976) of the use of contingency fees in American class actions).
3. A way to think about this is that we are looking for suitable variables to appear on the lefthand-side of a regression equation that has funding measures (possibly dummies) on the righthand-side. The models also indicate relevant control variables for such equations and, in principle, relevant estimation techniques (though we sidestep this last issue).
4. In addition, the model is arguably more suitable to individual (or, in Kritzer's (1990) phrase, 'ordinary') litigation as opposed to its commercial counterpart.
5. The cumulative distribution tells us the probability of encountering a plaintiff with damages below a given value of L. The density tells us the probability of damages lying between two given points. Thus, both capture that fact that D must consider many possible damage levels when assessing the claim brought by P.
6. This differs from for example the contribution of Visscher and Schepens in Chapter 2 of this book.
7. This also differs from Visscher and Schepens. One implication is that insurance is a strategic purchase, as defined by Kirstein (2000); see Heyes et al. (2004) for a version of the model where insurance is purchased by risk-averse litigants.
8. To confirm this last point, note that the settlement offer is higher for $\eta = 2$ than for $\eta = 1$ (which represents a lesser degree of responsiveness).
9. In this case, $H(S^*) = 0$, so $x^* = 0$: that is fees affect questions of equity (access to justice) and efficiency (deterrence).
10. See Rickman (1999) for an example where there are two periods of pre-trial bargaining and two potential types of plaintiff.
11. As mentioned earlier, it is also common to purchase 'after-the-event' insurance as protection against a successful D's costs; in recent years, the associated insurance premium has been recoverable from a losing D. Incorporating these would affect t and the objective functions.
12. It is worth noting that this contribution focuses on (econometric studies of) data drawn mainly from claim files and largescale databases. There are also some valuable survey studies of the use of fees in litigation. For example, Yarrow (1990) provides the first such study of conditional fee agreements' use in England and Wales while Moorhead and Cumming (2008) provide a thorough study of contingency fee use in employment claims in England and Wales.
13. Recall that CFAs allow the lawyer to collect hourly fees plus a percentage mark-up in the event of a win; but nothing if the case is lost. To protect the plaintiff against adverse costs (in defeat) they often involve an after-the-event legal expenses insurance policy.
14. See also Fenn and Rickman (1999).
15. Notably, this is often observed with contingency fee percentages.
16. An added complication is that the cross-sectional data are taken from judicial records,

where a case has clearly been filed, while the intertemporal data from Florida are taken from the inception of (medical negligence) claims. Arguably, the notion of 'dropping' differs across the two. Fenn and Rickman (1999) use actual recorded views about liability as a more robust measure of case strength.

17. Kritzer and several colleagues have been prolific contributors to this area for a number of years. The 1990 book is a valuable summary/extension of the previous research, but Kritzer has continued to publish in the area subsequently; in particular, see Kritzer (2004).

REFERENCES

Bebchuk, Lucian A. (1984), 'Litigation and settlement under imperfect information', *RAND Journal of Economics*, **15**(3), 404–415.

Danzon, Patricia M. and Lee A. Lillard (1983), 'Settlement out of court: The disposition of medical malpractice claims', *Journal of Legal Studies*, **12**(2), 345–377.

Fenn, Paul and Neil Rickman (1999), 'Delay and settlement in litigation', *Economic Journal*, **109**(457), 476–491.

Fenn, Paul, Alastair M. Gray and Neil Rickman (1999), *The impact of plaintiff finance on litigants' behaviour: An empirical analysis*, London: Lord Chancellor's Department Research Report, 5/99.

Fenn, Paul, Alastair M. Gray, Neil Rickman and Howard Carrier (2002), *The impact of conditional fees on the selection, handling and outcomes of personal injury cases*, London: Lord Chancellor's Department Research Report, 7/2002.

Fenn, Paul, Alastair M. Gray, Neil Rickman and Yasmeen Mansur (2006), *The funding of personal injury litigation: Comparisons over time and across jurisdictions*, London: Lord Chancellor's Department Research Report, 2/2006.

Gravelle, Hugh S. E. and Michael Waterson (1993), 'No win, no fee: Some economics of contingent legal fees', *Economic Journal*, **103**(1000), 1205–1220.

Helland, Eric A. and Alexander T. Tabarrok (2003), 'Contingency fees, settlement delay and low-quality litigation: Empirical evidence from two datasets', *Journal of Law, Economics, and Organisation*, **19**(2), 517–542.

Heyes, Anthony, Neil Rickman and Dionisia Tzavara (2004), 'Legal expenses insurance, risk aversion and litigation', *International Review of Law and Economics*, **24**, 107–119.

Kirstein, Roland (2000), 'Risk-neutrality and strategic insurance', *Geneva Papers on Risk and Insurance. Issues and Practice*, **25**(2), 262–272.

Kritzer, Herbert M. (1990), *The Justice Broker: Lawyers and Ordinary Litigation*, New York, US: Oxford University Press.

Kritzer, Herbert M. (1997), 'Contingency fee lawyers as gatekeepers in the American civil justice system', *Judicature*, **81**, 22–29.

Kritzer, Herbert M. (2002), 'Lawyer fees and lawyer behaviour in litigation: What does the empirical literature really say?', *Texas Law Review*, **80**, 1943–1983.

Kritzer, Herbert M. (2004), *Risks, Reputations and Rewards: Contingency Fee Practice in the United States*, Stanford CA: Stanford University Press.

Moorhead, Richard and Rebecca Cumming (2008), 'Damage-based contingency fees in employment cases: A survey of practitioners', *Working Paper, Cardiff Law School, University of Cardiff*.

Rickman, Neil (1999), 'Contingent fees and settlement in litigation', *International Review of Law and Economics*, **19**(3), 295–317.

Rosenfield, Andrew (1976), 'An empirical test of class action settlement', *Journal of Legal Studies*, **5**(1), 113–120.

Thomason, Terry (1991), 'Are attorneys paid what they're worth? Contingent fees and the settlement process', *Journal of Legal Studies*, **20**(1), 187–223.

Yarrow, Stella (1990), *The Price of Success: Lawyers, Clients and Conditional Fees*, London: Policy Studies Institute.

8. Financing civil litigation: the US perspective

Deborah R. Hensler

1. INTRODUCTION

Virtually every aspect of financing civil litigation in the United States differs from the European model, at least with regard to formal rules. In the US, in most civil litigation, each party is responsible for its own legal fees and expenses, without regard to the outcome of the litigation. Consistent with this principle, in most instances how the lawyer's fee is calculated is a matter of private contract between lawyer and client. Attorneys may represent clients on a contingency fee basis, on a flat fee basis, on an hourly rate plus expenses basis, or on any other basis that the lawyer and client contract for. Normally, in tort claims for money damages and in contract and other claims where there is a potential for tort-like damages, plaintiffs are represented by lawyers on a contingency fee basis. There are exceptions to these rules: in some categories of private civil litigation statutes specify fee arrangements, and in class actions and some other forms of group litigation judges decide the amount of fees to be awarded to attorneys who represent the class or group.

The origin of the American fee rule is unclear (Leubsdorf 1984). Notwithstanding the general rule, there are circumstances in which courts impose the winner's costs on the loser, commonly termed 'fee shifting'. A survey of state law conducted in the mid-1980s found almost 2000 state statutes mandating or authorizing one-way fee-shifting when plaintiffs prevail (Note 1984). According to the Federal Judicial Center, by the mid-1990s Congress had passed close to 200 statutes authorizing fee shifting, most limited to one-way fee-shifting for prevailing plaintiffs (Hirsch and Sheehey 1994, p. 1). Congress has authorized one-way fee shifting in claims brought under civil rights law (42 U.S.C. §1988 (1994), environmental law and in other circumstances where legislators deemed it appropriate to incentivize litigation (for example Equal Access to Justice Act, 288 U.S.C. §2412). In addition, under federal and state law judges may shift fees (either way) as a sanction for abusive litigation practices (see, for example, F.R.C.P. 11 authorizing sanctions including attorney fees for frivolous claims) or for equitable reasons, as when a lawyer orders a better-off divorcing spouse to pay the legal fees of his ex-spouse.

Other things equal, US litigation financing rules ought to facilitate citizens' access to court when they have meritorious civil damage claims, by minimizing the financial risk of plaintiffs who retain attorneys on a contingency fee and by allowing plaintiff attorneys to prosecute these claims without fear of adverse costs. By extension, the fee regime ought to heighten defendants' risk of being sued for common law negligence and statutory violations where money damages are allowable (for example, consumer fraud, securities violations, anti-trust). But the fee regime also permits defendants to make with confidence risk-benefit calculations about their own litigation expenditures, without fear of being required to also shoulder opposing parties' expenditures.

Some aspects of litigation financing rules that may facilitate litigation in other jurisdictions are not prevalent in the US. For example, in some jurisdictions civil litigants have access to publicly subsidized legal services and in some, legal insurance is widely available. In contrast, in the US, the government offers very little financial aid for civil litigation, and insurance to cover the cost of bringing litigation is rare. (The cost of defending policyholders against liability suits is included in personal, professional and commercial liability insurance coverage.)

Although not strictly part of the financing regime, certain other aspects of the US civil justice system facilitate access to courts and favor litigation, including lawyers' right to advertise, rules governing awards in tort claims, and the constitutional right to a jury trial in money damage suits. Lawyers have been permitted to advertise in the United States since the US Supreme Court's ruling in *Bates v. State Bar of Arizona*, 433 U.S. 350 (1977). Although lawyer advertising still stirs controversy in some quarters, efforts by attorney groups and state legislatures to prohibit certain forms of advertising have met with limited success. There is evidence that ordinary citizens find lawyers in part through advertising (Hensler et al. 1991, Table 5.9, p. 134). Advertising is regulated by state law and rules of professional conduct but generally lawyers are free to advertise their services as long as their advertisements are not 'false, deceptive or misleading'. Law firm advertising generated $575 million in TV revenues in 2006; in the same year, legal advertising accounted for an additional $2 million in web advertising. Personal injury lawyers are said to be responsible for the bulk of lawyer advertising (Aspan 2007).

In tort litigation, jury awards for economic loss that by state law disregard whether the plaintiff has been compensated through private or public insurance (the 'collateral source rule'), provide for non-economic loss ('pain and suffering') and occasionally permit punitive damages drive the expected value of damage claims higher than in jurisdictions that restrict awards in some or all of these aspects. Although the 'tort reform' movement has had considerable success limiting such aspects of tort awards (American Tort Reform Association, 30 June 2001), US tort values still appear to be substantially higher than in other jurisdictions. As a result, the expected value of plaintiff attorneys' contingent fees is higher than it might otherwise be. In addition, because defendants are exposed to higher liability awards and therefore more inclined to invest in a vigorous defense, their outside counsels' billings are likely also to be higher than elsewhere.

Finally, admission to the bar in the US may be less restrictive than in some other jurisdictions, producing a larger supply of lawyers, relative to demand. Bar passage rates in the US range from lows around 60 per cent (*California Bar Journal*, December 2008) to highs over 80 per cent (Qualters, 4 December 2008). These statistics are similar to those in some other jurisdictions, although markedly higher than others. For example, in Israel, in 2008, 88 per cent of law students who attempted the bar exam for the first time passed (Haaretz, 4 May 2009). In Switzerland in recent years about 60 per cent of those who sat for the avocat exam succeeded, but the total numbers of applicants were very small (personal communication 2009). In Italy in recent years about 50 per cent of those who sat for the written portion of the examination were advanced to the subsequent oral exam; generally about 80 per cent of those who were examined orally succeeded, yielding an overall success rate of about 40 per cent. Thousands of applicants sit for the Italian bar exam annually (Barzaghi 2007). In many jurisdictions there are multiple steps to licensure that render the percentage admitted at the final stage difficult to interpret as a measure of ease of access to the legal profession. For example, barristers in England must complete an undergraduate law degree and a bar vocational course and then find a 'pupilage' (training) position in a barrister's chambers. About 1500 complete the course each year – approximately half of those who apply – but only about 500 pupilages annually have been offered in recent years (English Bar Council 2009). In Poland similarly there are multiple steps to admission to practice; in recent years about 75 per cent of those who applied for training positions succeeded (Ministry of Justice 2009). In contrast, until 2001, the bar exam passage rate in Japan was about 3 per cent. After the establishment of post-graduate law schools, the bar exam passage rate is said to have increased to 30 per cent (Paul, 2005). This past year, lawyers in Japan have begun pressing for the bar passage rate to be lowered again (personal communication with Prof. Takao Tanase, February 2009). In Taiwan the bar exam passage rate is said to be 8 per cent (Chih-Chieh et al., 2010).

In sum, the US civil justice system seems designed to facilitate access to courts. Although controversial, the proposition that litigation is an appropriate tool for regulating private behavior in a society that has usually eschewed public law and public regulation as vehicles for achieving shared social goals provides the foundation for a civil justice system that favors private litigation.

In this article, I describe the operation of the US financing system in ordinary and complex civil litigation. Section 2 discusses financing for ordinary litigation between two or a few parties. Although the categories of civil litigation in the US are diverse, Section 2 focuses on personal injury litigation, because that area has been most thoroughly researched. Section 3 discusses financing class actions and other group litigation, including securities, anti-trust, employment discrimination, consumer protection, and personal injury and property damage cases. Section 4 discusses the evidence on Americans' litigiousness and considers how the US financing system affects litigation behavior. Section 5 concludes.

2.   FINANCING ORDINARY CIVIL LITIGATION

In ordinary civil litigation outside of the personal injury context and involving one or two parties on each side, parties generally pay lawyers on an hourly or flat fee basis. Flat fees are offered for simple matters, such as uncontested divorces (which must be submitted to the court for approval), and sometimes for straightforward events, such as representation at a court-connected alternative dispute resolution hearing (Hensler, Adler and Nelson 1983). Most lawyers who represent plaintiffs in personal injury litigation offer clients contingency fee agreements that generally specify that the lawyer will take one-third of damages if the case settles and 40–50 per cent if the case requires trial. A nationally representative survey of accident victims found that 87 per cent of people who hired lawyers to represent them in personal injury litigation signed contingency fee agreements, 4 per cent hired lawyers for a fixed fee, and less than 1 per cent agreed to pay hourly fees and expenses (Hensler et al. 1991, Table 5.11, p. 136). Some lawyers offer to represent clients before filing suit for a lower contingency fee rate (Heyman Law, n.d.). Anecdotally, it appears that some contingent fee attorneys charge the higher 'trial' rate for cases that go to mediation or other alternative dispute resolution hearing, notwithstanding the fact that most such proceedings require little preparation of expert evidence or trial advocacy skills. There is little evidence that contingency fee lawyers compete for clients by offering lower than average contingency fees and the one-third contingent fee appears to have persisted for decades. In a series of studies of civil litigation costs conducted in the 1980s, the researchers found price competition among plaintiff contingent fee lawyers only in the area of high-value aviation accident litigation (Kakalik et al. 1983; Kakalik and Pace 1986; and Kakalik et al. 1988).

A plaintiff represented by a lawyer working on a contingency fee agreement pays no fees upfront. The lawyer pays all of the litigation expenses, including any litigation-related medical expenses (for example the cost of medical tests conducted to evaluate the plaintiff's disability). Professional rules generally prohibit lawyers from helping plaintiffs pay for medical care, but a 1989 national survey of US accident victims found that one-third of victims who consulted attorneys said that the attorney recommended a specific course of health care, a specific health-care provider or both and 13 per cent said that the attorney offered to help them with expenses while their claim was being processed (Hensler et al. 1991, pp. 134–35).

A number of private companies offer represented plaintiffs cash in exchange for a property interest in their unresolved lawsuits; these enterprises advertise their services as a means of receiving quicker reimbursement of the expenses associated with accidental injuries. (See, for example, www.fundmysuit.com; www.getlegalfunds.com; www.americanlegalfunding.com; www.anylawsuits.com; www.litigationcapitalinvestors.com.) All of these enterprises appear to limit their advances to plaintiffs who have obtained legal representation, perhaps so as not to run afoul of ethical rules that forbid lawyers to split their fees with non-lawyers (most states no longer enforce the old English rules of champerty and maintenance that forbade contracts that advance payments to parties contingent on the outcome of a pending case). Perhaps to drive home this point, the firm 'Litigation Capital Investors' explains that it has no control over the case and does not participate in settlement negotiations. All of the enterprises offer cash in the form of an 'advance' on the settlement amount (often referred to as a 'non-recourse advance'). By structuring payments as contingent on case outcomes, these funding enterprises may also hope to avoid state usury law that might otherwise cap the percentages charged to successful plaintiffs (Hyman and Frumkin 2003). If plaintiffs do not obtain damages, nothing is owed to the funder (that is 'non-recourse'); if they do obtain damages, the funder receives a reimbursement and fee. Litigation Capital Investors explains that it only purchases a share of the recovery, generally 10–20 per cent and that generally it provides $2500–$20 000 but that it has advanced as much as $2 million in some cases. The firm offers multiple advances for high-value cases and monthly payment plans and also offers to pay off advances that the plaintiff has obtained from other such enterprises. Other companies offer cash for structured settlements obtained in a lawsuit that has already been resolved. (See, for example, www.fairfund.com; www.patriotsettlement.com; www.nomorewaiting. com.) The firms 'Patriot Settlement' and 'No More Waiting' offer cash advances not only for structured settlements but also for annuities and lottery awards, suggesting that enterprises perceive all these to represent similar investment opportunities.

When a plaintiff prevails by settlement or trial, her attorney bills her for legal fees and expenses, plus the contractually agreed-upon share of damages. Some plaintiff attorneys first compute their share of the total amount paid by the defendant and then subtract their expenses from the client's share; others first subtract expenses from the total amount paid by the defendant and then compute their share of the remaining amount.

Hourly billing prevails in corporate litigation generally including on the defense side in tort litigation, with fees ranging from an average of around $100/hour for small firms representing clients in low-stakes litigation to upwards of $1000/hour for top law firms representing clients in high-stakes matters (GAO 2001; Fortado 2005; Wall St. Journal Law Blog 2009). Insured defendants in tort litigation are typically represented by insurance defense counsel who contract with the insurance company.

Hourly billing by outside counsel is increasingly under attack. In an effort to reduce legal costs, corporations increasingly assign routine legal matters to in-house lawyers who are paid hourly salaries; enter into contracts in which law firms agree to take on a package of high-volume predictable legal work for a flat fee; and assign high profile matters to law firms that agree to charge lower hourly rates in exchange for success fees if defendants prevail or do better than usual in similar cases (ABA Commission on Billable Hours 2002; Weltman 2008; Inside Counsel 2007). Outside defense counsel may need to seek approval from clients for adopting expensive litigation tactics, such as expert research (Yeazell 2001). Corporate law firms and corporations are increasingly outsourcing legal work, particularly to India (D'Angelo 2008; Krishnan 2007). It seems likely that these arrangements will become more popular as a result of the global economic downturn. Still, in high-stakes cases defense legal costs may be enormous: in 2007, Merck reported spending more than $1 billion on legal fees and expenses to defend itself in litigation arising out of Vioxx, which it recalled from the market in 2004 (Seidenstein 2008).

Although large law firms and large legal fees command media attention, a large fraction of plaintiffs and defendants represent themselves in legal matters ranging from divorces to simple contract disputes to small value tort matters. In some instances, *pro se* parties appear in small claims courts where rules forbid lawyers to appear, even when one or both parties can afford them (Finney and Yanovich 2006). In other instances, an unrepresented party may find herself facing a lawyer for the opposing party. Some US state courts report upwards of 50 per cent of suits in divorce, landlord-tenant, probate and other civil matters involve one or more unrepresented parties There is little reason to believe that these parties avoid lawyers for ideological reasons, rather than lack of financial wherewithal (National Center for State Courts 2006). The high rate of unrepresented plaintiffs in combination with a relatively large supply of lawyers drives home the observation that the US legal services industry is sharply tilted towards large corporate parties (Galanter 2006).

3. FINANCING CLASS AND NON-CLASS MASS LITIGATION

While legal fees and financial arrangements in ordinary litigation are largely unregulated in the US, common law, court rules, and practice have imposed a regulatory framework on mass litigation involving large numbers of plaintiffs and sometimes large numbers of defendants. Mass litigation comprises claims arising out of alleged violations of securities and anti-trust (competition) statutes, common law and statutory consumer fraud, civil rights violations (including employment discrimination), and personal injury and property torts. In some instances, the litigation proceeds in class action form; in other instances, attorneys aggregate individual claims and litigate them in groups. In a few instances, mass claims have been litigated in US bankruptcy courts. With nationalization and more recently globalization of economic activity, the incidence and scope of mass litigation has increased dramatically (Hensler 2001; Hensler 2007). Mass litigation often proceeds in multiple fora, within and outside the US, in criminal, civil and bankruptcy courts, and at the behest of private and public parties, all at the same time. Coordinating such litigation imposes additional costs on both parties and courts. In the US, the increased risks of such litigation for plaintiff counsel and defendants alike has led to a legal culture that promotes settlement in virtually all cases.

3.1 Financing Class Action Litigation

Provisions for class actions – litigation in which one or more parties come forward to represent a group of like parties who are not formally before the court – have been part of US law since the country's inception (Hensler et al. 2000, Chapter 2). The groundwork for the American class action can be found in medieval English law, although true representative class actions are not permitted under contemporary English law (Yeazell

1987). In the modern era in the US, the most significant change in class action rules occurred in 1966, when Rule 23 of the Federal Rules of Civil Procedure was substantially amended. Accounts of the amendment process agree that the intent of the rule-drafters was to facilitate the use of class actions, particularly by claimants charging civil rights violations by public institutions (Hensler et al. 2000, Chapter 2).

Before a lawsuit can proceed in class form, Rule 23 requires that the judge assigned to a lawsuit claiming class action status certify that the litigation meets a variety of criteria, including that the class is adequately represented. Rule 23(a) specifies the threshold criteria for all class actions and Rule 23(b) identifies different circumstances that justify class actions and sets forth additional criteria for certifying damage class actions.

Although the language of Rule 23 refers to the adequacy of parties to represent the class, over time, judges increasingly interpreted the 'adequacy of representation' criterion as requiring an inquiry into the competence and experience of the class representative's legal counsel. As a result, the lawyer-client relationship, which in ordinary litigation is outside the purview of the court and governed mainly by rules of professional conduct, has come within the cognizance of judges assigned to class action lawsuits.

Because the outcome of a class action lawsuit binds all class members, whether the case is settled or decided by summary judgment or trial, the US class action regime contains a large number of provisions to ensure a fair process. In money damage suits (actions that proceed under Rule 23(b) (3)) the most important of these provisions is the opportunity for a class member to opt out of the litigation entirely and pursue her own individual suit. Extensive notification procedures (commonly termed 'notice') are required to ensure that the opt-out opportunity is a real one. But the rule drafters were also concerned about the consequences for absent class members who did not opt out of a settlement agreement between the class representative(s) and the defendant. As a result, Rule 23(e) requires that a judge first review (after a public hearing) and then approve a proposed settlement only if the judge finds, after hearing any objections from class members, that the settlement is 'fair, reasonable, and adequate.' The requirement that a judge review a settlement negotiated by private civil parties sets class actions apart from ordinary civil litigation in the US, where settlements are favored by public policy and not normally subject to judicial review.

Until recently, US class action rules were silent with regard to how class action attorneys were to be paid and how their compensation was to be determined. Except in cases where Congress mandated special fee rules, the normal US fee rule applied,[1] meaning that the class representative(s) and class action attorneys had no risk of adverse fees and therefore no requirement to post bond against such fees. The defendant similarly was responsible for paying its own fees, whether it won or lost. Some US statutes that provide for class actions contain one-way fee shifting rules, meaning that defendants are required to pay attorney fees for prevailing class members. But in most private damage class actions, no such statutes apply.

In the absence of statutes or formal rules, it was left to the courts to fashion a litigation financing scheme for class actions and other litigation in which a party acts on behalf of a group or public interest. A long line of US jurisprudence sounding in equity holds that when a common benefit or fund accrues to a group of parties as a result of litigation, the group's attorney's fees and expenses are paid by all of the group's members, not just the party who stepped forward to bring the lawsuit.[2]

Not only can courts require that all class members contribute to attorney fee compensation, a class action attorney is not permitted to enter into a fee contract with a class representative, on the theory that such a private contract might distort the representative's incentives to faithfully represent the interest of absent class members who are not parties to the contract.[3] This judge-made fee doctrine ensures that there is a source of funds to pay the attorney who acts on behalf of the class – at least when the class prevails – and that the cost burden is not assumed solely by the class representative(s), thereby eliminating the potential for free riding by other class members. (Unless the class counsel is a salaried employee of an NGO or other organization that funds class actions, if the class does not prevail the counsel receives no fees and must cover expenses herself.)

How a large number of class members – most of whom are not actively engaged in the litigation – could decide what the attorney is owed and how that payment should be apportioned among the class members poses an obvious practical challenge. The response in the US has been to authorize the judge to award fees and expenses to class counsel, acting in essence as a fiduciary for the class.[4]

Prior to 2003, when provisions specific to the appointment of class counsel and attorney fees were added to Rule 23, federal judges took their authority for reviewing and approving (or disapproving) fee requests in class actions from their settlement approval authority (Rule 23(e)). Even when counsel argued that they had negotiated the class settlement and attorney fees separately, judges held that the class counsel's fees were properly subject to review and approval[5]. By the early 2000s, concerns about collusive settlements – deals in which class counsel allegedly agree to less-than-adequate settlements for class members, in return for defendants' acquiescence to excessive fee requests – led the federal judiciary to amend Rule 23 to make explicit the judge's responsibility to approve fee requests. In addition, the Civil Rules Committee Advisory Committee encouraged judges presiding over class actions to require that class members be informed as to the attorney fee awards that are contemplated, so as to provide an opportunity for class members to object to fees, as well as to the merits of the settlement itself (Advisory Note to F.R.C.P. 23(h)). Consistent with this advice, model notices of pending class action settlements posted as judicial guidance on the Federal Judicial Center's website (www.fjc.gov) include not only the terms of the settlement (for example who is eligible to claim compensation, how much a class member can expect to obtain, and so on) but also the amount of fees requested by class counsel. And when objectors come forward, they often do contest class counsel fee requests, even when they have no objections to other settlement provisions (Hensler et al. 2000, footnote 18, pp. 93–99).

The question remains: how should judges determine the amount of fees and expenses that is appropriate to compensate successful class counsel. As a formal matter, the judge approves or disapproves the fees requested by class counsel (see F.R.C.P. 23(h)); as a practical matter, however, the judge sets the fee amount. Two approaches have emerged over time: the 'percentage of fund' approach and the 'lodestar' approach.

Historically, courts awarded attorneys a percentage of the common fund when plaintiffs prevailed (Federal Judicial Center 2004). For a time, this approach fell into disfavor, as critics argued that it produced 'windfall' profits out of proportion to the time and effort class counsel had invested in prosecuting the action on behalf of the class, thereby encouraging frivolous litigation. In response to critics, judges began to award fees on the basis of the hours and costs actually expended by class counsel – with hours valued at the going rate in the geographical area where the court sits – plus a premium (literally, a 'multiplier') for the results achieved, risks undertaken by class counsel, and other factors. (In large-scale national litigation, courts sometimes used a higher fee rate for lawyers who typically practice outside the court's geographical locale.) This type of calculation is termed the 'lodestar' approach, although just why it acquired this title is uncertain (Report of the Third Circuit Task Force 1985). The lodestar approach, in turn, fell into disfavor as critics argued that it rewarded lawyers for investing excessive time in litigation and as judges struggled to find the time to review and the expertise to evaluate the time records class counsel submitted and class counsel's claims for a fee 'multiplier'.[6] Today there is a division across the US appellate circuits with regard to whether judges are permitted or required to use one or the other approach, but the majority have returned to favoring the percentage of fund approach (Federal Judicial Center 2004). The lodestar approach continues to prevail in federal statutory fee-shifting cases, but the US Supreme Court has forbidden the application of a multiplier in such cases.[7]

In a court adopting the lodestar approach, if (as is common) multiple firms serve as class counsel, each firm submits its hours and expenses for review and a judge may assign a different fee rate and award a (different) multiplier to each. When a percentage-of-fund approach is used, the court is likely to leave the distribution of fees among multiple class counsel firms to private negotiation among those firms. In some instances in which counsel join together to bring a class action they may negotiate an expense-sharing arrangement among themselves before filing the lawsuit, as when a group of 60 plaintiff firms came together to file a nationwide class action against the big tobacco companies.[8] In that case, it was reported that each member of the plaintiff law firm committee contributed $100000 to join the law firm consortium.

Neither statutory nor case law has established bright-line rules for what percentage of a common fund a judge should award to successful class counsel or the appropriate multiplier a judge should apply to a lodestar calculation. Some federal appellate courts have suggested benchmarks for court guidance[9] but warned that they should not be applied 'mechanically'. Circuit courts of appeal have set forth various factors that should be taken into account in applying benchmarks for percentage-of-fund awards or multipliers for lodestar awards,[10] but have defined these factors imprecisely.

A study of published fee decisions from 1993–2002 found judges awarded a mean of about 22 per cent of the common fund in non-fee-shifting cases; the median was about 23 per cent, suggesting that the percentages awarded were distributed roughly normally (that is, without a skew to the high or low end of the distribution) (Eisenberg and Miller 2003, Table 1). In securities cases, which accounted for about half of the cases studied, the fee percentage averaged 24 per cent; in consumer cases, which accounted for roughly one-sixth, the fee percentage averaged 16 per cent.[11] The nominal amount of fees was strongly correlated with the nominal value of the settlement fund: as the size of the fund increased, so too did the amount of fees judges awarded to class counsel. But attorney fee awards, as a percentage of the settlement fund, declined somewhat as the size of the fund increased. For common funds up to about $10 million, fee percentages averaged around 25 per cent; for common funds from about $10 million to $38 million, fees averaged around 20 per cent; for funds ranging from $38 million to $190 million, fees averaged closer to 17 per cent; and for the largest settlement observed in the dataset, fees averaged 12 per cent (Eisenberg and Miller 2003, Table 7).

Although the Eisenberg and Miller dataset included both federal and state court cases, it was not a statistically representative sample of all class action cases in which judges award fees, as not all such awards result in published decisions. Typically, published decisions under-represent state court cases. How such under-representation might have affected the findings is unknown; in their dataset, Eisenberg and Miller found no statistical differences between average fee awards in federal and state court cases suggesting the state court under-representation may not be too important.

A more important caveat to the Eisenberg and Miller findings is that published court opinions provide no information about the actual amount of the common fund that class members collected, and therefore no way to gauge how much of the total settlement dollars paid went to class counsel. In recent years, private firms have emerged that for a subscription fee scan the legal landscape for class actions that have been resolved and file claims on behalf of clients who may unwittingly have become class members. (See, for example, www.claimscompensation.com.) But particularly in cases where class members' claims are for modest amounts, anecdotal evidence indicates that a large fraction of class members never come forward to claim the compensation owed them under the settlement. In such cases, the actual percentage of the total amount expended by the defendant to resolve the litigation may be far less than the amount suggested in published opinions.

Courts do not routinely monitor and report the fraction of class members who come forward to claim compensation or the total proportion of common fund dollars paid out to class members, so comprehensive data on this phenomenon are lacking. A 2000 analysis of ten mass tort and consumer class actions found five in which class members collected half or less of the total paid out by defendant to settle the cases and only three in which class members collected 70 per cent or more of the total paid out (Hensler et al. 2000, Figure 15.9, p.433). Such mismatches between the total per cent of the fund awarded to class counsel and the total per cent of the dollars paid that class counsel collect occur when settlement agreements provide that any dollars not claimed by class members are not owed by the defendant to anyone – so-called 'reversionary' settlements. Although widely criticized as a sign of collusion between plaintiff class counsel and the defendant (Hensler et al. 2000, pp. 79–85), reversionary settlements have been approved by federal and state judges. Moreover, courts have upheld the award of class counsel fees calculated as a share of the full common fund even when the settlement agreement specified that any unclaimed funds would revert to the defendant.

In the absence of bright-line rules for the appropriate percentage of a fund or the appropriate multiplier to award prevailing class counsel, some judges have turned to competitive processes, in which they invite all or a select group of class action firms to indicate prior to the inception of litigation what their fee structure will be. A proposal that courts *auction* class action representation to the highest bidder among law firms – that is, the firm willing to pay the most to represent a class in expectation of winning fees proportional to outcome – stirred considerable interest but also criticism in the judiciary and legal academia (Macey and Miller 1991). Modified versions of Macey and Miller's proposal have been adopted by some federal judges,[12] and the auction strategy was endorsed as one possible approach to selecting and paying lead counsel by a task force of the Third Circuit appellate bench, which judges have looked to for guidance on fee issues over the last several decades (Third Circuit Task Force on the Selection of Class Counsel 2002). Although the Civil Rules Advisory Committee declined to include specific authority for auctions in the 2003 Rule 23 amendments, there has been no significant challenge to federal judges' authority to require lead counsel to compete for their appointment.

The passage of the Private Securities Litigation Reform Act (PSLRA) in 1995 also seems to have encouraged price competition among class action firms. By awarding presumptive lead plaintiff status to the investor(s) with the largest financial stakes in a securities class action lawsuit, the act created incentives for plaintiff class action firms to compete for the support of these investors for class counsel appointments. (The PSLRA also banned incentive payments by class counsel to class representatives, outlawing in securities litigation the types of arrangements that have led to federal prosecution of some prominent class action lawyers.) The PSLRA is reported to have produced another outcome that has led to price competition among plaintiff class action firms: now more engaged in monitoring class actions (the explicit aim of the statute's lead plaintiff provision), institutional investors have begun to exercise opt-out rights to pursue individual litigation. Reportedly, many of these investors are soliciting bids from leading class action firms to represent them in this individual litigation, with price a key factor in firm selection (Toll and Reiser 2008).

No one knows how much profit plaintiff law firms realize from their class action practices. It seems likely that in some instances the profits are enormous, but class actions can be a risky proposition for law firms: a 2007 study of insurance policy holders' class actions against insurance companies found that only 14 per cent of class complaints were certified to proceed in class form; the rest were denied certification, dismissed or withdrawn or resolved by individual litigation that likely yielded much smaller amounts than would have the hoped-for class action (Pace 2007). Class action law firms invest their own resources in prosecuting class actions, and when they do not obtain a judgment or settlement for class members, they receive no compensation for their time or reimbursement of their expenses. The resources expended can run in the millions of dollars: one plaintiff attorney, who did not wish to be identified, told the author the firm had billed approximately $20 million worth of time and paid more than $3 million in expenses to others in a still-ongoing class action.

The practice of third-party funding of class litigation, which developed in Australia and has now migrated to Europe has yet to become widespread in the US. Instead, plaintiff law firms obtain lines of credit to finance their law firms' operations. The attraction for banks that provide these lines of credit is not a share of the litigation, but rather what it would be for any other business loan: the interest on loans and the attraction of holding the large sums deposited with them when the law firms are successful. In recent years, some banks have established specialized divisions that offer creative lending arrangements to firms with substantial portfolios of high-value cases (Yeazell 2001). With credit available to them on good terms, the best known plaintiff law firms have little incentive to turn to third-party funders who demand a significant fraction of the fees obtained when plaintiffs prevail. Media reports on the evolution of third-party litigation financing in the US suggests that smaller law firms are the most common recipients of third-party financing (Frankel 2006).

The dominance of well-capitalized law firms with good access to credit in class action practice in the US (and in sub-niches within, such as securities litigation) poses a special challenge for third-party funders seeking to enter the market: the most experienced and best known firms have little need to exchange a share of their fees for up-front funding and reduced risk and the lesser known, less experienced, firms that might be interested in such an agreement are less likely to succeed in the class action domain. This challenge may be exacerbated by the consequences of the PSLRA and by the more recent passage of the Class Action Fairness Act of 2005 (CAFA). After the PSLRA's passage, the largest and most experienced securities class action firms began to forge strong relationships with institutional investors, including pension funds, increasing the likelihood that when class counsel were selected they would be in the lead for the position. Rather than curbing the role of these class action firms in the prosecution of securities litigation (an unspoken but widely understood objective of the statute), it seems likely that the PSLRA enhanced their status and made more difficult the task of smaller less experienced firms who wish to break into the market. More recently, CAFA, which provides federal jurisdiction for multi-state class actions where there is minimal diversity between the class and the defendant, seems to have further strengthened the position of the largest class action firms, which have extensive experience in federal courts (Erichson 2008). Nonetheless, third-party funders might find a foothold in the market by investing in firms that spin off from large well-known firms when individual lawyers decide to seek their fortunes outside of these larger firms. Indeed, some third-party financers are said to be backed by principals from highly successful plaintiff law firms (Frankel 2006). A growing academic and practitioner-oriented legal literature arguing in favor of litigation funding and suggesting how funders (and lawyers who might benefit from third-party funding) might circumvent putative bars on third-party funding practices evinces the interest third-party funding has begun to garner in the US (Molot 2009).

In the absence of systematic empirical evidence on plaintiff law firm earnings, we can only assume that class actions, properly identified as such and prosecuted capably, earn substantial enough profits as to make the practice attractive. Class action practice likely also contributes significantly to the handsome profits-per-partners reported by the leading US corporate firms who represent defendants in such actions.

3.2 Financing Non-Class Mass Actions

In the US when many individual claims are aggregated together but proceed in non-class form, the court's authority to regulate fees is much reduced, by comparison to class actions. Non-class aggregation is typical of mass personal injury and property damage litigation in the US, where case law has long held that class certification is generally inappropriate for such claims (Hensler et al. 2000; Hensler 2007). In these moderate to high value tort cases, plaintiffs enter into individual representation contingency fee contracts with law firms whose practice is to bundle together hundreds or thousands of claims arising out of the same circumstances. The practice of aggregating claims was the key ingredient in the rise of mass tort litigation in the US (Hensler and Peterson 1993) and opened the doors to the courthouse for asbestos victims (Carroll et al. 2005) and other toxic tort claimants. Although plaintiff attorneys represent aggregated claimants as a group, they typically charge each of these clients the same contingency fee (roughly one-third) as they would if they were representing a client in truly individual litigation (Carroll et al. 2005, pp. 102–104). As with all contingency fee litigation, if the plaintiff does not prevail the client owes the law firm nothing and the firm is left to cover its own time and expenses.

Court involvement in managing financial arrangements in non-class mass tort litigation occurs when large numbers of cases are filed in multiple jurisdictions and then consolidated in a single court and assigned to a single judge under federal statute 28 U.S.C. § 1407 (the multi-district litigation (MDL) statute) or similar state rules that apply to mass litigation within a single state. This procedure has some similarities to the English Group Litigation Order (GLO) (Hodges 2001). In the last two decades, virtually all mass personal injury litigation filed or removed to the federal courts has been consolidated in this fashion (Hensler 2007). It is now common practice for judges assigned to manage such litigation to appoint a 'plaintiffs steering committee' (PSC) comprising the most prominent law firms from among those who are representing the plaintiffs. Although the federal statute that provides for coordination of mass tort cases formally applies only to federal cases, it has become common in recent years for federal judges who preside over multi-district litigation to coordinate with state court judges who are overseeing state cases that are part of the mass litigation and even to include lawyers litigating those cases in state courts on the federal court plaintiff steering committee (Federal Judicial Center 2004, pp. 405–407).

Having appointed some firms to lead the litigation – conduct discovery, draft and argue pre-trial motions and so forth – judges have felt a need to provide a mechanism for paying them. Judges have taken their authority for ordering fee arrangements from equitable fee doctrine, reasoning that the plaintiff steering committee members are creating a 'common benefit' by leading the litigation (Federal Judicial Center, Fourth 2004, pp. 405–407). Typically, the judge issues a fee order specifying how the cost of developing the litigation is to be shared among all of the lawyers who are representing plaintiffs before the court. Sometimes the judge's order specifies that the plaintiffs themselves will owe the plaintiff steering committee members a share of any settlement they obtain.[13]

If a fund is established early in the litigation and if individual lawsuits (or groups of lawsuits) are settled as time progresses, assessments against settlements yield payments into the fund that both reimburse steering committee lawyers for any expenses they have paid out up front and provide support for the on-going litigation. Funds may also be disbursed to other lawyers whose work benefits the ongoing litigation aggregate.

For example, in recent federal multi-district litigation that was coordinated with state litigation against a contact lens manufacturer, the federal judge issued a case management order establishing a steering committee fund to be subsidized by assessments against recoveries ranging from 4–6 per cent, depending on the nature of the claim. The assessments are to be withheld from all settlements the defendant may enter into and paid directly into the fund by the defendant. Lawyers in the parallel coordinated state litigation who choose to use the work product of the plaintiff steering committee in the federal case have agreed to subject their settlement recoveries to the assessment as well. The federal judge appointed a certified public accountant to manage the steering committee fund.[14]

In a few recent instances, judges presiding over consolidated mass tort litigation under the federal multi-district litigation statute have announced that they will scrutinize and perhaps limit the total fees paid to plaintiff lead counsel as a result of a mass settlement negotiated between those counsel and the defendant, reasoning that the case is a 'quasi-class action.'[15] It is still too early to say whether such a practice will become common in non-class mass actions.

Financing arrangements become even more complicated when class and non-class complaints are filed at the inception of mass tort litigation and consolidated in a single court before a single judge. In such instances, a judge may appoint a plaintiff steering committee comprising both putative class counsel and law firms representing aggregated plaintiff claims. In instances when such litigation is certified for the purposes of a class settlement, the judge's attorney fee order may award class counsel fees and also impose limits on the share contingency fee lawyers may take from class members' compensation from the common fund.[16]

4. DO US LEGAL FINANCING RULES LEAD TO EXCESSIVE LITIGATION?

The popular view in many circles outside the US is that the American legal financing system produces excessive litigation. To test this assumption one needs to know:

(1) How much civil litigation is there in the US?
(2) How much do financing rules contribute to explaining the amount of litigation?
(3) And is the amount of litigation in the US 'excessive'?

The answers to questions 1 and 2 are matters for empirical analysis. The answer to question 3 requires a value judgment but it too is often transformed into an empirical question by comparing US litigation to litigation elsewhere, apparently on the assumption that litigation rates outside the US are appropriate, rather than the converse.

Given the extent and heat of the rhetoric regarding Americans' 'litigiousness' it may be surprising to discover that all three of these questions are remarkably difficult to answer.

4.1 How Much Civil Litigation is There in the US?

About 17 million new civil cases were filed in US state courts in 2006 (the latest data available) (National Center for State Courts 2007), and approximately 260 000 more were filed in federal courts (Administration

Office of the US Courts 2007). Most of these lawsuits were in categories that are not the subject of public policy controversy: small claims, probate and estate. Small claims accounted for the largest share of these suits; many of these claims are collection cases filed by businesses. Viewed close up, the numbers of civil suits filed by 'litigious' Americans – that is to say suits in which parties chose to litigate a dispute rather than being required to do so by law or bureaucratic practices – are not as dramatic as observers outside the US assume: in 2006, about 1.25 million new contract suits and 400 000 new tort suits were filed in the 34 states that report detailed civil caseload statistics. About 61 000 new contract suits and 34 000 tort suits were filed in federal courts during that year. Rounding up to 2 million to account for unreported cases, for a country of 300 million, this amounts to 0.006 per capita. Put another way, if litigation was evenly distributed over the population and over time, a typical American would file a contract or tort claim once every 150 years.

Of course, litigation is not distributed evenly over the country's population. Indeed, available evidence suggests that businesses are more likely to file lawsuits than individuals (Dunworth and Rogers 1996; Public Citizen 2004; Galanter 2006). To measure disposition to litigate, it is necessary to calculate litigation *rates*. This is even harder than counting different types of cases as it requires knowing the number of circumstances in which people might file a lawsuit. The best data on litigation rates in the US relate to personal injury litigation, and were collected in 1989. In the first nationally representative survey of Americans who suffered financial or other losses due to accidental injuries, the Rand Institute for Civil Justice found that only 19 per cent of accidental injury victims even considered taking any steps to claim compensation from someone other than their own insurer, and only 10 per cent took such a step, usually consulting a lawyer. Four per cent hired lawyers and two per cent filed lawsuits (Hensler et al. 1991, Fig. 5.2, p. 122). Even when their injuries were quite serious, victims were unlikely to claim compensation from others. Only half of those whose injuries were objectively rated as serious (for example life-threatening, resulting in long-term impairment) considered claiming, and 43 per cent of those who required hospitalization or surgery immediately or subsequently considered claiming. Only one-third of those who themselves considered their injury to be 'extremely serious' considered claiming and only 19 per cent of these initiated some sort of claiming activity. Because millions of Americans have no health insurance or are under-insured and few have adequate disability insurance, in many instances failure to bring liability claims meant the households had to shoulder a substantial fraction of the costs of accidental injury themselves. In the aggregate, at the time of the injury compensation study, US households paid two-fifths of the costs of accidental injury out of their own pockets (Hensler et al. 1991, p. 174).

4.2 Do Legal Financing Rules Explain Litigation Behavior?

The reasons for the low litigation rates found in the 1989 survey had less to do with barriers to access to the legal system (difficulty finding lawyers to represent them, legal fees, and so on) than with the way victims viewed the causes of their accidents. A majority of accident victims attributed their accidents to some combination of 'bad luck' or 'chance' and human behavior, and of those who saw a human cause, more than half blamed themselves (Hensler et al. 1991, Table 6.3, p. 155). Most of those who attributed the accident wholly or partially to chance never even considered claiming. The minority of victims who mostly blamed others for their injury were 12 times more likely to consider claiming than those who mostly blamed themselves. Yet only a quarter of those who blamed others actually initiated some sort of claiming behavior, and only one-eighth got so far as to hire a lawyer. The 1989 survey of accidental injury victims has not been replicated but studies of medical malpractice claiming relying on record data have found similarly low rates of liability claiming and litigation, even for instances where medical specialists believed that such claims would be merited (Studdert and Brennan 2000; Baker 2005).

4.3 Are US Litigation Rates 'Excessive'?

Taken together, the data summarized above suggest that under ordinary circumstances, Americans are not as prone to litigating as many outside the US assume. Valid cross-national comparisons of claiming behavior are hard to come by. Detailed civil caseload data are even less available outside the US than within it, and studies that compare claiming to opportunities for claiming are rare. A comparison of the 1989 US data with data from a similar English survey conducted around the same time found similar patterns of claiming by injury circumstances but a substantially higher rate of claiming by Americans for automobile accident and non-work injuries; in contrast, the English survey respondents were more likely than Americans to claim for losses due to injuries at work. The latter difference was easily explainable by the differing structures of workers compensation in the two jurisdictions (Hensler et al. 1991, Figure 5.3, p. 123). A comparison of the 1989 US claiming and litigation rates in automobile accidents and more recent Japanese survey data on automobile accidents found that the Japanese accident victims were more likely than Americans to claim compensation from someone else involved in the accident, but that Americans, when they did claim, were more likely to turn to lawyers and the courts (Hensler 2009).

In summary, the available data on legal claiming situations other than mass injury do not support the conventional wisdom regarding Americans' litigiousness, either in absolute terms or by comparison to citizens of other nations. Moreover, to the extent that researchers have been able to explain litigation behavior in the US, it appears to be more strongly correlated with the circumstances of injury than with the US litigation financing regime. While Americans may be able to more easily find and secure the services of lawyers than citizens of other jurisdictions, individual Americans' thoughts do not seem to turn towards the litigation process nearly as often as is generally believed.

In mass injury circumstances, however, the story may be different. There has been no systematic analysis of claiming behavior in mass injury situations in the US but fragmentary data and sociological analysis suggest that claiming rates are higher than in ordinary litigation (Hensler and Peterson 1993). Still, the absolute number of mass litigation cases – class and non-class – is not huge, relative to the total size of the US civil justice system. A recent review of high-profile mass product defect litigation in the US over the past 35 years identified 45 lawsuits (about 1.3 annually) that had been litigated to near-completion and an additional dozen or so that appeared to be in a nascent stage. The cases ranged from a few thousand plaintiffs to hundreds of thousands and the settlements (when achieved) ranged from a few million dollars to billions (Hensler 2007). In the US there are accurate statistics on annual class action filings in federal courts but there are virtually no systematic data on annual class action filings in the 50 state courts. Because the majority of civil lawsuits are filed in state rather than federal courts this means that it is difficult to estimate the total class action caseload in the US today. Drawing on disparate sources, I estimate that about 6500 unique class action suits have been filed annually in US federal and state courts in the past several years, amounting to less than one per cent of all civil lawsuits in the categories of cases that typically give rise to class actions: contracts, torts and property (Hensler 2010).

5.   CONCLUSION

Although I have argued above that the US litigation financing system does not, by itself, incentivize individuals to bring ordinary civil litigation it unquestionably incentivizes lawyers to bring class and non-class mass litigation. Absent the potential for fee awards proportionate to damages obtained on behalf of class members – and the potential to secure large damages for the class – it is unlikely that vigorous class action practice would survive. And without the possibility of aggregating large numbers of individual claims represented on contingency fee contracts, it is unlikely that mass non-class practice would continue to flourish. The long history of individual litigation against tobacco manufacturers in the US demonstrates the futility of dispersed litigation by law firms and plaintiffs with limited resources against a determined well-subsidized party with much at stake (Rabin and Sugarman 1993). Along with other features of the US legal system, legal financing rules in the US have enabled class and non-class litigation. Absent public financing – which is highly unlikely – or more extensive use of private third-party financing than has so far emerged in the US, the current US legal fee regime is essential to the continuation of such litigation.

Should social policy support the continuation or indeed the growth of class and non-class mass litigation? The answer depends on an assessment of the merits of lawsuits and the utility of their outcomes, as well as more fundamental beliefs about the relationship between private and public law. Determining the merits of any single class action turns out to be surprisingly difficult: although many observers can easily retrieve a memory of a class action they thought frivolous, a close analysis of the circumstances underlying many class actions yields divided opinions. Judged up close, the merits are in the eyes of the beholder. Assessments of the merits of class and non-class mass litigation generally are even more difficult and are shaped significantly by the observer's political values. Those who are comfortable relying on market competition and public regulation to regulate corporate behaviour, and on corporate beneficence and government welfare programs to compensate citizens for loss, place a low value on class actions and other forms of mass litigation. Those who are less willing to trust in the market, corporate actors, legislatures and government bureaucracies are likely to endorse an expansive role for private class actions and other forms of mass litigation. But while class actions and non-class mass actions may offer the *promise* of regulation and redress, the reality of such outcomes is more uncertain. Assessing the utility of class actions and mass litigation generally requires a more comprehensive and more systematic analysis of litigation outcomes than scholars have conducted to date.

NOTES

1. *Alyeska Pipeline Serv. Co. v. Wilderness Soc'y*, 421 US 240 (1975) (holding that absent a specific statutory exception to the 'American Rule' regarding fees, each party bears its

own fees, even when plaintiffs are acting as 'private attorneys general' protecting public interests).

2. *Boeing Co. v. Van Gemert*, 444 US 472, 478 (1980) (Noting '(s)ince the decisions in *Trustees* v. *Greenough*, 105 US 527 (1882), and *Central Railroad & Banking Co.* v. *Pettus*, 113 US 116 (1885), this Court has recognized consistently that a litigant or a lawyer who recovers a common fund for the benefit of persons other than himself or his client is entitled to a reasonable attorney's fee from the fund as a whole.')

3. The widely reported prosecutions of Melvyn Weiss, former named partner of Milberg, Weiss, Bershad & Shulman and William Lerach, founder and former named partner of Lerach Coughlin Robbins & Stoia (and Weiss' former partner at Milberg, Weiss), resulted from charges that the lawyers had secretly contracted with class representatives to funnel additional funds to these representatives, over and above what they were due as class members. The two lawyers claimed that these were at most 'ethical lapses' that did not harm class members; they pleaded guilty to conspiracy charges and were sentenced to substantial time in prison (Perino 2008). There are widespread concerns about the potential effects of payments to class representatives (Jones 2008).

4. *In re Copley Pharm., Inc.*, 1 F. Supp. 2d 1407, 1409 (D. Wyoming 1998).

5. See, for example, *Strong v. BellSouth Telcoms.*, 137 F.3d 844 (5th Cir. La. 1998) (holding that district court judge has authority to review attorney fee agreement even when fees were not to be paid from the 'common fund') and *Welch & Forbes, Inc. v. Cendant Corp. (In re Cendant Corp. Prides Litig.)*, 243 F.3d 722 (3d Cir. N.J. 2001). (Ruling on an appeal of the district court's award of attorney fees, the court wrote 'Our interest and supervisory role is pervasive and extends not only to the final fee award but also to the manner by which class counsel is selected and the manner by which attorneys' fee conditions are established'.)

6. *In re Copley Pharm., Inc.*, 1 F. Supp. 2d 1407 (D. Wyoming 1998).

7. *Burlington v. Dague*, 505 US 557 (1992).

8. *Castano v. American Tobacco Co.* 160 F.R.D. 544 (E.D. La 1995).

9. See for example, *Camden I Condominium Ass'n v. Dunkle*, 946 F.2d 76 (Eleventh Cir. 1991) (suggesting 25 per cent as a reasonable benchmark).

10. See for example *Johnson v. Georgia Highway Express, Inc.*, 488 F.2d 714 (5th Cir. 1974). Although *Johnson* was not a common fund case, judges have frequently turned to it for guidance in common fund cases.

11. The confidence interval around these estimates is about plus/minus 10 per cent for consumer cases and about plus/minus 7 per cent for securities cases.

12. Judge Vaughn Walker of the Northern District of California has been the foremost proponent of the use of auctions in securities class actions. See, for example, *In re Oracle Sec. Litig.*, 132 F.R.D. 538 (N.D. Cal. 1990) and *In re Quintus Sec. Litig.*, 148 F. Supp. 2d 967 (N.D. Cal. 2001).

13. *In re Silicone Gel Breast Implant Litigation,* Order 13, Establishing Plaintiffs' Litigation Expense Fund to Compensate and Reimburse Attorneys for Services Performed and Expenses Incurred for Common Benefit, N.D. Ala, 23 July 1993 (on file with author).

14. Pretrial Order No. 15 (Amended), *In re Bausch & Lomb,* C/A No. 2:06-MN-77777-DCN (D.S.C. 2006) and Order Appointing CPA, *In re Bausch & Lomb,*, C/A No. 2:06-MN-77777-DCN (D.S.C. 2006).

15. *In re Zyprexa Prods. Liab. Litig.*, 424 F. Supp. 2d 488 (E.D.N.Y. 1988) (in non-class mass tort litigation, capping fees at 35 per cent and ordering that fees be paid from the mass settlement fund, not from individual plaintiff compensation); *In re Vioxx Prods. Liab. Litig.,* MDL 1657 (E.D. Louisiana, 27 August 2008), available at http://vioxx. laed.uscourts.gov/Orders/o&r082708.pdf (capping individual plaintiff attorney's fees at 32 per cent of plaintiff damages obtained as a result of a mass settlement in a case denied class certification).

16. *In re Copley Pharm., Inc.*, 1 F. Supp. 2d 1407, 1412 (D. Wyoming 1998); *Walker v. Bayer Corp.*, Order Concerning Certain Claims for Attorney Fees (18 February 1998)

(limiting fees to contingency fee lawyers representing individual class members in class action brought on behalf of HIV-infected hemophiliac).

REFERENCES

Administrative Office of the US Courts (2007) 'Judicial Business of the United States Courts', www.uscourts.gov/judbus2007/tables/S07Sep07.pdf (accessed on 27 July, 2010).

American Bar Association Commission on Billable Hours (2002) 'Report', www.abanet.org/careercounsel/billable/toolkit/bhcomplete.pdf (accessed on 27 July, 2010).

American Tort Reform Association (2001) 'ATRA Issues: Collateral Source Rule Reform', www.atra.org/show/7344 (accessed 30 June, 2001).

Aspan, Maria (2007) 'Getting Law Firms to Like Commercials', *New York Times*, www.nytimes.com/2007/06/19/business/media/19adco.html (accessed on 12 June 2007).

Baker, Tom (2005), *The Medical Malpractice Myth*, Chicago: University of Chicago Press.

Barzaghi, Alessandro (2007) 'The Italian Bar Exam', *Santa Clara Journal of International Law*, Symposium, www.scu.edu/scjil/global/BarzaghiArticle_ItalianBar.shtml (accessed on 27 July, 2010).

California Bar Journal (2008) 'Bar Exam Pass Rate Jumps Nearly 6 Per Cent', *California Bar Journal*, http://archive.calbar.ca.gov/Archive.aspx?articleId=94709&categoryId=94606&month=12&year=2008 (accessed in December 2008).

Carroll, Stephen J., Deborah R. Hensler, Jennifer Gross, Elizabeth M. Sloss, Matthias Schonlau, Allan Abrahamse and J. Scott Ashwood (2005), *Asbestos Litigation*, Santa Monica, US: Rand.

Chih-Chieh, Lin, Liu Shang-Jyh and Chen Chih-Hsiung (2010), 'Taiwan's Legal System: Three Most Important Things', *International Association of Law Schools Conference*, www.ialsnet.org/meetings/enriching/chih-chieh.pdf (accessed on 27 July, 2010).

D'Angelo, Carlo (2008), 'Overseas Legal Outsourcing and the American Legal Profession: Friend or 'Flattener'?', *Texas Wesleyan Law Review*, **14**, 167–195.

Dunworth, Terence and Joel Rogers (1996), 'Corporations in Court: Big Business Litigation in US Federal Courts, 1971–1991', *Law & Social Inquiry*, **21**, 497–592.

Eisenberg, Theodore and Geoffrey Miller (2003) 'Attorneys Fees in Class Action Settlements: An Empirical Study', papers.ssrn.com/sol3/papers.cfm?abstract_id=456600 (accessed on 27 July, 2010).

English Bar Council (2009) 'The Statistics', www.barcouncil.org.uk/CareersHome/TheStatistics/ (accessed on 27 July, 2010).

Erichson, Howard (2008), 'CAFA's Impact on Class Action Lawyers', *University of Pennsylvania Law Review*, **156**, 1593–1627.

Federal Judicial Center (2004), 'Manual for Complex Litigation'.

Finney, Tal and Joel Yanovich (2006), 'Expanding Social Justice Through The 'People's Court', *Loyola Law Review*, **39**, 769–784.

Fortado, Lindsay (2005), 'Hourly Rates Continue to Rise', *National Law Journal*, ed 12 December 2005, www.law.com/jsp/article.jsp?id=1134122711101 (accessed on 27 July, 2010).

Frankel, Alison (2006), 'Helping Underfunded Plaintiffs Lawyers – At A Price', *Law com*, ed 13 February 2006, www.law.com/jsp/law/LawArticleFriendly. jsp?id=1139565913200 (accessed on 27 July, 2010).

Galanter, Marc (2006), 'Planet of the APs Reflections on the Scale of Law and Its Users,' *Buffalo Law Review*, **5**, 1369–1417.

Haaretz (Israeli daily newspaper), 'The Marker', 4 May 2009.

Hensler, Deborah R. (2001), 'Revisiting the Monster: New Myths and Realities of Class Action and Other Large Scale Litigation', *Duke Journal of Comparative and International Law*, **11**, 179–213.

Hensler, Deborah R. (2007), 'Has the Fat Lady Sung? The Future of Mass Tort Litigation', *Review of Litigation*, **26**, 883–926.

Hensler, Deborah R. (2009), *Claiming in US Auto Accidents*, Paper presented at Meiji University, Tokyo, March 2009.

Hensler, Deborah R. (2010), 'Using Class Actions to Enforce Consumer Protection Law', in: Geraint Howells, Iain Ramsay and Thomas Wilhelmsson (eds), *Handbook of Research in International Consumer Law*, Cheltenham, UK and Northampton, MA, US: Edward Elgar.

Hensler, Deborah R., Jane Adler and Charles Nelson (1983), *Simple Justice: How Litigants Fare in the Pittsburgh Court Arbitration Program*, Santa Monica, US: Rand.

Hensler, Deborah R. and Mark Peterson (1993), 'Understanding Mass Personal Injury Litigation: A Socio-Legal Analysis', *Brooklyn Law Review,* **59**, 961–1063.

Hensler, Deborah R. et al. (1991), *Compensation for Accidental Injuries in the United States*, Santa Monica, US: Rand.

Hensler, Deborah R., Nicholas M. Pace, Bonnie Dombey-Moore, Elizabeth Giddens, Jennifer Gross and Erik Moller (2000), *Class Action Dilemmas: Pursuing Public Goals for Private Gain*, Santa Monica, US: Rand.

Heyman Law, Robert, 'Frequently Asked Questions', www.robertheyman.com/faq.php.

Hirsch, Alan and Diane Sheehey (1994), *Awarding Attorneys' Fees and Managing Fee Litigation*, Washington DC, US: Federal Judicial Center.

Hodges, Christopher (2001), *Multiparty Actions*, Oxford: Oxford University Press.

Hyman, J. Leonard and Paul Frumkin (2003), 'Contingent Advances; Are They Subject to Usury Law?', *Michigan Bar Journal*, **82**, 28–31, www.michbar.org/journal/pdf/pdf4article613.pdf (accessed on September 2003).

Inside Counsel (2007), 'Managing Litigation Expenses', *Lexis*, ed April 2007, Chicago, Illinois: Summit Business Media.

Jones, Robert (2008), 'The Ethical Impact of Payment to Lead Plaintiffs', *Georgetown Journal of Legal Ethics,* **21**(3), 781–794.

Kakalik, James S, Patricia A. Ebener, William L.F. Feistiner and Michael G. Shanley (1983), *Costs of Asbestos Litigation*, Santa Monica, US: Rand.

Kakalik, James S. and Nick Pace (1986), *Costs and Compensation Paid in Tort Litigation*, Santa Monica, US: Rand.

Kakalik, James S., Elizabeth M. King, Michael Traynor, Patricia A. Ebener and Larry Picus (1988), *Costs and Compensation Paid in Aviation Accident Litigation*, Santa Monica, US: Rand.

Krishnan, Jayanth (2007), 'Outsourcing and the Globalizing Legal Profession', *William and Mary Law Review,* **48**, 2189–2246.

Leubsdorf, John (1984), 'Towards A History of the American Rule on Attorney Fee Recovery', *Law and Contemporary Problems***, 47**, 9–36.

Macey, Jonathan and Geoffrey Miller (1991), 'The Plaintiff's Attorney's Role in Class Action and Derivative Litigation: Economic Analysis and Recommendations for Reform', *University of Chicago Law Review*, **58**(1), 1–118.

Ministry of Justice, Poland, 'Statistics on Admission to the Bar' (in Polish) (2009), www.ms.gov.pl/ogloszenia.php#akt091026 (accessed on 27 July, 2010).

Molot, Jonathan (2009), 'A Market in Litigation Risk', *University of Chicago Law Review*, **76**, 367–439.

National Center for State Courts (2006), 'State Court Pro Se Statistics, 2006', www.ncsconline.org/wc/publications/memos/prosestatsmemo.htm#statecourt (accessed on 27 July, 2010).

National Center for State Courts (2007), 'Examining the Work of the State Courts', www.ncsconline.org/D_Research/csp/2007_files/Examining%20Final%20-%20 2007%20-%201%20-%20Whole%20Doc.pdf (accessed on 27 July, 2010).

Note (1984): 'State Attorney Fee Shifting Statutes: Are We Quietly Repealing the American Rule?', *Law & Contemporary Problems*, **47**, 321–346.

Pace, Nicholas (2007), *Insurance Class Actions in the US*, Santa Monica, US: Rand.

Paul, Annie (2005), 'Land of the Rising Lawyer?', *Legal Affairs* www.legalaffairs. org/printerfriendly.msp?id=859 (accessed on 27 July, 2010).

Perino, Michael (2008), 'The Milberg Weiss Indictment: No Harm, No Foul?', *AEI Legal Center for the Public Interest*, Briefly ed 1 May 2008, www.aei.org/ publications/pubID.28060/pub_detail.asp (accessed on 27 July, 2010).

Public Citizen (2004), 'Frequent Filers: Corporate Hypocrisy in Accessing the Courts', www.citizen.org/pressroom/release.cfm?ID=1799 (accessed on 27 July, 2010).

Qualters, Sheri (2008), 'Bar Exam Pass Rates Climb In Several States' ed 4 December 2008, www.law.northwestern.edu/career/markettrends/2008/2poa3oepoubr.pdf (accessed on 27 July, 2010).

Rabin, Robert L. and Stephen D. Sugarman (1993), *Smoking Policy: Law, Politics, and Culture*, New York: Oxford.

Seidenstein, Robert (2008), 'The Vioxx Hit: Merck's Big Ticket Defense', *New Jersey Lawyer*, ed 10 March 2008 Lexis.

Studdert, David and Troyen Brennan (2000), 'Beyond Dead Reckoning: Measures of Medical Injury Burden, Malpractice Litigation, and Alternative Compensation Models from Utah and Colorado', *Indiana Law Review*, **33**, 1643–1686.

Third Circuit Task Force (1985), *Report*, 108 F.R.D. 237 (Special).

Third Circuit Task Force (2002), *Report on the Selection of Class Counsel*, http://www.ca3.uscourts.gov/classcounsel/final%20report%20of%20third%20 circuit%task%20force.pdf (accessed on 27 July, 2010).

Toll, Steven and Julie Reiser (2008), 'Opt-Outs: Making Private Enforcement of the Securities Laws Even Better' *18 CADS Report (Class Action and Derivative Suits reporter, ABA Section on Litigation)*, ed Winter-Spring 2008, http://www. reedsmith.com/-functions/download.cfm?use_id=o&fde_id=8066.

US Government Accounting Office (2001), 'Hourly Fees paid by various Federal Agencies to Private Attorneys for Legal Services', www.gao.gov/new.items/ d01887r.pdf (accessed on 27 July, 2010).

Wall St. Journal Law Blog (2009), 'I'm a trial lawyer. I bill by the hour. This has to be fixed', wwwblogs.wsj.com/law/2009/01/07/im-a-trial-lawyer-i-bill-by-the-hour-this-needs-to-be-fixed/ (accessed on 27 July, 2010).

Weltman, Stuart (2008), 'How to Manage Your Litigation Costs', *The Corporate Counselor*, ed 12 May 2008, www.yourdon.com/?loc=litigation&gclid=CKeOn eqWjZkCFQlrgwodFyVFaA (accessed on 27 July, 2010).

Yeazell, Stephen (1987), *From Medieval Group Litigation to the Modern Class Action*, New Haven, US: Yale University Press.

Yeazell, Stephen (2001), 'Re-financing Civil Litigation', *De Paul Law Review*, **51**, 183–217.

9. New trends in financing civil litigation in Europe: lessons to be learned

Mark Tuil and Louis Visscher

1. INTRODUCTION[1]

Civil litigation serves a multitude of goals, many of which were explicitly touched upon in the previous chapters. Civil litigation in the first instance is a way of resolving conflicts. Depending on the type of conflict at hand, the plaintiff for example may want the court to issue a declaration regarding the unlawfulness of the defendant's behaviour, or he may want the defendant to restore the *status quo ante*, to refrain from further infringements, to perform his contractual duties, to compensate his losses, or to restitute illegitimate benefits. In essence, civil litigation is a way to realise rights and entitlements, without having to resort to vigilantism.

In addition, civil litigation is a driving force behind legal development. The continuous flow of cases forces (or maybe better: enables) courts to find new solutions for existing problems. An ever-changing society is confronted with conflicts which legislators cannot all foresee *ex ante*. However, the *ex post* character of civil litigation enables courts to seek solutions to the arisen issues.

Furthermore, even though the conflict-resolving goal of civil litigation in essence is retrospective to the conflict at hand, the legal norms which are created by the courts in deciding the cases may very well have an *ex ante* impact on the parties involved in the conflict, as well as on other actors. Put differently, civil litigation may also serve the goal of deterrence, because it shows prospective norm violators which sanctions could result from their lawbreaking behaviour.

2.   THE PROBLEM OF FINANCING CIVIL LITIGATION

Irrespective of the goals which one ascribes to civil litigation, these goals can only be reached if litigation indeed takes place. However, many obstacles to bringing a civil claim exist. For example, the potential plaintiff may not know that a norm violation has occurred, he may fear that he will not be able to meet the required standard of proof, or he may decide to wait for others to bring a claim so that he can take a free ride on these efforts.

The obstacle that forms the main topic of this book consists of the costs of bringing a civil claim. If these costs outweigh the expected benefits of the civil claim to the plaintiff (both costs and benefits may be monetary and/or non-monetary), it is very likely that the potential plaintiff will decide not to bring a claim at all. In economic terms, he remains *rationally apathetic* (see Chapter 2 by Visscher and Schepens and Chapter 4 by Keske, Renda and Van den Bergh). This problem is exacerbated if a potential plaintiff is risk-averse so that he does not want to run the risk of having to pay high legal fees (possibly including the legal costs of the opposing party, should the plaintiff lose), if the funds for bringing legal claims are limited or in case of widespread, small losses (trifle damage or so-called 'scattered damage').

This financing problem may be combated in many different ways. Two instruments which lie outside the primary scope of this book, are publicly subsidised legal aid and public rather than private enforcement. Cutbacks on legal aid are exactly one of the reasons why the issue of financing civil litigation is becoming more and more important. Besides, as Faure, Fernhout and Philipsen point out it does not provide a solution to the financing problem for the so-called 'sandwich-class', that is the people too wealthy for subsidised legal aid but not wealthy enough to be able to self-finance civil litigation. Public enforcement strictly speaking is no solution to the problem of financing civil litigation, because it removes the need for civil litigation in the first place. It lies beyond the scope of this chapter and book to go into details into the reasons why public enforcement is no perfect solution. In many areas of law, public and private enforcement coexist, showing the need for private enforcement and hence the importance of solutions to the financing problem. Even in some settings where public enforcement until now has been the paramount form of enforcement, private enforcement is gaining in importance (see Chapter 4 which deals with private enforcement of competition and consumer law).

3. THE POSSIBLE SOLUTIONS DISCUSSED IN THIS BOOK

This book focuses on several possible ways to deal with the issue of financing civil litigation, other than subsidised legal aid and public enforcement. Specifically, the following methods are discussed:

- *Cost Shifting or Fee Shifting*: different ways in which the costs of litigation are divided between plaintiff and defendant are analysed. In this respect a dichotomy is created between the 'American Rule' (where each party bears its own legal expenses) and the 'English Rule' (where the losing party pays the litigation costs of the prevailing party, also called the 'loser-pays-principle'), although it should be noted that in practise most jurisdictions, including the American and English, use a mix between the two extremes. Also other rules, such as 'one way fee shifting' are treated;
- *Fee Arrangements*: in many of the chapters in this book, the issue of lawyer's fees appears. Hourly fees, contingency fees and conditional fee arrangements all influence the costs to the plaintiff of bringing a civil claim. Especially 'no cure, no pay' or 'no win, less fee' arrangements may reduce the hurdle of bringing a civil claim. However, fee arrangements turn out to affect much more than only the costs of bringing the claim, as is shown in several contributions;
- *Legal Expense Insurance*: Before-the-event insurance (BTE) and After-the-event insurance (ATE) reduce the financial burden of civil litigation to the parties involved. Especially in Chapter 5 Van Boom analyses the strengths and weaknesses of these instruments in overcoming the financing problem;
- *Group Litigation*: in Chapter 4 Keske, Renda and Van den Bergh discuss a different approach to the financing problem: group litigation. In essence, through sharing (some of) the costs of litigation by bringing similar cases collectively in one procedure, the costs per plaintiff dramatically decrease, which reduces rational apathy. However, other problems such as principal–agent problems between the lawyer and the represented parties may occur and obviously, the collective claim has to be financed. Hence, the topics of cost shifting, fee arrangements and legal expense insurance are also relevant in a setting of group litigation;
- *Public Funds*: Keske, Renda and Van den Bergh as well as Faure, Fernhout and Philipsen discuss several 'contingency style litigation funds', which cover plaintiffs' costs. Plaintiffs only pay a fee to the fund in case of success, but the fund retains the lawyer on the basis of the existing fee arrangements (often hourly fees);

- *Assignment and Securitization of the Claim*: in Chapter 6 Pinna analyses yet another avenue which could be taken. An injured party could, at least in theory, assign the claim to a third party. The price received can be regarded as his compensation, which he receives even before liability and the extent of the losses have been established by means of litigation. The assignee could securitize the claim, which – again at least in theory – could solve the financing problem.

The chapters in this book target the topic of financing civil litigation from a legal, an empirical and an economic perspective. By combining the three approaches, we believe that a better picture of the financing problem can be painted than by focussing on only one of these perspectives. The economic approach can, on the basis of the assumptions that are made regarding human behaviour, predict the effects of the different instruments on issues such as the level of claims, the quality of the claims, the duration of trial, the possible misalignment of incentives of plaintiffs, lawyers and/ or insurance companies, et cetera. The empirical approach can provide valuable information on which instruments are actually used in practice, test the theoretical hypotheses derived from the economic theory, and indicate the relative size of the predicted, sometimes opposing, effects. The legal approach can show which instruments are actually available and can expose relevant legal differences between the various forms of the instruments, which from a non-legal perspective may look the same at first glance. It can also show the purpose of a rule and the principle on which the rule is based and thus indicate the 'no-go-areas'.

Besides the contributions of European authors, which discuss the new trends that are visible in Europe, Hensler provides an American perspective on the topic of financing civil litigation. This is especially important as in European discussions regarding aspects of civil litigation, for example, contingency fees or class actions, the 'American situation' is being used as an example of how *not* to proceed. Hensler's contribution shows that the fear for the 'American situation' is often ill-founded.

The fact that the goals of civil litigation can only be reached if financing problems are overcome shows the societal importance of analyzing the potential solutions. This holds even more now private enforcement is becoming more important in the European context, and the budgets available for subsidised legal aid become tighter. In Chapter 7 Fenn and Rickman explicitly deal with empirical research regarding the relationship between a decrease in public funding and an increase in other solutions to the financing problem, such as conditional fee arrangements.

As becomes apparent from several chapters in this book, the instruments under discussion may provide an additional benefit besides improving access to justice. They may also entail a selection effect towards higher quality claims, which would result in especially more meritorious claims being brought. The way in which the various instruments influence access to justice, quality of the claims, the interplay between the parties involved et cetera, will be subsequently discussed in more detail below.

4.   COST SHIFTING

Cost shifting, also called 'fee shifting' (but we use the term cost shifting to avoid confusion with the alternative instrument of 'fee arrangements') considers the question of which party bears which legal costs. Under the American rule each party bears its own costs, while under the English Rule the costs are shifted to the losing party. In practise, there is a 'gray area' between the American and the English Rule, now often not *all* costs are shifted under the English Rule (see also Pinna), for example because they are regarded as excessive (also see the judgment of the European Court of Human Rights from December 15, 2009, in the case *Financial Times Ltd and others v. the United Kingdom*).[2]

Visscher and Schepens describe the effects of cost shifting on the basis of a review of mostly theoretical literature. Whether the level of suit will increase under the English Rule as compared to the American Rule depends among others on the assessment of the plaintiff of his chances to win (in which case he does not bear his litigation costs) and on his degree of risk aversion (under the English Rule risk-averse plaintiffs will sue less often, given that the stakes now also include the litigation costs. Van Boom discusses the way in which after-the-event insurance in a sense forces the losing party to finance the risk aversion of the winning party, now he also has to reimburse the insurance premium). The fact that losing plaintiffs under the English Rule have to bear all litigation costs in theory discourages potential plaintiffs to bring weak claims, while the fact that winning plaintiffs do not bear any litigation costs stimulates bringing high-quality claims. The existing, albeit limited, empirical research seems to corroborate this hypothesis. Cost shifting therefore could be regarded as an instrument which lowers the financing problem, especially for meritorious claims. However, the overall effect of cost shifting measures also strongly depends on the fee arrangement in place.

With regards to group litigation, Keske, Renda and Van den Bergh argue that the English Rule may hinder this form of litigation due to the increased risk it entails. They doubt, however, that a shift to the American Rule would lead to more representative actions being brought by, for example, consumer associations, because the decision of whether or not to sue does not only depend on the costs, but more importantly on the expected benefits. They also argue that the increased risk caused by the English Rule in group litigation may be mitigated by the use of contingency fees or conditional fee arrangements, because such an arrangement shifts the risk from the plaintiff to his lawyer. One-way fee shifting would encourage litigation even more in a setting of contingency fees, because if the case is won, the losing party pays the litigation costs, and if the case is lost, due to the contingency fee the plaintiff(s) pay(s) nothing anyway.

5.   FEE ARRANGEMENTS

Many chapters in this book devote attention to the payment structure of lawyers. Legal fees form a substantial part of the costs of civil litigation and hence of the financing problems. Under hourly fees, the lawyer has to be paid on the basis of the time he has spent on the case, irrespective of the outcome. This may form a substantial hurdle to civil litigation being brought. However, arrangements that link the payment to the outcome of the result could overcome this hurdle.

This book illustrates the need for clear definitions. Faure, Fernhout and Philipsen analyse the main forms of fee arrangements. 'Contingency fees' are a combination of 'no cure, no pay' and *quota pars litis*. Hence, if the case is lost the lawyer is not paid, and if the case is won the lawyer receives a percentage of the proceeds. A 'conditional fee arrangement' (CFA) in their definition entails that a losing lawyer receives nothing while a winning lawyer receives a success fee (a flat fee or an additional percentage on top of the regular fee). Some of the other contributions in this book apply the same concept. Keske, Renda and Van den Bergh, however, define a CFA as an arrangement where a losing lawyer only receives his basic fee while a winning lawyer also receives the success fee. This shows the need for clear definitions, because the conclusions reached by these authors when comparing contingency fees with CFA are strongly influenced by their definition of CFA. We do not argue here that one definition is better than the other, but as Faure, Fernhout and Philipsen rightfully state, 'the rather liberal use of concepts such as "contingency fees", "no cure no pay", "no win no fee" and "success fees" may give rise to many misunderstandings', which would cloud the already complicated debate. The last form of fee arrangements which Faure, Fernhout and Philipsen distinguish is the 'Dutch agreement', which is a combination of 'no win, less fee' and either *quota pars litis* or an unrestricted success fee. In our view, the CFA of Keske, Renda and Van den Bergh forms an example of such a 'Dutch agreement'.

Contingency fees reduce the financing problem, because a losing plaintiff bears no litigation costs, while a winning plaintiff finances these costs out of the proceeds of the claim.[3] In a sense, the lawyer pre-finances and insures these costs so that (especially risk-averse) plaintiffs may bring suit where they would not have done so under hourly fees. The hourly wages of contingency fee lawyers will be higher than those of hourly fee lawyers because the former will charge a premium for their financing and insurance service. Fenn and Rickman indeed find empirically that under result-based fees, the plaintiff's net reward is lower than under hourly fees. Hensler shows that many victims in personal injury cases prefer contingency fees over hourly fees or flat fees despite the lower reward. Whether the improved access to justice due to result-based fees leads to an increase in the level of suits depends on many factors, such as the impact of the threat of litigation on the behaviour of actors and, very importantly, on the role of lawyers as gatekeepers. After all, lawyers receive incentives to better screen the cases which they are willing to take, because their remuneration depends on winning the case (see Visscher and Schepens, Faure, Fernhout and Philipsen, Keske, Renda and Van den Bergh, Fenn and Rickman and Hensler). This gate-keeping role has the potential to increase the fraction of high-merit cases, so that result-based fees increase access to justice especially for meritorious claims. Empirical research verifies this gate-keeping role, but it also shows that cases with a relative low value are often turned down. The fear of a flood of litigation and for many meritless cases being brought seems unwarranted, both from a theoretical and an empirical perspective. The contributions of Faure, Fernhout and Philipsen and Hensler show that many forms of result-based fees are applied on both sides of the Atlantic, without any of the alleged problems as a result. Fenn and Rickman argue that CFA is becoming more and more important in England and Wales (the countries which they have studied) as legal aid disappears as a result of policy.

Fee arrangements do not only impact the possibilities of financing civil litigation, but they also may impact the incentives provided to the relevant actors in civil litigation. Under an hourly fee system, the payment of the lawyer depends on how many hours he puts in. Under result-based systems, however, it is the result which is decisive for the remuneration. Under the first system, spending more time on the case directly benefits the lawyer (of course, reputational effects and legal ethics may pose limits to this mechanism), while under the second system this is only the case if the additional efforts are made up for by a better outcome. This line of reasoning touches upon the topic of *principal–agent* problems. Ideally, the interests of lawyers are perfectly aligned with those of his clients and of society. In practise, this is not the case. Under hourly fees, lawyers may put in more hours than is in the interest of their clients and of society.

Result-based fees reduce this problem and better align the interests of lawyer and client, because both now have an interest in winning the case. This reason, which is an advantage from the point of view of agency theory, is exactly mentioned as a problem in many legal debates regarding the introduction of contingency fees. Faure, Fernhout and Philipsen show that in many European countries where contingency fees are not allowed, mainly or partly on the basis of this argument, other forms of result-based fees *are* allowed and used, apparently without (major) problems.

Another way in which contingency fees may combat the principal–agent problem is that lawyers may use the fee as a way to signal their quality (Visscher and Schepens, Faure, Fernhout and Philipsen, Keske, Renda and Van den Bergh). Hensler however states that there is little evidence that lawyers indeed compete through their fee and that only in high-value aviation accident litigation is there evidence of price competition between lawyers.

Result-based fees, however, do not perfectly address the principal–agent problems. Where hourly fees may lead a lawyer to spend too much time on a case, contingency fees may result in the opposite problem. After all, the lawyer bears the full costs of additional efforts, but only receives a percentage of the additional benefits (Visscher and Schepens, Faure, Fernhout and Philipsen). In addition, under the assumption that a lawyer can better assess the quality of a case than the client (especially if the latter is a one-shotter), lawyers may negotiate a too-high percentage when taking a case on a contingency fee basis, or they may give biased advice regarding the decision of the client to opt for hourly fees or contingency fees. Furthermore, the fee arrangement may impact the incentives to settle. Theoretically it can be argued that contingency fees lead to more and earlier settlements than hourly fees, because the lawyer secures his fee with fewer efforts. However, literature that includes lawyer's efforts in the analysis argues that contingency fees on the opposite lead to fewer settlements, because lawyers spend less time on the case during trial. Rejecting settlement offers can also be a strategic move: by signalling confidence in the case if it were to go to trial, a lawyer may extract a better settlement offer in subsequent rounds. Empirical research seems to corroborate the finding that contingency fees lead to fewer settlements (for higher amounts) than hourly fees, and that limitations on contingency fees decrease the probability that a case proceeds to trial. However, Fenn and Rickman also discuss empirical research which shows the opposite result. As Faure, Fernhout and Philipsen state, more empirical research is needed to yield more definite answers. They do recognise the problem, which is also mentioned by Fenn and Rickman, that it may be hard to acquire the necessary data for this.

6. LEGAL EXPENSE INSURANCE

In Chapter 5 Van Boom focuses on legal expense insurance, both in the form of 'Before-the-event insurance' (BTE) and 'After-the-event insurance' (ATE). These forms of insurance may overcome the financing problem, because the insurance company now bears the risk of having to bear legal expenses. Under BTE a risk-averse actor purchases insurance against legal expenses he may have to bear if he would become involved in a conflict. Under ATE, the policy is concluded after a conflict has occurred which will likely lead to litigation. Van Boom describes how the development of legal expense insurance depends heavily on domestic institutional factors, such as the extent of publicly funded legal aid (also see Fenn and Rickman) and the intensity of regulation of legal services. Also the rules on cost shifting, fee arrangements (Faure, Fernhout and Philipsen describe for several countries how the availability of legal expense insurance affects the development of result-based fees) as well as cultural factors are relevant.

Because BTE solves the financing problem and covers the risk of having to bear large costs, one may expect an increase in the number of suits. This holds even more now through adverse selection mainly high-risk actors would take out insurance and they may exhibit moral hazard so that more conflicts may arise. However, the insurance industry seems quite able to limit these effects. Moreover, insurers may function as gatekeepers, screening the cases on their merits, so that predominantly meritorious claims would be covered. There is no clear empirical support for this theoretical possibility (Visscher and Schepens).

Just as with fee arrangements, the interests of all parties involved may not be perfectly aligned, leading again to principal–agent problems. Van Boom discusses the European Directive on legal expense insurance, which tries to neutralise potential conflicts of interest between insured and insurer, which calls for implementation of arbitration or ADR procedures to quickly settle such conflicts, and which requires a free choice of council. The extent to which insurers are able to keep the costs of litigation low, depends among other factors on whether they can have in-house lawyers or whether they need to retain external lawyers. The difference in financing (the insurer has already received the benefits through the premium and now wants to limit the costs, whereas the remuneration of an external lawyer may depend on the number of hours put in or the result achieved) provides different behavioural incentives, with all the agency problems that come along. Van Boom therefore argues that the free choice of council should be reconsidered. Also the interests of the insurer and the insured may be opposed. The insured may want to litigate more (also the lower quality claims) and settle less (because trial costs are covered)

and for higher amounts (because the threat to go to trial is more credible). The insurer can try to limit these problems by using deductibles,
merit tests, maximum coverage, et cetera (Visscher and Schepens). Fenn
and Rickman mention that settlement delay in England and Wales was
lower under BTE than under other forms of litigation funding, which
suggests that indeed insurers are successful in countering principal–agent
problems.

Van Boom distinguishes two forms of ATE arrangements: ATE funding
and ATE insurance. ATE *funding*, also called 'third party funding',
means that the provider finances all costs involved in the claim against a
'premium' (varying with the value of the claim and the stage at which the
dispute is ended) which is only paid if the case is won. The provider investigates the merits of the claim and only finances viable claims. It is especially
used for commercial claimants with high value claims with a high probability of success. Given these characteristics, Van Boom argues that ATE
funding looks more like contingency fees than like insurance.

The combination of ATE *insurance* and CFA results in an instrument
which is very beneficial to claimants (also see Fenn and Rickman on this
combination). Due to CFA, a losing defendant does not have to pay his
own legal costs, but due to the English Rule he does have to pay the legal
costs of the prevailing party. The ATE insurance covers those costs. If the
claimant wins, he can recover both his legal costs (which due to the CFA
success fee may be substantial) and his ATE insurance premium from the
defendant. Hence, losing defendants also bear the costs which risk-averse
plaintiffs make to cover their risk. The only thing a plaintiff may lose is his
ATE insurance premium if he loses. Van Boom describes a recent development which even removes this last risk: a self-insured deferred premium.
The premium is only paid if the case is won, and it is then paid by the
losing defendant. This instrument induces lawyers and insurers only to
take cases on this basis if there is a large enough probability of success.
The defendant may receive a (too?) large incentive to settle such cases,
given the large financial consequences of losing in court. Therefore, this
instrument, although it is very able to overcome the financing problem,
may come at the cost of excessive litigation and over deterrence.

7.   GROUP LITIGATION

Keske, Renda and Van den Bergh discuss the possibilities to amelio-
rate the financing problems through the use of several forms of group
litigation, which is especially relevant in cases of scattered damage (where
the problems of rational apathy and asymmetric information play an

important role). In group litigation, either an informed individual party or an association initiates the proceeding. The superior information, as compared to that of uninformed individuals, tackles the asymmetric information. Rational apathy is addressed because it is no longer an individual victim with relatively low losses as compared to the costs of litigation who has to start the suit. The costs are either divided among more plaintiffs, or borne by for example a representative organization.

If group litigation in the form of a collective action or class action takes place, the extent to which rational apathy is solved depends on the way in which the collective is formed. Under an opt-in regime the problem may persist, because individuals have to become active in order to join the group. Under opt-out and mandatory forms, rational apathy is better overcome. An often-heard resistance against opt-out and mandatory collective actions is that it would deprive individuals from 'their day in court', so it would frustrate access to (individual) justice. In our view it is important to realise that in many instances the problem of rational apathy would avoid most individuals from bringing a claim anyway so that this argument is often an empty shell. Collective actions in a sense increase access to justice rather than frustrate it because as a member of the group, the individual victim may receive some compensation where individually he would not have brought a claim. And even if the individual would not receive individual compensation, for example because a *cy pres* system is applied, the possibility of collective claims may provide deterrent incentives to potential wrongdoers so that potential victims still benefit from reduced risks.

A drawback of group litigation may be that it introduces several forms of principal–agent problems. A representative organization or a lawyer litigating on behalf of a group of victims may have different interests at heart than the victims themselves. Especially in cases where the value of each individual claim is limited, victims will not spend much effort on monitoring the agent. Keske, Renda and Van den Bergh give examples of class action settlements which are rather beneficial to the lawyers and/or the defendant, but not so much for the plaintiffs, for example the so-called coupon settlements (also see Hensler on this issue). In Section 5 above it already became clear that fee arrangements may influence the agency problems. This holds even more in group litigation, now the plaintiffs have fewer incentives to monitor their representative. Hensler discusses Rule 23 of the Federal Rules of Civil Procedure, which contains instruments to combat agency problems (such as the requirement that the class is adequately represented and that proposed settlements have to be approved by the court).

The possibility of group litigation may also lead to frivolous suits: low (or even 'no') quality claims being brought in order to distract a settlement, because for the defendant settlement may be cheaper than trial (especially when potential reputational effects are incorporated), even in case of success.

Representative actions by, for example, consumer associations in the view of Keske, Renda and Van den Bergh do not solve the financing problem as good as class actions (which are almost always combined with contingency fees). The association's budget may not be large enough to finance the desired amount of litigation. Government funding could improve the situation, but also public budgets are limited. Furthermore, public funding may make the association too dependant on the government. Given the remaining financing problems, Keske, Renda and Van den Bergh advocate introduction of result-based fees. They also argue that agency problems may not be solved by representative actions, because the association may very well have interests which depart from those of the consumers at large. They suggest that agency problems are better solvable under collective actions financed via contingency fees. Due to the characteristics of collective litigation, result-based fees stimulate collective litigation even more than individual litigation, so that it is a powerful tool to overcome the financing problem.

8. PUBLIC FUNDS

Faure, Fernhout and Philipsen, as well as Keske, Renda and Van den Bergh give their attention to yet another way of financing civil litigation: contingency-style public funds. For example in Hong Kong, the Supplementary Legal Aid Scheme (SLAS) after a merit test may take on a case on a contingency fee basis. Hence, the fund pays all costs and the plaintiff only pays a contribution to the fund if he prevails. The lawyers, however, are paid by the fund on the basis of hourly fees. The fund, being a repeat player, is better able to monitor the lawyers than one-shot plaintiffs would be, so that this solution may reap the fruits of contingency fees (financing civil litigation, especially for the sandwich class) while avoiding the agency problems that normally come along.

Keske, Renda and Van den Bergh argue that the success of such funds depends, among others, on the design of the fund (for example the percentage to be paid in case of success and the formalities involved in applying) and on the cost shifting rules which are in place. They describe a successful Canadian fund as well as less successful Canadian and Australian funds. The SLAS discussed by Faure, Fernhout and Philipsen also seems successful in addressing the problem of financing civil litigation.

9. ASSIGNMENT AND SECURITIZATION

Pinna discusses the possibility of transferring one's claim to a third party. This way the victim receives an amount of money (the price paid by the assignee) even before any litigation has commenced. In a sense this is therefore no solution to the financing problem as a whole, but it removes the financing problem for the potential claimant altogether, because he does not bring the claim anymore. The price would depend on the value of the claim, the probability of success, the expected legal fees and a risk premium and it accounts for the time difference between the payment of the price and the outcome of the trial. The price would hence be lower than the losses of the victim, but the latter does not run a risk and bears no costs. It may therefore be an attractive scheme for victims who prefer receiving a lower amount now over the possibility of a higher amount later.

Pinna discusses potential legal hurdles regarding assignment of claims, such as the English prohibition of assignment of 'mere rights of action'. He also shows that assignment of the *proceeds* of the claim is allowed under tort law (Hensler discusses some American examples of this idea), and under contract law assignment is allowed if the assignee has a genuine commercial interest. In France assignment is allowed, but if this is done after the claim is already brought to court, the defendant can extinguish the claim by refunding the assignee the price he paid for the claim. This greatly limits the possibilities for securitization, so the possibility for the assignee to sell his claim to another party, either through a succession of assignments or by setting up a special purpose investment vehicle.

The advantages of assignment in Pinna's view are manifold. First, the injured party receives compensation quickly, without costs and risk. Second, it may benefit the assignee because he regards it as an investment. Differences in risk attitude between the victim and the investor, as well as differences in time preference and access to capital can make assignment attractive to both. Third, it could accommodate group litigation in jurisdictions which do not allow class actions. Even where they are allowed, assignment introduces less severe agency problems than class actions, provides higher awards for the victims and avoids the strict conditions surrounding class actions.

The main disadvantage according to Pinna is that assignment is only possible on a voluntary basis. In our view, the fact that the victim will never receive full compensation should be mentioned as a potential problem. Of course, in other situations where the plaintiff bears litigation costs himself he is also not fully compensated, but instruments such as legal expense insurance or cost shifting could be more attractive to plaintiffs. Another problem which is not discussed by Pinna is the fact that the assignee, when bringing the case to court, may have to obtain information from the victim in order to, for instance, meet the burden of proof. The fact that the victim has already received his money may make him less inclined to spend time and other resources on the case.

10.   LESSONS TO BE LEARNED

Financing civil litigation is a topic which appears to have a much broader impact than merely the question of how to finance the costs of civil litigation. In various contributions to this book it became clear that the separate instruments may not only affect access to justice, but also the quality of the claims that are being brought, the behaviour of plaintiffs, defendants and legal representatives in settlement negotiations and during trial, as well as possibly the behaviour of parties before conflicts have arisen.

The complexity of the analysis further increases if one realises that many instruments are used in various combinations. Keske, Renda and Van den Bergh have given explicit attention to the differences between class actions and representative actions when combined with contingency fees or CFA, under various cost-shifting rules. Faure, Fernhout and Philipsen analyse the SLAS, which combines public funding with result-based fees. Van Boom discusses the potential pitfalls of the combination of ATE and CFA. Fenn and Rickman analyse the development in the use of various combinations in England and Wales, especially as a result of declining legal aid.

The theoretical predictions discussed in the contributions are not unambiguous and empirical research is not providing unambiguous results either (due to limited availability of data or differences in methodology). Several authors therefore call for more empirical research in order to better assess the effects of the alternatives schemes.

Notwithstanding the need for additional research, we believe that this book can already contribute to the debate on alternative ways of financing civil litigation in Europe, besides the traditional form of subsidised legal aid. At this place, we would like to isolate two remarkable conclusions, or lessons for the future, which appear from the different contributions.

First, when discussing the financing problem, one should not separate this from the other effects that solutions to the financing problem may have. Especially the potential of fee arrangements, cost shifting rules and insurance schemes to screen cases on their quality is an interesting aspect. By improving access to justice especially for meritorious claims, the goals which are served by civil litigation may be better reached. One should, however, keep a critical approach to avoid undesirable effects, such as those of the combination of ATE and CFA, discussed by Van Boom.

Secondly, the substantial resistance in Europe against financing instruments in general and against US-style class actions and contingency fees specifically should be replaced by a more positive, open approach to these instruments. Faure, Fernhout and Philipsen show that many forms of result-based fees already exist in several European countries, apparently without causing substantial problems. Visscher and Schepens discuss the theoretical arguments pro and con contingency fees, where the arguments pro seem to outweigh those con. Keske, Renda and Van den Bergh argue that especially for scattered losses, class actions and contingency fees may be exactly what we need in order to enable effective private enforcement in the first place. The overall picture which emerges therefore is that allowing contingency fees in Europe as a way to secure access to justice should be seriously considered.

This development should not be rejected with a simple reference to 'the American situation', because, as is shown by Hensler's contribution, much of the resistance to this alleged situation is based on a misunderstanding or an incomplete assessment of this situation. Similarly, a reference to the traditional legal opposition on the bases of arguments such as that the lawyer should not have an own interest in winning the case or that contingency fees cause a flood of litigation, under-appreciates or even neglects the theoretical arguments in favour of contingency fees, the empirical research which seems to corroborate the theoretical findings and the fact that the system of hourly fees may cause principal–agent itself, which could be more serious than those of a contingency fee system. We therefore feel that those who still want to reject the instruments that have been discussed in this book have to provide ample reasons for their position.

This does, however, not mean that we advocate an unrestricted introduction of these instruments. First of all, as has become apparent, the effect of the introduction of these instruments depends on other rules regarding litigation costs, the availability of other instruments and legal culture. We therefore feel that the instruments should only be introduced after a careful legal and economic analysis of their potential effects and subsequential empirical research. Similarly, we do advocate that existing instruments are carefully scrutinized and in the case where these instruments seem to be particularly problematic, these instruments could be further regulated or in extreme cases banned. Some forms of the CFA + ATE contracts reported on by Van Boom could serve as a good example.

This book does not solve all problems and does not answer all questions. We do think that, by combining legal, empirical and economic approaches, it has provided new insights and arguments in the legal debate regarding financing civil litigation. By doing this, it has also shown the direction in which future research could (or maybe: should) go. In other words, it shows *New Horizons in Law and Economics* of civil litigation: more legal research into the peculiarities of existing and newly developing instrument to finance civil litigation, more (theoretical) economic research to derive hypotheses about the way in which these instruments influence human behaviour, and more empirical research to test those hypotheses in practice.

NOTES

1. The authors would like to thank Michael Faure for his concluding remarks at the Conference, which were very useful for this chapter.
2. Application no. 821/03.
3. Other forms of result-based fees also have the potential of reducing the financing problem, although less distinct in a case where a losing plaintiff still bears some costs.

Index